FROM NAPOLEON TO LENIN

FROM NAPOLEON TO LENIN

Historical Essays

A. J. P. TAYLOR

HARPER TORCHBOOKS ♦ The Academy Library
Harper & Row, Publishers
New York

FROM NAPOLEON TO LENIN

First HARPER TORCHBOOK edition published 1966 by
Harper & Row, Publishers, Incorporated
49 East 33rd Street
New York, New York 10016.

Contents

NOTE

THE essays in this book, the first of three projected volumes of A. J. P. Taylor's essays, have been selected from collections previously published under the titles *From Napoleon to Stalin*, *Rumours of War*, and *Englishmen and Others*. The purpose of this rearrangement is to facilitate the use of these essays as supplementary reading in European history courses. This first volume contains the major essays in European history from Napoleon to the outbreak of the First World War. The second volume will contain those essays on recent history and contemporary politics, and the third, the essays on English history and on historiography in general.

FRITZ STERN

I

NAPOLEON

(1) *On Himself*

A LIFE of Napoleon written by himself! The appeal seems irresistible. Mr. de Chair, the editor,[1] describes it as "the voice of the giant himself." The conversation of giants, then, must be very dull. The proclamations and bulletins of Napoleon show him to have been a propagandist of genius; so, too, was Goebbels. Yet the Memoirs of the one are as dreary as the Diaries of the other. In fact, the Memoirs of Napoleon—undoubtedly a genuine product of his mind—convinced me that the Goebbels' diaries were genuine; if Napoleon could write as boringly as this, Goebbels could also. Both works are, of course, full of lies; that was to be expected. It is the drabness, the fatuity, the commonplaceness of mind, that are surprising. What, for instance, could be more idiotic than Napoleon's explanation of polygamy in his chapter on Egypt? It occurs, he says, in countries inhabited by men of several colours and "is the only means of preventing them persecuting each other," since every man can have a black wife, a white one, a copper-coloured one "and one of some other colour." He proceeds to recommend it in the French colonies as the solution of the colour question, so that every man can have "one white, one black, and one Mulatto wife, at the same time."

Napoleon knew well that he was not a brilliant author; and he protected himself by speaking contemptuously of writers, as he did of his other enemies. Just as he described the English as "men who were continually at table, almost always intoxicated, and of uncommunicative disposition," so he dismissed writers as men of no practical sense.

He was not concerned to compete with those detestable

[1] *Napoleon's Memoirs*. Edited by Somerset de Chair.

ideologues; he had no interest at all in creating a work of art—his life in action had been creation enough. His reminiscences were written, or rather dictated, for effect. They were to launch a legend, the legend of Divine Caesar. Cold and aloof like a marble statue in classical robes, they are without personality; and it was a great error of judgment by Mr. de Chair to substitute the first person singular for "Napoleon," "the Emperor," "the general" of the original text. For Napoleon's statue is not vocal even after the fashion of the statue in *Don Giovanni*; and the essential purpose of these writings is in their remoteness from life. Napoleon the man was finished; Napoleon the institution had to be perpetuated.

It is not surprising therefore that the only section of Memoirs which Napoleon completed and finally polished is the part dealing with the campaign of Waterloo. A defeat of such finality needs a good deal of explaining away. Napoleon had an excuse in Grouchy's failure to come up with Blücher on June 18; and he repeats this excuse again and again. But he is pulled up by an uneasy sense that the real failure lay in the faulty orders which Grouchy received from his Supreme Commander; and Napoleon swings off on the other tack that Waterloo was an indecisive battle, the effect of which could have been undone by a further campaign. This line, too, has its dangers; for the failure to continue the war could be explained only by the war-weariness of the French. This was not an argument with which to appeal to posterity. The only way out is to assert that his strategy was throughout correct and that Wellington and Blücher committed "every conceivable mistake." Thus Napoleon persuaded himself that he had in fact won the battle of Waterloo and his Memoirs end with an expression of sympathy for the people of London "when they learnt of the catastrophe which had befallen their army."

The main section of the record, which runs from the siege of Toulon to the battle of Marengo, lacks the finish of the Waterloo narrative. Napoleon dictated these chapters haphazard to two amanuenses; and the two rivals kept their work separate when they published it after Napoleon's death. Mr. de Chair has sorted out the two sources and pruned away the asides with which Napoleon relieved the tedium. In this story of his early success Napoleon had less to explain away; all the same he never missed a chance to heighten the emphasis on the unique character and achievement of "the Emperor." Thus Paoli, the Corsican patriot, "used frequently to say of the young artillery officer [myself], 'He is a man for a Plutarch's biography.' " With this unlikely anecdote Napoleon blots out the story of his equivocal behaviour in Corsican affairs. Entertaining, too, in their way are the passages on naval warfare, in which Napoleon proves that it is much easier to win battles at sea than on land; Trafalgar is successfully rubbed out of existence. But for the most part the principles of Plutarch are observed all too seriously. There are accounts of Italy and Egypt which could have been taken from any gazeteer; even the military narrative lacks spirit. This served Napoleon's purpose. "The general" remained without a rival figure; and Napoleon could conclude with an account of Marengo, which conceals that he had lost the battle and slides, almost without mention, over Desaix who had come to Bonaparte's rescue. It is a fitting end to a narrative which is unreliable from beginning to end.

Can Napoleon have supposed that this dull and lying record would really secure his fame? This puzzle is the only point of interest raised by this book. Some part of the explanation may be found in the decline of his faculties. The only exciting passages are the quotations from the proclamations which Bonaparte wrote as the young general of the Army of Italy; these still ring with life, and their author could not have written dully however hard he tried. Success corrupts; and Napoleon had achieved success without parallel in modern history. The spare, beautiful artillery officer had become fat and coarse; and his mind became coarse at the same time. Besides, Napoleon had expected everyone to sacrifice himself for the Empire; and the first sacrifice had been his own personality. The young Bonaparte had been vital, though no doubt unattractive; Napoleon had squeezed the life out of him. Flashes of personality persisted, even at St. Helena. These make Napoleon interesting to history; they did not interest Napoleon himself. He was concerned only with his public performance. Stendhal found the key to Napoleon, when he described Julien Sorel, after his first night with Mme. de Rênal, asking himself: "*Ai-je bien joué mon rôle?*" Sorel, like Napoleon, was dominated by ambition; he lacked inner life and so fails to hold the reader's sympathy or even attention. Napoleon's was a more complicated case. He had begun as a romantic figure in the spirit of Rousseau; he ended as an abstraction from Plutarch. To use the clumsy contemporary phrase, this destruction of Napoleon by himself was the last triumph of the Classical over the Romantic. The essence of the Romantic movement was the elevation of individual sentiment and of individual character; yet Napoleon, with a more remarkable character than any, was ashamed of possessing it and returned to a Classical worship of the external world.

The explanation of this outmoded artificiality is simple; and Napoleon himself hints at it in the early pages of his Memoirs. He could have been genuine—"romantic"—only as a Corsican patriot; once he deserted his natural cause, he could only play parts and to do this he had to crush out his individuality. Sometimes, as when he played at being a French patriot or even a French Emperor, the part came off; at others, as when he played at being a Moslem in Egypt or wished to play at being the liberator-general after Waterloo, the pretence was too blatant. But, for a man who claimed to possess a sense of reality, Napoleon's judgment was strangely unreliable from start to finish. The eighteenth of Brumaire was as wild an adventure as the Hundred Days; in neither case did Napoleon have any clear idea what he was doing—he was simply "playing his role." For that matter Marengo was as much a gamble as Waterloo. It implanted in Napoleon the belief that he had truly mastered the external world; this gave him the necessary self-confidence for his career, though it ultimately brought him to disaster. Traditional ideas and traditional institutions had lost their force. Losing faith in God, men sought a human saviour. The first of these human gods was Napoleon; and the condition of his fame was the confident readiness to attempt the impossible. Napoleon believed in himself; he continued to believe even when reality had shattered the basis of this belief, and he supposed that others would believe too. Hence he even believed that readers could be found for his Memoirs.

All the same, despite Napoleon, a human being is buried in these writings. Napoleon no doubt thought that he was building a monument to his future fame. Most of the time, in reality, he was fighting his battles over again simply for the pleasure of it; and this time without risk of failure. No reader can be persuaded that the catalogue of divisions and the description of obscure skirmishes serve any literary purpose. Napoleon had ceased to think of the reader. He had escaped from the unpleasant reality of St. Helena and was manœuvring imaginary armies. There once more he could exercise the devotion to detail and the implacable demands for speed that had been the secret of his success (though also of his failure). Bending over the map of Lombardy, he could once more forget that Josephine had been unfaithful to him immediately after marriage (and he expected the reader to forget it too). In fact, if only he exerted his will strongly enough, he might again master the external world: St. Helena would disappear and Lombardy, or Paris under the Consulate, become once more reality. It was this belief in the human will, at any rate his own, that made Napoleon the representative and culmination of the French Revolution.

The essence of the Revolution was belief in man. Once you believe that man is naturally good, you must believe, too, that he can do anything. Napoleon certainly held this belief about himself. And no doubt man can do anything, if he goes the right way about it. The right way, as the events of the last century and a half have shown, is the way of science: the improvement of technique. The men of the French Revolution, and Napoleon with them, supposed that they could master the world by will alone. Hence the Napoleonic armies, for example, marched faster than other armies simply by the compelling force of Napoleon's command; modern armies move faster by train or aeroplane. Napoleon killed his secretaries by over-work; with the dictaphone and the typewriter they would have survived quite easily. Napoleon was following the wrong course; the further his will carried him, the greater was bound to be his final catastrophe. He supposed that events could be made; in the end events took their revenge on him. There was no essential difference between Napoleon in victory and in defeat (hence his own bewilderment at Waterloo): he always asked the impossible, and sometimes it was granted him. This is the real basis of the Napoleonic legend (as it will be for the legend of Hitler). Napoleon is the hero of all those who resent reality, of all those who will not trouble to master "the art of the possible." Napoleon is the supreme example of the human being who became more than life-size; and those who admire Napoleon are really flattering the human being in themselves. Yet what did this wonderful human being end in? A querulous sick man on a sub-tropical island dictating a drab and meaningless record to wile away the time. The Memoirs of Napoleon suggest that there is something to be said for not thinking that you are God.

(2) *The Verdict of History*

Events are well enough in their way; what historians write about them is much better. Who really cares about the later Roman Emperors, about Dutch William, or even about Pericles? These survive by grace of Gibbon, Macaulay and Thucydides. The greatest figure of modern times made himself such by providing a myth which would provide endless fascination for historians. Napoleon knew the secret of survival: *quel roman que ma vie!* His own literary gifts were those of an amateur—characteristic of one who carried that second-rate tear-jerker, *The Sorrows of Werther*, in his hip-pocket; the Napoleonic legend would never have taken hold had it depended on Napoleon's own writings. Napoleon's great stroke was to provide raw material for works of genius, so that French historians wrote about Napoleon inevitably, as every Greek playwright interpreted the story of the Trojan wars. Of course there is always a certain amount to be discovered about Napoleon, as no doubt matter of archæological interest can be found by grubbing in the ruins of Troy. But the profundities of the human spirit are to be found in what men have made of the legend, not in the archives and the rubble. The career of Napoleon is the greatest of modern legends.

This fact, once noticed, seems obvious and inescapable; and it is surprising that no one has had the idea long ago of discussing what French writers have made of Napoleon. To discover the obvious which no one else has thought of is the speciality of Professor Geyl,[1] one of the great historical minds of our time. It would be unfair to say that he demolishes the reputations of the great French historians; though he exposes their flaws, there remains, in his words "what life and energy, what creative power, what ingenuity, imagination and daring!" These words are a reminder of peculiar value for the English reader. Every continental student of history, even if he be a German, knows that the French are the greatest practitioners of the art. English historians have never recovered from the fraud put over on us by Acton (or perhaps Carlyle) and still suppose that serious history—scientific history as it is called—was perfected in Germany. But what tawdry stuff the German historians are compared to the stars of Professor Geyl's book—and how long-winded!

Professor Geyl gives a plain analysis of what French historians from the Restoration to the present day have written about Napoleon. He starts with Chateaubriand and ends with Georges Lefebvre. Each writer is summarized with the painstaking detachment with which a newspaper correspondent gives a summary of the foreign press. There are no graces of style, no novelty in the point of view; the general effect is humdrum, almost dull. It is like listening to a conversation where tones are never raised, where there is never a flicker of emphasis nor even, one supposes, of interest. As the conversation proceeds, it gradually becomes clear that Professor Geyl, far from being the club bore, declines to raise his voice simply because he is discussing the most profound topics of human experience. It is rare enough to find a work of history which is interesting, let alone exciting. This book is vastly more, an infinite consolation to the professional historian: it shows that history is a subject which can provoke thought. For my part,

[1] *Napoleon: For and Against.* By Pieter Geyl.

I would rather have written Professor Geyl's book than invented Existentialism or the new fashion in academic philosophy—what is it called? The subject, at any rate, which now spends its time debating whether it was once correct to describe itself as logical positivism. Professor Geyl's book enables the historian to look the philosopher in the face without cringing for quite a week.

His book teaches one, in the first place, a great deal about Napoleon. French historians have found in Napoleon infinite variety; and all of it was there. It is impossible to read this catalogue of their judgments without realizing that Napoleon really was a most extraordinary man, probably the most extraordinary figure that has ever appeared in the world of politics. Sorel saw him as the man who devoted his life to the defence of the natural frontiers; Bourgeois as the man who lived only for the creation of a great Empire of the Middle East; Driault as the restorer of the Roman Empire in Europe, the greatest of the Caesars; Vandal even discovered in him the pacifier of the world—no wonder he spoke of "the ultimate justice and grandeur of his aim." The same variety and the same vastness are revealed in the descriptions of Napoleon's work as a civilian ruler—the heir of the Revolution, the restorer of order, the architect of the Code Napoleon, the founder of the French Empire, the protector of the Catholic Church. All these things happened in Napoleon's time; yet the cumulative effect of them is not to increase admiration for Napoleon, rather to rouse doubts.

Here Professor Geyl, as it were, turns the tables on Napoleon: for his book, despite its cool tone and its scholarship, is an anti-Napoleonic tract, the most formidable ever composed. He has given the legend a good showing in order to show that it is a legend, that it over-reaches itself by its very absurdity. He quotes the rhetoric of Thiers, the brilliance of Vandal, the sophistication of Sorel; then brings them to earth with a gentle query—the murder of the Duke of Enghien? the breach of the Treaty of Amiens? the oppression and exploitation of Europe? the stifling of French Liberalism? Above all, the lies, the intrigues, the dishonesty? Professor Geyl has no doubt of his own verdict:

> He was a conqueror with whom it was impossible to live; who could not help turning an ally into a vassal or at least interpreting the relationship to his own exclusive advantage; who decorated his lust of conquest with the fine-sounding phrases of progress and civilization; and who at last, in the name of the whole of Europe, which was to look to him for order and peace presumed to brand England as the universal disturber and enemy.

This is not, however, only the verdict of a dispassionate Dutch observer. The historians of the legend do not exhaust French writings on Napoleon. Indeed, all Professor Geyl's criticism of the admirers of Napoleon is based on the work of French scholars; and his analysis of the two attitudes, *for* and *against*, is a splendid contribution to the study of French ideas. The cleavage is, in the first place, political. In England admiration for Napoleon has often (perhaps usually) been found on the "left"—a line running from Lady Holland to Hilaire Belloc and (dare I say it?) Bernard Shaw. What English admirers of Napoleon have in common is simple: they are all "agin the government" and, since Napoleon was also against the British Government, they suppose that he was on their side. In France, however, the "establishment" has been on the left, especially in the time of the Third Republic; and Napoleon has been the hero of the Conservatives. They did not need to pretend that Napoleon cared for liberty: they were delighted that he had destroyed it and wished to follow his example. They echoed the phrase of Barrès: "Napoleon, Teacher of Energy," and praised, perhaps exaggerated, those qualities which made Napoleon the precursor of Fascism. Moreover, unlike English writers, they did not conceal that Napoleon was the enemy of England, not merely of the British Government; for, since England represented the principles of liberty, of constitutional government, and of agreement between the nations, she was their enemy also. This tradition, though strong, was the school of a minority in France. French writers who cared for liberty, who opposed militarism, had no illusions about Napoleon and exposed the errors of those who had. French Liberals in the nineteenth century, and Socialists in the twentieth, stood unanimously for "the other France" which repudiated Napoleon with his gospel of energy and violence.

The cleavage *for* and *against*, as well as being political, is also professional; this is a point of peculiar interest fully worked out by Professor Geyl. The men of letters, with the exception of Taine, have been for Napoleon, and Taine was only against Napoleon because he recognized in Napoleon himself; the men of learning have been against him. The men of letters have often been distinguished scholars, as Vandal and Sorel were; but, in the last resort, they were concerned to produce an effect, to write a work of literary genius. It is a very different Napoleon who appears in the school text-books. Indeed one is almost driven to postulate the general rule: the better written a book, the more unreliable as history. But there is more in it than that. Tocqueville said of Napoleon: "He was as great as a man can be without morality"; and the truth is that all men of letters, that is all who care for good writing, are, in this sense, immoral. They will always subordinate reality to effect and facts to phrases. Paine's judgment on Burke will serve for every French writer on Napoleon whose works one reads for pleasure: "He pities the plumage but forgets the dying bird." Nothing is stranger than the delusion of our time that men of letters are, by nature, champions of political, or even of intellectual liberty. If Professor Geyl's book is not evidence enough to the contrary, consider the famous writers who made the pilgrimage to Mussolini. Of course, scientists are even worse—but then one hardly expects political sense from them. It was only when reading Professor Geyl's book that I realized that professors of history, at any rate in France, are so much better. Their record of integrity has been almost unbroken. Even in the Second Empire the committee of scholars, employed to publish the correspondence of Napoleon I, was too resolutely honest to please Napoleon III; it had to be replaced in 1864 by a committee of literary men (including Sainte-Beuve) which set out to publish only what Napoleon "would have made available to the public if he had wished to display himself and his system to posterity." Still, the achievement of the French professional historians cannot necessarily be counted to the general credit of the trade. What German historian stood out against the cult of Bismarck, at any rate until Bismarck had failed? And what chance is there that any

German historian will stand out against the coming cult of Hitler? As for English historians, they have hardly escaped from the Anglican sycophancy which marked the universities until the beginning of this century. Chaplains of the pirate ship, they have extolled the British Empire as persistently as the French men of letters extolled the Empire of Napoleon. The French professors represented a general "university" culture which hardly exists outside France. As Professor Geyl says: "The scholarliness of their method . . . disciplines their mental attitude. But it would be foolish to overlook the fact that these authors came to Napoleon with their own, with different, *a priori* ideas, that they measure him against standards of spiritual freedom, of culture, of humanity, of social progress, that politically they are as a rule of the left. With some of them anti-clericalism is predominant, with others liberalism, or socialism." What a wonderful country of which these things can be said of university professors!

The last quotation is a reminder that Geyl's book, as well as being a book about Napoleon and about French historians, is about clerical values (using the word in Benda's sense). Geyl concludes his praise of the professional historian, Georges Lefebvre, in whom he finds the most convincing version of Napoleon, with criticism: "I should like to see the eternal postulates of respect for the human personality, of the feeling for spiritual freedom, of lofty idealism, of truthfulness, taken into account when the final reckoning is made." This is a startling evocation of the shade of Acton; and it leaves me wondering whether the virtues of a historian and those of a "clerk" are the same after all.

II

NAPOLEON AND GENTZ

How has the continent of Europe escaped political unification? Everything in Europe seems to call for it; everything, that is, except the temperament and traditions of its peoples. More uniform in climate than China, less diverse in religion than India, less diverse in race than the United States of America, Europe has had for centuries a single culture and a common social structure. Landowner and peasant, merchant and banker, factory owner and factory worker, artist and scholar, would nowhere find themselves in an alien world in moving from one part of the Continent to another. There is a European way of thinking and of living; even a uniform pattern of meals—England and Russia, both outside the Continent, are both marked off from it by their times for eating. For a thousand years men have dreamed of European union; yet for a thousand years this most uniform of continents has defied political unification. The most recent attempt at it we have just lived through and successfully opposed; and it is too soon, perhaps, to estimate the historical place of Hitler's New Order. Yet as it slips into history we can already begin to see how little of it was original, how much of it (like most German political activity) a perverse aping of an earlier French achievement. Hitler was Napoleon's Caliban. The French came as liberators and offered to Europe far more than did their German imitators; yet in the Napoleonic Empire, too, appear the defects—one is tempted to say the inevitable defects—of attempting to force Europe into a single political mould.

"L'Empire de Napoléon,"[1] of which M. Madelin writes, is the Empire of 1811, the year of calm and grandeur before the great storm which was to blow the Empire out of exist-

[1] *Histoire du Consulat et de l'Empire*. X. L'Empire de Napoléon. By Louis Madelin.

ence, the year when the Empire extended from the Baltic to the confines of Greece. It was, above all, the year of the dynasty. The Austrian marriage had already announced Napoleon's changed role from that of the continuator of the revolution to that of the champion of monarchical order against "the disorderly spirit" of the *canaille*; with the birth of a son he became the originator of the Holy Alliance. Previously Napoleon's sentiment had been for his brothers and sisters—the family sentiment of a Corsican. Now the thrones of the Bonapartes were endangered—Louis dismissed from Holland, even Joseph given only a breathing-space in Spain. Napoleon imagined that he had founded a dynasty and had become indeed the successor of Louis XIV. Yet, with the strange realism which redeemed the vulgarity of his character, he saw through his own pretences. He said to Molé: "We are the monarchy of a week"; and, again: "All this will last as long as I do, but, after me, my son will perhaps think himself fortunate if he has 40,000 livres in the funds." Sometimes he consoled himself with the thought that his son, "probably an ordinary man, of moderate gifts," would be "the constitutional King *tout trouvé*"; for Napoleon knew that "in the long run, the sword is always vanquished by the spirit"; that he himself had had neither time nor patience to build up a new system of institutions.

But Napoleon refused to be shaken by his own scepticism. He accepted his destiny. The revolution had repudiated the legacy of history and had made the gigantic attempt to build a system of social life on the basis of abstract principles. Napoleon, profoundly sceptical and deeply experienced in practical affairs, knew well that society could not be based on reason alone; the only alternative he could hit upon was trickery. He invented institutions in which he did not believe, but which he was naïve enough to suppose would deceive others. His own imperial title, the new nobility, the wearisome court ceremonial (imitated from the German courts, not from Versailles)—even these tawdry pretences were given a false animation by the energy with which Napoleon threw himself into the masquerade. Lacking belief and lacking purpose, Napoleon tried to solve all his problems by the same means: ever more activity. As long as he kept driving forward and driving others forward, he could hope to escape the failure which his own mind told him to be inevitable. Hence the pell-mell of ideas, which made Narbonne exclaim: "What a man! What great ideas! What dreams! Where is the keeper of this genius? The whole thing is scarcely credible. We are between Bedlam and the Panthéon." Hence, too, by 1811 the weariness which overcame Napoleon, even occasionally the longing for an obscure family life which made him so much exaggerate the virtues of the dumpy Marie Louise.

Napoleon's latest invention was the Empire of the West, with its second capital at Rome. But this led him inevitably into conflict with the Papacy and so to the destruction of his most genuinely conservative work, the Concordat. Napoleon believed the Catholic religion to be useful for his Empire; he was *plus catholique encore que chrétien*. The French hierarchy owed their security and greatness to Napoleon; good Bonapartists, the last thing they wanted was to quarrel with the Emperor. Yet they, too, had to follow the logic of their position. At the Council of Imperial Bishops Napoleon's own creations, even his uncle the Cardinal Fesch, were driven reluctantly and feebly, but inescapably, to adopt the attitude of martyrs. The quarrel with the Church was the final proof that a conservative system could not be built on reason and human energy. The Empire, at its height, had no convinced supporters—not even Napoleon. The régime was composed of all those who had profited from the Empire; but they supported it only so long as they could enjoy their profits, and would turn against it the moment that it demanded sacrifices from them. Napoleon had tried to make a collective system out of individual interests; he could not blame the deserters of 1814. Not that there was opposition in 1811. Talleyrand, the wisest man in France, and perhaps Fouché, waited for the blunder which they knew that even Napoleon would make; but for the most part men dared not look into the future.

The most fortunate were the younger men who had not yet made their fortunes and to whom had fallen the administration of the Empire outside France. Here ceaseless activity, ceaseless levelling, still seemed a substitute for genuine creation. Since there could be only one form of rational government and since that government had been achieved in France, all Europe was to be remade on the French pattern. Napoleon himself defined the aim of Imperial policy: "I must have a European code, a European Court of Cassation, a common coinage, common weights and measures, and common laws; I have to make of all the peoples of Europe one single people, and of Paris the capital of the world." Fontanes, the head of the University, put it more dramatically: "We must be able to say: 'At this very moment all the students of the Empire are at work on the same Latin passage.'" The first stage of French government was liberation—the destruction of privileges, of abuses, of traditional inefficiency. It was welcomed with gratitude by the people and with enthusiasm by the local philosophers. Hegel, ever an admirer of successful power, wrote of Imperial rule: "It is enough that it be the will of Heaven, that is, of the French Emperor." By 1811 this first stage was past. The peoples, liberated from the old, were being driven into the new; and they were stiffening their backs. All over Europe the Imperial system was sticking in the mud of human reluctance to be turned into perfect beings; and, from Napoleon downwards, human energy flagged and faltered.

M. Madelin is puzzled by the failure of the French system to take roots. For the failure of a rational system he seeks a rational cause. Conscription and the continental system, he concludes, were the two disadvantages which outweighed the benefits. Yet these seem to him rather forced on Napoleon by the wilful opposition of England and Russia than springing inevitably from the Napoleonic system. It shocks him that Napoleon should have declared his principle to be *La France avant tout*; but it shocks him even more that the peoples of Europe should have been reluctant to have their lives run for them by the French. M. Madelin concludes that they would have got used to Napoleon with time: "It was only time that he lacked." But time was lacking for what? Only to organize an even greater catastrophe. Tocqueville was wiser. He said of Napoleon: "He was as great as a man can be without morality." What Napoleon and his Empire lacked was not time, still less energy, but belief. Frenchmen can rule with grace and France had a real civilization to offer; therefore Napoleon's rule was more tolerable than Hitler's. But, ultimately, it broke against the same obstacle: the unwillingness of European peoples to be fitted into a uniform system.

The Imperial cause did not even inspire the French. The reality in the Napoleonic Empire was French national consciousness; and Napoleon, thinking to found the United States of Europe, became in fact the greatest of French national heroes. The national pride of France pointed the way which the rest of Europe would follow. The great revolution of 1789, with its rationalistic philosophy, did not transform the French into Europeans but made them more assertively French. Throughout Europe the French were successful in destroying the traditional order; and even where they did not conquer, that order destroyed itself by its rigidity and decay. The outcome was the rise of nationalism in Europe, the only way, once historical differences were lost, by which men could be different. The rejection of uniformity was the one thing uniform to the inhabitants of Europe. This conclusion, implicit in the fall of the Napoleonic Empire, has been emphasized again after Hitler's New Order. Unexampled destruction has been followed by unexampled nationalism. And by a simple process: when men lose everything, the nation remains their sole possession.

Europe could not be brought together by destruction and by the rule of a single people, either in Napoleon's time or in Hitler's. But could there not be another way—the way of preserving something of the historic forms and bringing men together in voluntary co-operation? This great question is asked now, as it was asked in the age preceding and following the fall of Napoleon. This question dominated the mind of Metternich and led him to devise the "system Metternich." It dominated, too, the mind of the man from whom Metternich learned his system, Friedrich von Gentz[1] (the noble title was a gift from the legitimist King of Sweden), a man who with

[1] *Secretary of Europe*. The Life of Friedrich Gentz, Enemy of Napoleon. By Golo Mann. Translated by William H. Woglom. *Friedrich von Gentz*. Defender of the Old Order. By Paul R. Sweet.

many human faults had probably the most interesting mind of his day. Vain, snobbish, a cadger and a spendthrift, Gentz was the first great commentator on current affairs; and the heart of anyone who has ever attempted that speculative role must warm to him in success and still more in failure. His two biographers sort out the facts of his life; both fail to straighten out his ideas. And this is not surprising: Gentz would have been hard put to it to straighten them out himself. In 1814, when arguing against the deposition of Napoleon, he answered his own pamphlet against recognizing Napoleon, which he had written in 1804. What was more damaging, in 1820, when Gentz was advocating the censorship of the German Press, some German liberals reprinted the pamphlet against Press censorship which he had written in 1797. These inconsistencies are to Gentz's credit rather than the reverse. The enemy of perfectionist ideas, he sought the practical and the moderate: something that would not ask too much of human beings. Like Burke, though in even stormier times, he set habit against reason; or rather, tried to make a compromise between the two.

It is easiest to understand his opposition to Napoleon, though it made him for many years a solitary figure. Hegel, Goethe, all the great German figures of the day, expected Napoleon to make a new world for them. Only Gentz held from the start that nothing lasting could come from conquest and arbitrary rule. Napoleon was condemned to pursue ever greater success until it turned to failure; that was obvious afterwards, not so easy to predict in 1804 or even in 1807. But what cause should be set against the cause of the dictator? This was the search to which Gentz devoted his journalistic life, the question to which he never found a satisfactory answer. Certainly not the cause of German nationalism. This cause he dreaded even more than the cause of Napoleon. France, he believed, would, after defeat, come to accept an equal place among the Great Powers of Europe; in this belief he successfully advocated a peaceful policy towards Louis Philippe in 1830. But national Germany would be content with no place but the first: it would drive towards an even more perilous ascendancy than that of Napoleon and destroy what remained of the European order. Gentz cared for historic Germany and abandoned Prussia, the state of his birth, for the more traditional Austria; he failed to see that this historic Germany had been destroyed almost as much by the Habsburgs as by Napoleon himself. War accelerates political developments; it does not cause them. In our own time the two German wars have obscured the economic crisis which springs everywhere from the rejection in men's minds of economic individualism. So the Napoleonic wars obscured the political crisis which sprang from the decay of traditional political obligations. The restorations of 1815 were not real but sham-Gothic.

Gentz at the end of his life confessed this. He said in 1830: "Were I to write the history of the last fifteen years, it would be a continuous accusation of Metternich"; and he condemned most strongly the steps which Metternich had taken on his advice. The emptiness of the "system Metternich" was made clear to Gentz by the Austrian restoration of absolutism in Naples after the revolution of 1821. The King of the Two Sicilies was a *reductio ad absurdum* of legitimist policy, just as the King of Greece is a *reductio ad absurdum* of democratic policy a century or so later. Words and reality were not in tune; and Gentz at least had the honesty to admit it. After all, what could be more absurd than to preserve irrational abuses on rational grounds? Once the political institutions have become subject for argument, the traditional must give way to the rational. Gentz came to admit this; he only asked that the giving way should not be too rapid. Hence he believed that both he, as a Conservative, and the Liberals were doing a useful work; they demanded reforms—he slowed them down. Like Canning opposing Parliamentary reform, he thought that someone should defend the old order, even when its destruction was certain.

In international affairs, too, Gentz came to admit that he had defended "a lost cause." This lost cause was the Habsburg monarchy; more deeply the cause of the historic European States (including the Ottoman Empire); and most deeply of all the cause of European union. During Gentz's lifetime Europe had been offered the chance of union either under

Napoleon or against him. It took neither: Europe would not accept Napoleon's Empire, but failed to overthrow it. The liberation of Europe came from without, from England and Russia: Europe had been unable to solve its own problems or to determine its own destinies. European union demanded, and demands, co-operation between France and the principal Germanic Power, whatever name that may bear. But legitimist Austria would not accept the supremacy of Napoleon; liberal France would not work in partnership with Metternich's Austria; Stresemann's Germany would not take an equal place in the French order devised by Briand; and, least of all, will the France of the Fourth Republic become the junior partner of a revived Germany. The "good Europeans" who began with Gentz, Metternich and Talleyrand ended with Laval. Gentz saw the alternative; he regretted it, but believed that, like the victory of liberalism, it was inevitable. Europe failed to achieve her own union or freedom; therefore not union, but peace and a stable order of States had to be imposed from without. At the Congress of Westphalia all the Powers were European; at the Congress of Vienna the European Powers were three against two; now Europe has dwindled to a doubtful one among five.

Europe could not be united on a revolutionary programme; that was the lesson of the failure of Napoleon. Europe could not be united on a conservative programme; that was the lesson of the failure of Metternich and Gentz. Europe prized diversity; this had to be paid for by others. When Napoleon failed to cross the Channel, still more when the Grand Army perished in the snows of Russia, the fate of Europe passed from European hands: England and Russia became the trustees of European independence. In the nineteenth century the two trustees quarrelled over their private concerns; but, as 1914 and 1941 showed, they could not escape their trust. Now, as at all times since the Congress of Vienna, the security of Europe depends not on an impossible reconciliation between France and Germany, but on a lasting co-operation between England and Russia. The Congress system of Gentz's day was destroyed by Anglo-Russian disputes over Constantinople; the system of the United Nations would not survive a second Crimean war. To reconcile British and Russian interests in the Near East—this (as Metternich realized after Gentz's death) was the essential condition for European security. The passage of a century has only reinforced the need.

III

METTERNICH

MEN live after their own deaths in the minds of others. Samuel Butler thought that this was the only form of immortality. For most men it is a wasting asset. Memories fade; causes change. Who now cares what Gladstone said in 1868? Occasionally the historian acts as a resurrection-man. He discovers that some forgotten figure was the real saviour of his country or maker of empire. Our nineteenth-century Prime Ministers, for instance, are being pushed aside; and their fame is being usurped by civil servants, hitherto obscure. There is another, and more lasting, way to survival. The historical figure is turned into a symbol. The man becomes a myth; and, though his real deeds are forgotten, he is mobilized in defence of some cause which might have surprised him. The founders of the great religions have all enjoyed this fate. Millions of men repeat their names, while knowing nothing of the details of their lives. The carpenter's son of Galilee blesses the grandeurs of the Papacy; and the tyranny of the Politburo is carried out in the name of a crabbed German scholar.

Metternich knew this success, even in his lifetime. His name was the symbol of resistance to the revolution—abused by the radicals, praised, though more rarely, by conservatives. His fall in 1848 was the decisive sign that 'the springtime of peoples' had begun. Soon he was being treated as the great opponent of German unity, his immortality turned to ridicule by Treitschke, only his interminable 'five metaphors' remembered. Every textbook of history rejoiced that 'the system of Metternich' had been overthrown; and the most humble politician assumed that any future settlement would improve on the work of the Congress of Vienna. The peace-making of Versailles began the disillusionment. Metternich crept back into favour as the exponent of a less idealistic diplomacy. The Balance of Power seemed a more sensible and a more effective principle than the League of Nations. But Metternich had to wait for his full restoration until the present cold war of creeds. He has re-emerged as 'the rock of order', and every renegade liberal in America discovers an admiration for this desiccated aristocrat. Metternich is again to fight the Jacobins, but this time with the big battalions on his side. Nationalism is frowned on; and Western Union is to replace 'the mouldering edifice' of the Habsburg monarchy, which Metternich lamented that he had spent his life in propping up.

The new saint of conservatism is a long way from the Metternich of history. He was a very silly man. This is revealed even in the flattering portrait by Lawrence. Vain and complacent, with fatuous good looks, his first thought in a crisis was to see whether his skin-tight breeches fitted perfectly and the Order of the Golden Fleece was hanging rightly. Even his love-affairs—and he had many—were calculated for their political effect. He sought influence on Napoleon through the Queen of Naples and learnt the secrets of Russia from Countess Lieven. It must have been disturbing when he whispered political gossip in bed. He never made a clever remark. His thoughts, like those of most conservatives, were banal and obvious. 'Things must get worse before they get better'; 'after war Europe needs peace'; 'everyone has his allotted place in society'. Most men could do better than this when shaving. As he grew older, he grew more sententious. His deafness gave him an irresistible hold over his visitors. Bismarck wisely slept during his discourse and so won the old man's favour. There are those whom we would recall from the dead. Metternich is not among them. Even Mr. Viereck and Professor Morganthau would blench if he appeared on their doorstep, his empty sentences already phrased.

He was good at his job, though it was not so difficult a job as is often supposed. His job was diplomacy and, in particular, to maintain the greatness of the house of Habsburg. He was spared the greatest difficulty of the diplomat, which is to convince his own employer. The Emperor Francis gave Metternich a free run so long as Austria was kept out of war; and even the Austrian generals counted on being beaten. He liked to present himself in later life as the symbol of resistance. In reality he had been the greatest of appeasers. His first stroke was 'the Austrian marriage', by which he hoped to buy off Napoleon with an Austrian arch-duchess. Far from being the enemy of Napoleon, Metternich was the most anxious of allied statesmen to compromise with him. He hesitated to enter the last coalition; strove for an agreed peace; and regretted Napoleon's downfall. He justified his policy by fear of

Russia; it was pointless, he argued, to overthrow one tyrant of Europe if another took his place. The truth is that he wanted others to do the fighting for him. Besides, he supposed that a plump arch-duchess would turn Napoleon into a harmless, almost legitimate monarch and that the man who had grown great through the Revolution would now tame it. It made the delusion no less absurd that Napoleon sometimes shared it.

Metternich did not invent the Balance of Power, nor do much to develop it. The Great Powers of Europe existed without his assistance; and his only initiative at the Congress of Vienna was to project an unnecessary war over Poland—a war which others had too much sense to fight. In international affairs, too, he offered a series of platitudes. 'All I ask is a moral understanding between the five Great Powers. I ask that they take no important step, without a previous joint understanding.' Even the United Nations would work if Metternich's request were granted. But what if the Great Powers disagreed? Metternich offered only lamentations and reproaches. He abused Canning for putting British interests first; yet was ready to wreck his conservative partnership with Russia for the sake of Austrian interests in the Balkans. In the usual way of statesmen who rule over a decaying empire, he urged others to preserve the Austrian monarchy for their own good. He invented an Austrian 'mission' and assured his foreign visitors how unwillingly he had added Lombardy to the empire in 1815. It is, of course, rare for upholders of empire ever to admit that they get advantage or profit from it. And as Metternich went from one palace to another or pocketed the rewards which other sovereigns as well as his own showered upon him, the cares of office were no doubt the only thought in his mind.

He played some diplomatic problems competently, though Palmerston, his contemporary, did better with less fuss. The two shared the credit for a peaceful outcome to the eastern crisis of 1840. But ten years earlier Metternich might have muddled the Belgian alarm into a war, if it had not been for Palmerston's firm handling. Again, Metternich put years of wasted effort into attempts at intervening in the Spanish civil wars. His most original move in Austrian policy was to concentrate her strength on Italy. Though himself a German from the Rhineland, he encouraged Austria's withdrawal from Germany. He did not assert her supremacy in the German confederation nor even grudge Prussia her private score of the Zollverein. Yet he was too much a man of Western Europe to be content with the Balkans as compensation. For him Asia began at the road eastwards from Vienna. Italy alone seemed worthy to be the Habsburg prize. And Metternich taught the doctrine—quite erroneous, as it turned out—that the Habsburg monarchy could remain great only so long as it continued to dominate in Italy. All his diplomatic combinations centred on the Italian provinces. Yet he knew both that the Italians hated Austrian rule and that France would not tolerate it indefinitely.

This double threat was in itself an attraction to him. It was always his aim 'to fight the revolution on the field of international politics'. He had no faith in principles or ideas despite his theoretical posturing. Though he claimed to be a disciple of Burke, he doubted whether historical institutions would hold against radical ideas. In any case, there were no historical institutions in Central Europe except for the Hungarian parliament; and this Metternich never managed to control. The kings and emperors were almost as new as Napoleon, who had indeed created many of them. The Habsburgs had laid their hands on the historic states of Hungary and Bohemia; and Poland, the greatest historic state of all, had been eaten up by Metternich and his two conservative partners of the Holy Alliance. If tradition was useless, concession was dangerous. Metternich never wearied of explaining that moderate liberalism inevitably opened the door to extreme radicalism—a judgement repeatedly belied by events. Indeed, he argued in a perverse way that extreme radicalism, being less concealed, was somehow less alarming, even less destructive, than moderate reform.

His only answer to either liberalism or radicalism was, in fact, repression. If people were not allowed to think for themselves, they would be satisfied with material prosperity—and even this could be neglected. Since he had no genuine conservative ideas himself, he denied that radical ideas were genuine; and solemnly maintained that discontent everywhere was the result of 'a conspiracy'. When Confalonieri, the Italian patriot, was brought as a political prisoner to Vienna, Metternich wrangled with him for hours in the hope that 'the conspiracy' would at last be revealed. His view of radicalism was exactly that of Senator McCarthy. The good conservative must look under the bed every night. One day he will find a radical lurking there. A conspiracy needs a centre; and Metternich found it in Paris, as his present admirers find it in Moscow. How much easier to forget men's political grievances and to raise the cry of foreign war. But Metternich had more sense than those who now tread in his footsteps. Though he advocated a conservative crusade against France and 'the revolution', he proposed that it should be fought by others. Austria did her duty to civilization by existing; it was for others to keep her going. He said in old age: 'Error has never approached my spirit.' And certainly he never made the error of getting into the front line if he could avoid it. In this way at least he set an example to us all.

IV

1848

(1) *Year of Revolution*

"We are making together the sublimest of poems." Lamartine embodied the revolutions of 1848 in speech and in deed; and his grandiose phrase was echoed by every Radical in the revolutionary year. Heaven on earth seemed nearer in 1848 than at any other moment in modern history. Eighteen forty-eight was the link between the centuries: it carried to the highest point the eighteenth-century belief in the perfectibility of man, yet, all unexpectedly, launched the social and national conflicts which ravage Europe a century later. Socialism and Nationalism, as mass forces, were both the product of 1848. The revolutions determined the character of every country in Europe (except Belgium) from the Pyrenees to the frontiers of the Russian and Turkish empires; and these countries have since shown common characteristics not shared by England, Russia, the Balkans, or Scandinavia. Politically speaking, a "European" is an heir of 1848.

The moment of the revolution was determined by the financial crisis of 1846 and by bad harvests in 1846 and 1847. These caused food riots in the towns and sharpened the long-standing grievances of the peasants in Eastern Germany and in the Austrian Empire. Economic discontent gave force to revolts; only the moral upheaval turned these into a revolution. Eighteen forty-eight was the victory of the "ideologues," as Napoleon had contemptuously named them. Respect for traditional beliefs and forms of government had broken down; as a German poet wrote, "Monarchy is dead, though monarchs still live." Even the rulers had lost faith in themselves. The King of Prussia received the revolutionary poet Herwegh in order to bow "before a worthy opponent," and Metternich denounced "the rotten edifice" which it was his duty to uphold.

The revolutions repudiated "throne and altar"; equally they repudiated existing State frontiers and the treaty settlement of the Congress of Vienna. After forty years of peace and stability men were bored: they wished to translate into real life the poetry of Victor Hugo and the music of Berlioz. Most of the radical leaders were between thirty-five and forty years of age; they represented the generation which had caught only the echoes of the Napoleonic Empire and which wished to hear again through Europe the thunder of the guns —though this time on the barricades. The barricades, built in every city in Europe and often erected even when there was no fighting, were the symbol of 1848. The ideologues had evoked the masses for sixty years; in 1848 the masses at last took their call.

The ideas of 1848 were the ideas of the French Revolution, applied now without doubt or reserve. The men of 1789 had been concerned with freedom from arbitrary government and equality before the law; though they used democratic phrases they restricted "the people" to the property-owning middle class—even Robespierre only brought in the skilled artisan and petty shopkeeper. The men of 1848 had infinite faith in "the people," whom they identified with themselves; and every little radical club spoke for "the nation," as, say, the British Communist party speaks for the British "working class." The liberals, prizing the rights of 1789, saw these endangered by the intrusion of the masses and were thus driven on to the side of the counter-revolution; indeed, in most of Europe, the defeat of the revolution was achieved by liberals, to their own subsequent ruin. In the enmity between liberal and radical, too, 1848 created a political pattern peculiar to the continent of Europe.

Though the masses certainly broke on to the political stage, they did not fill the humble parts which had been allotted to them by the ideologues. The urban movements were revolts against hard conditions of life and work; caused not by the Industrial Revolution but by its absence. They were "Luddite" in character, seeking to destroy the new machines (especially seeking to destroy the railways which were being built by British capital and labour in western Europe). With the general increase of population, towns were growing; these, as yet, lacked the cheap goods of mass production which make urban life tolerable. The less industry, the more revolution. Belgium, the only industrialized country in Europe, escaped revolution; Italy, with no modern industry, had seven.

Marx, prophesying revolution for the rest of his life, was in fact foretelling the revolution of 1848 which he had experienced as a young man (prophets always foretell what has already happened); but he drew the wrong conclusion. Far from industrial development producing revolution, it was a protection against it; a century later the most advanced industrial countries are the least in danger from Communism. The urban masses of 1848 had no Socialist programme; they demanded "the right to work," the programme of Napoleon III and, subsequently, of Hitler. Their "social republic" was not Social Democracy; it was a longing for the days of mercantilism. Still, "the right to work" challenged "the rights of property," which had been the essential revolutionary condition for the middle class; it was the claim by the disinherited of the great revolution that they, too, had rights, and so announced the class struggle between capitalists and proletarians.

Social conflict broke the unity of "the people" within the nation; national conflicts broke the unity of "the people" throughout Europe. The French Revolution had preached nationalism; it meant by this only the right of existing nations to succeed to the inheritance of their kings. The revolution of 1848 aspired to destroy existing States and to create new ones in accordance with the national principle. This doctrine was destructive of existing monarchies; it menaced also the preponderance of France, the existing Great Power. The "historic nations," Italy, Hungary and Poland, announced their claims in 1848; they were overshadowed by Germany, where the revolutionary idea reached its highest point. The German movement was at once the most romantic and the most radical; and 1848 ushered in "the German century," which has left Europe torn in pieces.

The "historic nations" all had a past, a literature and an intellectual class; their appearance was expected. The surprise of 1848 was the appearance of the "unhistoric nations," the submerged Slav peoples of east-central Europe. Emancipation of the peasants brought to life nations without aristocrats or burghers—their only spokesmen the educated sons of peasants —and therefore at one bound most under the leadership of ideologues. The historic nations, challenging the traditional order of Europe, were themselves challenged by the unhistoric nations. Slovenes and Croats disputed the historic claims of national Italy; Slovenes, Croats, Serbs and Rumanians (not a Slav people, but with similar social conditions) repudiated Great Hungary; the Czechs questioned German predominance in Bohemia; the Poles fought in both camps—they resisted the claims of the Germans in Posnania, yet to the east their own "historic" claims were challenged by the Little Russians or Ukrainians. In the words of Professor Namier: "With 1848 starts the Great European War of every nation against its neighbours." Metternich's Europe, in spite of its dullness, lasted more than a generation; the Europe of Lamartine never came into existence.

The sovereignty of the people was the cardinal doctrine of 1848; all frontiers were to be redrawn and all political institutions remade in its name. Hence the great practical expression of 1848 was direct universal suffrage, practised for the first time: the people were not to be limited in their sovereignty, nor was the power of the people to be weakened by any intermediary. France set the example for the political events of the following hundred years. The sovereign people were offered the "ideologues"; they chose Louis Napoleon. Proudhon, a democrat without illusions, drew the lesson: "Universal suffrage is counter-revolution." This lesson was applied by Bismarck and, later, by Hitler and Mussolini. Hitler, incorporating the General Will of the German people, united Nationalism and Socialism and redrew the map of Europe according to the German principles of 1848. Like the German Radicals of 1848, Hitler ran against the rock of Slav resistance; and the Slav peoples were the residuary legatees of 1848.

(2) *The French Revolution*

February 24, 1848, was the last day of great France, the last day of the France which had overshadowed the rest of Europe and had called the tune in political ideas. It was the last time when France sneezed and the rest of Europe caught a cold; henceforth France caught colds from others, as in the recent malady of Vichy. In 1848 the radicals of all Europe still looked to Paris, as the Communists now look to Moscow. Paris was the mother of revolutions; but in 1848 her progeny got out of control. Though there had been previous outbreaks in Galicia and in Sicily the revolution in Paris gave the signal for the real storm, and the street fighting which overthrew Louis Philippe brought down, too, Metternich and the absolute monarchy in Prussia. Yet the revolutions which swept Europe did not remain under the spell of French ideas; still less did they restore French hegemony in Europe, as the French Radicals had expected. Instead the French began to realize that the victory of the national principle, which they had launched, far from restoring Napoleon's domination of Europe, would destroy French security and would bring France under the threatening shadow of a Germany more powerful than herself.

Once a revolution is successful the revolutionaries become conservative in their turn. This is the key to French history in the hundred and fifty years since the Great Revolution. In 1789 the rights of man were subversive of the existing order and had to be fought for; later they became the existing order and had to be defended, until to-day the adherents of the rights of man are the most conservative element in European politics. The transition from one attitude to the other took place in France between February and June, 1848; on both occasions the radicals fought—but on different sides of the barricades. The revolution of February 24 had no deep-seated cause; as Proudhon said, it was made "without an idea." The demand for an extension of the franchise, which was its excuse, could have been met without a revolution; indeed, Louis Philippe had already granted it before his fall. But peaceful reform would have seemed a drab outcome, unworthy of the traditions of revolutionary France. The revolution was, in fact, its own object; the emotional experience provided the satisfaction of a religious conversion. A Radical journalist expressed this: "My hopes are in an act of providence, in a religious transformation to regenerate society." The revolutionaries repeated the attitudes of 1789, as in 1939 the French tried, in vain, to recapture the inspiration of 1914. Tocqueville, sitting in the Chamber when it was invaded by the mob, was puzzled that he felt no fear; suddenly he realized that he was watching men striking postures which they had seen in an old print, not a spontaneous revolution—it is difficult to be frightened of a musket which was loaded sixty years before and has become a theatrical prop.

The radicals established a Provisional Government; this was hard put to it to find a programme. Lamartine describes the members of the Provisional Government sitting round and racking their heads in vain for some great symbolical act which should make the revolution worth while. He solved the problem by proposing the abolition of the death penalty; within four months it was restored for political offences and applied wholesale to those who had won the battle of February for the Provisional Government. Though the radicals proclaimed the sovereignty of the people, they feared it in practice. They had no agrarian programme with which to win the allegiance of the peasants, who made up the majority of the population. The revolution of 1789 gave the peasants their land, free of feudal duties; the revolution of 1848 compelled the peasants to pay their debts and increased the taxation on land. For the Radicals of 1848 tried to combine revolution and a stable currency; not surprisingly, the peasants preferred Louis Napoleon, distinguished by his debts as well as by his great name. The radicals knew that universal suffrage would go against them; yet they insisted on perishing from their own principles. Lamartine declared: "The people must be left free to make mistakes." This mistake was the Second Empire.

Before 1848 the radicals had thought little of internal affairs. Their greatest grievance had been against the humiliation of the Congress of Vienna, and they expected to escape from their problems by renewing the glories of revolutionary war. Lamartine reserved his highest rhetoric for the circular dispatch in which he declared that France no longer recognized the treaties of 1815. Still, though France wished to see these treaties disappear, she would not herself make the effort to destroy them. Besides, on reflection it was not in the interests of France to replace the weak States across the Alps and the Rhine by a united Italy and a united Germany; and—in spite of past lip-service to the idea—even Radical Frenchmen saw the defeat of Italian and German nationalism with some relief. The army originally prepared to go to the assistance of revolutionary Italy went off in 1849 to restore the Pope. There could be no such practical arguments against aiding Poland, and war for Poland was the slogan with which the extreme radicals, Blanqui and Barbès, attempted to overthrow the Provisional Government on May 15. In 1848, as in 1939, France could aid Poland only by resuming the mastery of Europe which Napoleon had won and then lost; the task was already beyond her. Hence the defeat of Blanqui and his associates marked the turning-point in France's position in the world, as well as being the crisis of the revolution.

Still, behind the revolutionary echoes a true revolution existed. This was the movement of the town working-classes, especially in Paris. The Great Revolution had found no place for them; rather it had established an alliance of peasants and *bourgeoisie* against them. Now to the traditional rights of man they claimed to add "the right to work." This demand sprang from handicraft workers, threatened by the machine, not from factory workers, enslaved to it. In England at the same time the workers, more mature, were demanding the right to work less. "The right to work" was a demand for recognition rather than an economic programme; it was rejected by all those who had profited by the Great Revolution. The result was the June Days, the most formidable slave-war of modern times. The workers of Paris fought without leaders and without hope against a united front of nobles, middle class and peasants. Reactionaries and radicals, estranged since the execution of Louis XVI, were reconciled over the bodies of the Parisian workers. The June Days showed that radicalism would not satisfy the working-class; they became, and remained, an alien body in the French Republic. The radicals of 1848 had tried to be a "third force"; instead the June Days drove France into the arms of Napoleon. A hundred years later, the shadow of the June Days, and of its sequel, still lies across French political life.

(3) *Vienna and Berlin*

On March 13, 1848, revolution reached Vienna: Metternich was driven from power after thirty-nine years of office. The Vienna revolution was the central event of 1848, as significant as the fall of the Bastille in 1789. The Bastille was an antiquated fortress, virtually without a garrison; Metternich a feeble old man without supporters. Yet both symbolized the old order and brought it down with them. Monarchical authority over "subjects" lost its divine sanction on July 14, 1789; dynastic rights over peoples lost its hold on March 13, 1848. The Rights of Man triumphed in the streets of Paris; the rights of nations in the streets of Vienna. It was the end of government based on tradition. Henceforth peoples could be ruled only by consent—or by force. European history of the following hundred years recounts the oscillations between these two methods.

Though the Habsburg dynasty maintained a precarious existence in 1848 (and indeed for another seventy years) the fall of Metternich ended its independent position. Previously it had stood above the peoples; thereafter it manœuvred between them. The Vienna revolution was the cardinal date in the history of both national Hungary and national Italy; it was a victory for Kossuth and Mazzini. National Italy sought only separation from Central Europe (a separation never fully achieved from the days of the Triple Alliance to the Axis or the present). National Hungary hoped to remain a great State without the Habsburgs, or rather to substitute the Magyar landowners for the dynasty as the ruling authority in Central Europe. This aim was subsequently realized, though in association with the dynasty, in the period of

Dualism (1867–1918); in the end it brought "thousand-year-old" Hungary to ruin.

Once the dynasty lost its traditional appeal, Central Europe needed some other principle of association. The Slav peoples (who were in the majority) would not accept German and Magyar hegemony which was offered them as an alternative. Against this they raised the demand for their own national freedom and thus prepared the way for the national States of 1918. Still, they wished also for association; and the few far-sighted Habsburg ministers, after Metternich's fall, saw that the Empire could be saved only by invoking the peasant masses against the disruptive Liberalism and Nationalism of the middle classes. This was the significance of the emancipation of the peasants on September 7, 1848, the enduring achievement of the Austrian revolution. Aristocrats and liberals alike accused the Habsburg ministers of "Communism." A century later the same programme is being operated, though by the heirs of the Romanovs, not of the Habsburgs.

Still, the Vienna revolution found its greatest immediate impact in Germany. National Germany, too, was born in the streets of Vienna. If Hungary and Italy were to shake off the Habsburgs the remaining Austrian dominions could also follow the national principle: the way seemed open for Greater Germany. This faced the Hohenzollerns, the only other real power in Germany, with a problem of existence. If they resisted German nationalism they would be swept aside; if they went with it they would be submerged. Frederick William IV, astute though neurotic, avoided the dilemma and, with unconscious genius, stumbled on the programme of Little Germany. The revolution of March 18, 1848, in Berlin, though a victory for liberalism, did not break Hohenzollern power; the Army remained confident and intact. Frederick William IV granted a Constitution with a semblance of goodwill; this was his bid for German leadership. He announced: "Prussia merges into Germany." The phrase was fraudulent. Prussia continued to exist with an independent strength; the German liberals were invited to accept Berlin as the capital of Germany, solely in virtue of Frederick

William's word. The revolutions in Vienna and Berlin offered to Germany alternative solutions. The Vienna revolution aspired to a Greater Germany, based on radical violence, which would embrace all Germans and extend German supremacy throughout south-eastern Europe. The Berlin revolution was the first announcement of a more limited Germany, based on an alliance of moderate liberalism and Prussian military strength, and which would repudiate the German inheritance in the south-east. Berlin anticipated Bismarck, and Vienna Hitler.

In 1848 neither programme won unreserved acceptance. National Germany rejected both Vienna and Berlin, the two seats of power; it looked to Frankfurt, symbol of unification by consent. The greatest event in the history of German liberalism was the meeting of the National Assembly at Frankfurt on May 18, 1848. The Frankfurt Parliament hoped to give Germany freedom and unity; but above these it rated power (Macht). When German claims were challenged in Bohemia and in Posen, German liberals forgot the Rights of Man and invoked the right of the stronger; they expected the Austrian and Prussian armies to provide the strength which they themselves did not possess. They applauded the Habsburg victory in Prague over the Czechs and sought to use Prussian power against the Poles. In November the Frankfurt liberals even welcomed the victory of Frederick William IV over the Prussian Parliament, which they regarded as an impudent rival.

These victories did not help liberal Germany; it became the next victim of the power which it worshipped. In April, 1849, delegates from Frankfurt went humbly to Berlin to offer the Imperial Crown to Frederick William IV: liberal Germany was willing to merge into Prussia. The offer was rejected by Frederick William IV, and the Frankfurt Parliament was soon after dispersed by Prussian soldiers. Nevertheless Bismarck took up the offer, on terms still more favourable to Prussia, twenty years later.

Two great negatives were the legacy of the German revolutions of 1848. Dynastic power could not survive unless it took on a national colouring; on the other hand the Germans could not maintain the hegemony over Poles and Czechs on which the liberals most of all insisted unless they compromised with the possessors of power. This compromise is still sought by the Germans a century later; equally the foreign Powers who have replaced the dynasties compete for the favour of German nationalism.

March 13 will not be celebrated this year in Germany; it is the symbol of Greater Germany and so of Hitler's vanished Empire. The Russians have decreed March 18 as Germany's "day of freedom": like Frederick William IV they hope to pass off a spurious revolution as the real thing and, succeeding the Hohenzollerns as rulers in Berlin, announce that Prussia merges into Germany. As in the days of Bismarck, Little Germany is the best outcome for the Russians—a protection at once against Greater German power and against the West. The Western Powers follow in the footsteps of the Liberals of 1848 to Frankfurt; they, too, will find themselves embarrassed by frontier disputes with Poland and by the agitation of Germans from Bohemia. Disappointment awaits those who seek national Germany at Frankfurt; as in 1848, Frankfurt is the symbol of the Germany of the idea, peaceful, liberal, contented—and non-existent.

(4) *The Slav Congress*

The Slav Congress which met in Prague on June 2, 1848, was the least expected event in the year of revolutions. The Slav peoples of Central Europe had not been allowed for in radical calculations. Engels wrote of the Czechs and Croats (he was unaware even of the existence of the Slovaks): "The natural and inevitable fate of these dying nations was to allow the process of dissolution and absorption by their stronger neighbours [Germany and Hungary] to complete itself." Exception was made only for the Poles, as an historic nation, not as Slavs; the German radicals proposed to push Poland against Russia and then to jettison her later (the reverse of Russia's Polish policy a century later). Since Bohemia had been included in the Holy Roman Empire, it was assumed that it would become part of the new national Germany, and distinguished Bohemians were invited to join the preliminary meetings at Frankfurt. Palacky, the first historian of Bohemia and the recreator of Czech national consciousness, refused the invitation; he repudiated allegiance to Germany—"I am a Bohemian of Slav race"—and looked instead to the Habsburg dynasty as the protector of the Slav peoples from German tyranny. "If the Austrian Empire did not exist, it would have to be created in the interest of Europe and of humanity." This famous sentence launched the programme of Austro-slavism, the idea of maintaining a modest national existence under the wing of the most clerical and traditional dynasty in Europe.

In 1848 the dynasty seemed too shaken to act as the sole bond of union between different peoples, and those who feared incorporation in Greater Germany sought some more popular alternative. They thought to have found it in their Slav race. This was more than crude racialism: it assumed that all peoples with a Slav language had a common cultural background. In reality most Slav peoples outside Russia had been submerged by the culture of their conquerors, German, Hungarian, or even Turkish; hence the importance of ethnography in the Slav movement—the evidence for a common Slav "folk" had to be found in the designs on peasant costume or pottery. The Slav Congress was intended as a gesture against the German National Assembly at Frankfurt. This threatened directly only the Czechs and the Slovenes —another reason for draping Slav "folkdom" round the practical political issue. The Slavs of Hungary (Croats, Serbs and Slovaks) were indifferent to the German menace; the Czechs wished to avoid a conflict with Hungary, yet would not repudiate the Slovaks, who alone could swell their numbers.

The real stumbling-block for a common Slav policy came from the Poles. The Poles of Galicia were indisputably Slavs and indisputably Habsburg subjects; yet Russia was their only enemy, and they welcomed both Greater Germany and Great Hungary. The Poles, who were threatened by the Germans, were under Prussian rule in Posnania. To exclude them would weaken the struggle against Frankfurt decisively;

to include them would trespass beyond the frontiers of the Habsburg monarchy and so make nonsense of Austroslavism. In fact, the Slav Congress had stumbled on the Polish problem. The Poles of the Austrian Empire would not work with the Czechs nor against the Germans; the Poles of Posnania would work against the Germans, but equally emphatically would not work with Russia. The Czechs insisted that Poles from outside the Austrian Empire should attend the Congress only as guests; the Poles would not recognize the frontiers of the Polish partitions, and when the Polish section of the Congress met it made the Poles from Posnania full members, one of them, indeed, becoming its chairman.

This intrusion of non-Austrian Slavs had a further embarrassing consequence. No one minded the presence of Serbs from Turkey: the solidarity of the "master nations" did not yet extend to the Turks. But if the Slav Congress was to include all Slavs it was impossible to exclude the greatest branch of the Slav race, and the revolutionary Bakunin imposed himself upon the congress as the solitary, self-appointed representative of the Russian people. Bakunin had no patience with the cautious Austroslavism of Palacky; he demanded both the destruction of the Habsburg Empire and revolution in Russia. His goal was a federation of free peoples, based on the natural democracy of the Slav peasants. Like later versions of Pan-Slavism, Bakunin's vision rested on the dogma of virtues innate in Slav peoples which would save them from the failings of others.

Pan-Slavism evoked no response from the Slav Congress; indeed, Pan-Slavism had sense only as a translation into racial mysticism of the Byzantine and Orthodox heritage shared by some Slav peoples, and almost all those present at Prague were Western and Roman Catholic. The Slav Congress produced two contradictory programmes. The Poles drafted a manifesto to the Peoples of Europe which recognized the existence only of the "historic nations"—Poland, Germany, Hungary and Turkey—and politely invited these to treat their minorities better. The Czechs drafted an address to the Austrian Emperor which asked for the remodelling of the Austrian Empire into a federation based on national units.

Perhaps the most concrete effect of the Congress was its division into three sections—Polish-Ukrainian, Czechoslovak and South Slav—for these anticipated the "national amalgamations" which served as the basis for pseudo-national States (Poland, Czechoslovakia and Yugoslavia) in 1918.

All these programmes received only preliminary statement. The Congress met for the last time on June 12. Then fighting broke out between the Prague radicals, both Czech and German, and the Imperial forces; and on the suppression of the rebellion the Congress was dissolved. In its ten days of activity it had stated all the solutions for the problem of Central Europe which have been attempted from then until now. The Czechs followed Austroslavism for half a century after 1848; its essential condition, a federation of free nationalities, was granted by the Habsburg Emperor only on October 16, 1918, when the Empire was already in ruins. The last echo of Austroslavism was heard in the Slovakia of Tiso and the Croatia of Pavelic. The Poles tried to act as the partners of Greater Germany and Great Hungary in the days of Colonel Beck, and thought that they had reached their aim when they established a common frontier with Hungary in March 1939—six months before their destruction. Bakunin's first demand was fulfilled with the dissolution of the Habsburg monarchy in 1918; failing the establishment of democracy in Russia, the Slavs had to look for support from the Western democracies and suffered ineffaceable disappointment at the time of Munich. Now fear of Germany makes them pretend that Bakunin's second condition has been fulfilled, and the "democracies of the new type" rest on the double pretence of Russian democracy and Slav solidarity.

V

1848: OPENING OF AN ERA

ROBERT OWEN, on a visit to Paris, described his economic system as "the railway which will take mankind to universal happiness." His phrase crystallized the spirit of the year of revolutions. Movement, and a conviction that Utopia could be reached, were the essence of 1848: underlying these was a faith in the limitless goodness of human nature. The revolutionary cry, "All change!" sounded across Europe. Hope lit the dawn of a new Europe; and mankind clambered into the trains of political and social upheaval, all of which claimed to be directed to the same terminus—the Kingdom of Heaven on Earth. New faiths, new nations, new classes announced their arrival; each was the confident possessor of an exclusive truth. Before 1848 the rights of individuals and of States were a matter of history and of settled law; the revolutions substituted the rule of abstract principle. Louis Phillipe said bitterly of the revolution of 1830 which brought him to the throne: "What perished in France in 1830 was not respect for a dynasty, but respect for anything." This was demonstrated anew in France in 1848 and, for the first time, was demonstrated throughout Europe as well. Reason took the place of respect; and self-interest the place of tradition.

Movement was both the cause of the revolutions and their outcome: the revolutions threw down established landmarks that were already ruinous. In the preceding fifty years tumultuous development had taken the place of imperceptible change. There was an unprecedented growth of population, an unprecedented advance in the methods of industry and of transport, and an unprecedented novelty in the world of ideas; the three together composed the background to the revolutions. The old order had assumed stable populations; these ensured stability between classes and stability between States. For half a century before 1848 the increase of population had been gathering strength, and this contributed more than anything else to the illusion of progress. The increase was less in France than elsewhere in Europe; and the wise student of population figures might already guess that France, hitherto the greatest European Power and the most revolutionary nation, would soon become the most conservative and the least great of the Powers. The universal growth of population had profound consequences. Where the peasant was already free, as in western Germany, the surplus was being pushed into the towns. In the Austrian Empire the peasants could no longer tolerate the burden of feudal dues and of feudal subordination; moreover, with the increasing demand for food, the great landowners could no longer operate their estates by the traditional methods. Both lords and peasants turned against the old order of settled obligations; both demanded freedom of movement and the rule of the market. Almost the first act of the liberal parliament in Hungary was to abolish the old agrarian social order; and the Austrian Constituent Assembly followed suit (its only effective act) on September 7. The destinies of fifty million people were affected. The more prosperous peasants got the chance of survival; the poorer peasants lost their last traditional protection and were the victims both of the richer peasants and of the capitalistic great estates. The way was clear for the emigration to the towns and overseas which characterized the second half of the century. It was no accident that England and Russia, the only countries of Europe to escape the revolutions, had already found the way of emigration before 1848: the road to Siberia had been open since the beginning of the century, and the emigrant-steamers took the life out of Chartism when they began to sail from Liverpool in 1844. The rest of Europe had lacked the technical and social conditions for mass emigration: peasant emancipation came in 1848, and railways followed. These provided a safety valve which postponed further European explosions until the twentieth century. Modern industrial America, as well as modern industrial Europe, would have been impossible without the revolutions of 1848.

The idea of 1848 spread later to Russia; and the Russian

revolutions of the twentieth century were in the true spirit of 1848. In fact, Russia, missing the disillusionment which followed the failure of 1848, alone retained faith in the revolutionary course. America was already democratic, and therefore for her, though there was no need for revolution, there was no need for disillusionment either. For a generation after 1848, and even longer, America offered to the peoples of Europe the economic and political prizes which failure had denied them in Europe. Still, 1848 left no tradition in either Russia or America. Eighteen forty-nine has some meaning in the history of both countries. For Russia it brought a victorious repression of revolution in Hungary; for America it marked the discovery of gold in California. To the present day, the one Great Power offers Europe repression, the other material wealth. Neither can offer the liberty of spirit which was the true aim of 1848.

The staggering growth of towns throughout Europe was a consequence of the revolutions. Still, even before 1848, the swelling towns amazed and alarmed contemporaries; and their isolation—urban islands in a rural continent—emphasized their revolutionary character. The conscious revolutions of 1848 were all exclusively urban. "The German revolution" is a misleading generalization for the Berlin revolution and the Vienna revolution; "the Italian revolution" still more misleading as a title for the revolutions in Venice, Milan, Florence, Rome, Naples and many more. The contrast was sharpest in France. The great revolution of 1789 had been the movement of a people, the revolution of 1848 was a movement of Paris against the rest of the nation. Isolated in place, the revolutions were equally insular in idea: they had no agrarian programme and offered the peasants—troglodytes, in Marx's phrase—nothing but extinction. For the first time news of a revolution passed from one town to another by telegraph; it no longer needed to filter through, and so to affect, the countryside. The revolutionaries travelled by train from one revolution to the next; they had neither eyes nor thoughts for the country through which they passed. The revolutionaries equated revolutions with street-fighting. Their occasional forays into the countryside—from Hecker's raid on Baden in April 1848 to Garibaldi's march across Italy in July 1849—were the organized hikes of town dwellers.

Even the largest towns lacked industrial development. Labour had arrived before capital was ready for it. Only Belgium had experienced an industrial revolution; and therefore, despite its urban character, enjoyed an unique freedom from revolutionary danger. The revolutions elsewhere were not revolts against the machine; they were demands to be employed by it. The slogan of "the right to work" was a symbol of immaturity; an industrial proletariat would have demanded the right to work less—as indeed the English working-class had already done with success in 1847. "The right to work" was a protest as much against social inequality as against harsh living condition. Nevertheless, by formulating this protest in economic terms, it launched the idea that liberty and political equality were negligible, or indeed valueless, in comparison with food and clothing. This idea was not intended by the social revolutionaries of 1848, who took up economic grievances principally in order to add greater force to their political demands. All the same the damage had been done. Continental Socialism, which had its origins in 1848, wrote off political democracy as *bourgeois* and accepted the doctrine that violence and intolerance were a small price to pay for social change. Class war took the place of the struggle for political liberty, and the Rights of Man were a casualty of "the right to work."

The announcement of an economic programme was certainly the startling novelty of 1848; nevertheless the revolutions were not simply the product of economic circumstances. These determined the moment of revolution, not that it should occur. The economic upheaval and the upheaval in men's minds were two aspects of the same process. Certainly the age of coal and iron enforced daring political schemes and made them possible; but equally it needed a daring mind to think of the railway and the blast furnace. The great towns of modern Europe could not have been maintained without railways, steam power and a revolution in agriculture; but the movement to the towns depended just as much on the spread of new ideas which prised men away from their traditional beliefs and traditional surroundings. The railways found people ready to move; otherwise they would have run empty. Reason was the great dissolvent force. This made men dissatisfied with their traditional homes and with their traditional place in society just as much as with the traditional methods of production. The radicals of 1848 were the heirs of eighteenth-century enlightenment: sublimely confident in human nature (except that of their fellow revolutionaries), they believed that their only task was to shake off the hold of established beliefs and established institutions. Their common programme was "to strangle the last king with the bowels of the last priest." The natural goodness of man would do the rest.

The old order, thus dramatically threatened, claimed to depend on habit, on history and on established rights. No historical conflict is, in fact, fought on these easy terms. The old order was itself more rational and artificial—just as the revolutionaries were more traditional—than either side liked to admit. Revolutionary ideas had affected the upper classes before they spread to the masses; and the impact of the great French revolution had long shaken the foundations of the European system. Men were argued into conservatism as they were argued into revolution. The kings who were threatened by the movements of 1848 had less than a century of possession behind them, and many more were the creations of Napoleon. Even the house of Habsburg, the only genuine historic dynasty, had acquired a new title and new territories a generation previously and had knocked all life out of historic institutions everywhere in its dominions except in Hungary —and there from lack of strength, not of will. The "old aristocracy" was a creation of the eighteenth, or occasionally of the seventeenth century. Most of all the territorial settlement of the Congress of Vienna was as artificial as the Empire of Napoleon which it replaced. The peace which followed the Napoleonic wars sprang from exhaustion, not from belief or from content; and the society which perished in 1848 had no moral justification other than the desire of the possessing classes to enjoy their privileges.

The kings, aristocrats and states of the Vienna system had not even given themselves the trouble of being born; they had been conjured up ready-made by conservative theorists. Thus Metternich, to give historic character to the Austrian Empire (which had acquired legal existence only in 1804), proposed to invent for the Emperor a traditional ceremony of coronation. Metternich, symbol and chief exponent of Conservatism, claimed to be building a dam against revolution. In reality, his effort to set up a universal "system" of political ideas and institutions was typical of an eighteenth-century doctrinaire. He approached politics in the spirit of Robespierre: the only difference was in his employer. The dissolvent of reason could have been resisted only by communities with a living history; few such existed on the continent of Europe, and these few (Switzerland, Hungary and perhaps the Low Countries) did not accord with Metternich's conservatism. As a result, the system of Metternich was not overthrown in 1848; it collapsed. This collapse astonished contemporaries, other than Metternich himself: he had always appreciated the artificiality of his own system and had never felt the faith which he demanded in others.

In 1848 Europe broke consciously with its past. This was the indelible achievement of the year of revolutions. Yet more than destruction was intended. Bakunin, most extreme representative of the spirit of revolution, once declared that if his plans succeeded he would at once begin to pull down again everything he had ever made; this did not take the zest from a lifetime of planning. The radicals of all schools were as convinced as Metternich of the need for belief; and, unlike Metternich, themselves believed in the systems which they expounded. Their systems, too, were universal and dogmatic. All assumed that reason was adequate as the sole guide in human affairs; and they assumed also that there was no limit to what reason could do. The revolutionaries differed as to the means by which the human race might be made perfect; none disputed that the goal would be attained. The radical systems provided new Absolutes for old and gave final answers in politics, in society and in international affairs. The sovereignty of the people overthrew the sovereignty of kings; nations took the place of states; and intellect ousted heredity as the source of authority.

Though the sovereignty of the people had already served as inspiration to the French revolution of 1789, its operation had been restricted. The distinguishing mark of 1789 had been the confidence that universal principles could be limited in their application and a revolution arrested in its course. This expectation was not proved false until 1848. When all hereditary rights were repudiated, the right of private property had remained inviolate and was indeed reinforced; and the dogma of the sovereignty of the people was used to justify the franchise of the property-owning middle class. In 1848 the term of this compromise expired; and the *bourgeoisie*, once the leaders of revolution, became the symbol of conservatism. Almost the first act of the victorious revolution in France was to abolish the property qualification and to proclaim universal suffrage. This became everywhere the most concrete expression of the revolutionary programme. Only Hungary, which combined—or perhaps stifled—revolutionary principle with historic institutions, held out against universal suffrage until the twentieth century. The events of 1848 challenged also the economic privilege of the owners of property. The June Days in Paris gave dramatic announcement of the arrival of a new revolutionary class, "the proletariat." The June rising was not fought to promote any practical economic change; it was a social war, a slave revolt, and its repudiation of the moral superiority of the *bourgeoisie* could not be wiped out by all the executions and deportations which followed defeat. Before the June Days private property had been regarded as essential for liberty; after the June Days it became the symbol of oppression, and the capitalist took the place of priest and noble as the object of democratic hostility. Henceforth the *bourgeoisie* was morally on the defensive, ashamed and anxious. This was true not only of the French *bourgeoisie*, who had genuinely experienced the "social peril." The alarm of the June Days spread across Europe; indeed, apprehension increased as the reality of danger became more remote. The middle classes outside France abandoned the revolutionary cause almost before they had taken it up and sought for allies against a proletariat which was still imaginary. Thus, the October Revolution in Vienna, though it had a programme with no social implications, sent the German-Austrian middle classes over to the side of absolutism; and within a few years of 1848 German liberalism came to regard universal suffrage as its mortal enemy. The French *bourgeoisie* had pride enough to remain radical though they ceased to be revolutionary and adhered to the sovereignty of the people in the sense that they took into partnership the French peasants who had saved them in the June Days. Though universal suffrage, the work of the revolution of 1848, became everywhere a mainstay of conservatism, in France it sustained at least the Third Republic and later, in the Dreyfus case, upheld the Rights of Man. In Germany, however, it was the instrument of Bismarck and in Austria it became in 1907 the last prop of the Empire of Francis Joseph.

In the world of nations, too, the revolutions of 1848 ended the compromise which had been the outcome of the revolution of 1789. The French revolutionaries had launched the national principle; they supposed that this would operate to the sole advantage of France and that when all else of the old order was destroyed the predominance of France would remain unchallenged. France liberated other nations as the French *bourgeoisie* liberated the French people: freed from their hereditary rulers, they were expected to welcome French leadership instead. The Empire of Napoleon expressed the French version of the national principle: German, Italian, Polish and even South Slav nationalism were evoked as auxiliary weapons for the French cause. France was the only one who knew how to wield the national appeal, and remained the greatest single power in Europe even after the fall of Napoleon; the other Great Powers of the Continent were states, not nations, and therefore without the strength of popular enthusiasm. Thus the French nation claimed the cultural and political heritage of Louis XIV, despite the guillotining of Louis XVI and the renewed expulsion of the Bourbons in July 1830. This cultural headship was recognized for the last time at the beginning of 1848, when the other nations of Europe waited for the February Revolution in Paris before starting their own. Thereafter it was no longer enough to have taken the trouble to be born French. The laws of inheritance were repudiated between nations as much as between individuals. The lesson was not lost on the French themselves; henceforth the French nation was as much imperilled as, say, the dynasty of Habsburg by European upheavals, and France—previously the promoter of change—became the principal advocate of conservatism and of the *status quo*.

In 1848 every nation followed the example set by the French in 1789. Each claimed to be perfect: each, therefore, was entitled to lay down its own limits or, if it preferred, to recognize none. Moreover, each nation asserted a purity and greatness of character which made it an example to Europe and justified its bringing other less noble people under its own rule. Thus, Poland had long announced herself as "the Christ among the nations," and her liberation was regarded as the first object of the revolutionary cause; this liberation did not, however, extend to the Ukrainians under Polish rule. Similarly Mazzini, despite his denunciations of French arrogance, set up Italy as "God's word in the midst of the nations." Rome was to be the capital of a new federation of nations, all duly humble, which were to be cut and shaped to suit Italy's convenience. Kossuth, too, insisted on the unique civilization and political gifts of the Magyars. Though partly Slovak by birth, he denied the existence of a Slovak nation, and, since he could not deny the existence of the Serbs, proposed to root them out with the sword.

Magyar exclusiveness was relatively harmless, except to the subject nations of Hungary. The will to dominate was a more dangerous matter when it was taken up by the Germans, already the most numerous nationality in Europe. The revolutions of 1848 discovered "the German mission." This mission was simple: it was, simply, to be German. Europe was corrupt —French sophistication, English materialism, outworn institutions were all to be redeemed by the irruption of the clear-eyed, healthy German barbarian:

Und es soll am Deutschen Wesen
Noch einmal die Welt genesen.

A unique character was found in the German spirit (*Deutscher Geist*), and for that matter even in German rivers and trees—the one wetter and the other more arboreal than any others. Other nations based their claims on superiority of culture, as in the case of France or Italy, or at any rate on superiority of class—as Polish and Magyar nationalism sprang from their landed nobility. German nationalism was the first to depend solely on language: the future Germany was to extend wherever German was spoken. The *Volksdeutsche* were an invention of 1848. Since Germany had no "natural frontiers"—or none that gave such an easy excuse for expansion as the Rhine to France or the Alps to Italy—national Germany used a simpler argument and claimed whatever was necessary to her existence. Thus Bohemia, despite its Czech majority, could, according to Engels, "only exist henceforth as a part of Germany"; and the German liberal spokesman at Frankfurt said of western Poland: "Our right is that of the stronger, the right of conquest." This phrase supplied the basic theme of German history, until it turned against Germany a century later.

Resistance to German claims was not delayed until the twentieth century; it was the motive of the Slav Congress which met at Prague on June 2, 1848. The Slav peoples of eastern Europe were individually too small to hold out against German pressure; therefore, improving on the German model which had made language the basis of nationality, they tried to find a bond of alliance in ethnography and philology. The Slav Congress had practical motives of defence against German nationalism and had no time to trouble about the virtues of the Slav character. Still, even at Prague, Bakunin, one of the inventors of Slav solidarity, found in the Slavs "an amazing freshness and incomparably more natural intelligence and energy than in the Germans"; and he expected them "to renew the decadent Western world." The Slavs of the Austrian and Turkish Empires had enough to do renewing themselves and thereafter quarrelling with each other. The only contribution Russia made to the Western world in 1848–49 was to crush the revolution in Hungary. But the spirit of radicalism was not permanently arrested at the Russian frontier; and Pan-Slavism, which evoked little response outside Russia, became the delayed gift of 1848 to the Russian intellectuals. In the twentieth century they escaped from this ethnic intolerance only with the aid of class intolerance, which was the other legacy of 1848 to mankind.

The revolutions of 1848 dispelled the Utopian dreams of the eighteenth-century rationalists. These had supposed that mankind would attain universal happiness if traditional beliefs were abandoned and traditional authorities overthrown. The experiences after 1789 did not destroy this idea. Social concord accompanied the rule of the *bourgeoisie*, and a true international order was established with the Empire of Napoleon; it could plausibly be argued that achievement fell short of the ideal only because success was incomplete. Had the tricolour really "toured the world," universal happiness could have been expected to follow. In 1848 no bounds were drawn against revolutionary victory: no European country, except Belgium, escaped, and the established system lost its traditional authority for ever. The outcome was conflict, not concord. The June Days announced class war; the record of the German, Italian and Hungarian revolutions announced war between nations. Peaceful agreement and government by consent are possible only on the basis of ideas common to all parties; and these ideas must spring from habit and from history. Once reason is introduced, every man, every class, every nation becomes a law unto itself; and the only right which reason understands is the right of the stronger. Reason formulates universal principles and is therefore intolerant: there can be only one rational society, one rational nation, ultimately one rational man. Decision between rival reasons can be made only by force. This lesson was drawn by the greatest political genius who observed the events of 1848: "The great questions of our day will not be settled by resolutions and majority votes—that was the mistake of the men of 1848 and 1849—but by blood and iron." After 1848, the idea that disputes between classes could be settled by compromise or that discussion was an effective means of international relations was held only in England and America, the two countries which escaped the revolutions.

The liberals, the moderate men, shirked the problem of authority; it was faced by the radicals. They found a substitute for tradition in "the religion of humanity," just as their nationalism took the place of the decayed loyalty to kings. Above all, they found a substitute for the hereditary governing class in themselves. "The aristocracy of intellect" had a limitless confidence in its right to govern; for it spoke "in the name of the people." The radical leaders nominated themselves to this post: none of the great revolutionaries—not Marx nor Engels, Bakunin nor Blanqui—ever secured election by a democratic constituency, and, for the matter of that, none of them was sure of a majority even among the circle of his close associates. The greatest radical effort in France was the demonstration of March 16, which demanded that elections to the Constituent Assembly be postponed until the people were fit to exercise the franchise, that is, until they were willing to vote for the Radical leaders. Blanqui, when asked how long the postponement should be, answered: "For some months, or perhaps years." By democracy the men of 1848 did not mean the rule of the majority; they meant rather the rule of the discontented, a reversal of the previous order of society. The essence of 1848 was belief in movement; therefore only those elements of the population who desired change were democratic. The theoretical justification for this outlook was provided by Marx; it was his great contribution to history. Marx found the motive force of history in economic change; and this force was now impelling mankind from capitalism to socialism. Since movement and democracy were synonymous, only those who desired socialism were "the people." Marx could thus eliminate the peasants from his calculations, though they made up the great majority everywhere in Europe; and democracy could be turned into "the dictatorship of the proletariat." Marx was a man of the Enlightenment. He held that every man would recognize his own interest and follow it; therefore every proletarian would be a socialist. The proposition could be more usefully reversed: anyone who was not a socialist was not a proletarian. But the dictatorship was not really to be exercised even by those working men who accepted the theories of the learned Dr. Marx. The workers were to be led by the communists, "everywhere the most resolute and progressive element of the working class." Since the communists in 1848 consisted of Marx and Engels, this was a satisfactory conclusion—and has proved a satisfactory conclusion for communists ever since. The radical theorists were led inevitably from belief in the people to belief in themselves; and so to advocacy of authoritarian government. Marx was more self-satisfied and despotic than Metternich, the other system-maker from the Rhineland.

Yet these resolute and progressive leaders never displayed their talents in a revolution. The original outbreaks had no recognized leaders; and no one knows the names of the leaders of the June Days in Paris nor of the October Revolution in Vienna. The name of an individual leader in the rising of May 15 in Paris has been preserved; he is thought to have been a police spy. Only Kossuth and Mazzini experienced the practical tasks of revolutionary government; and the experience of Mazzini was not very serious. For the most part the self-styled spokesmen of the people were always trying to catch up on revolutions which had taken them by surprise, as Marx and Engels were still correcting the proofs of their revolutionary programme, the *Communist Manifesto*, when the first barricades were already built and the first shots were being fired. Bakunin distinguished himself by arriving in time for the Dresden revolution of May 1849. This was an accident—he was leaving Dresden for an imaginary revolution elsewhere and was prevented from reaching the railway station by unexpected barricades.

There would have been no revolutions in 1848 if it had depended on the revolutionary leaders. The revolutions made themselves; and the true heroes of 1848 were the masses. The Radical intellectuals had supposed that, once tradition was overthrown, the masses would acknowledge instead the claims of intellect. Nietzsche expressed later this great illusion of 1848: "Dead are all Gods. Now the superman shall live." The masses never responded to the ambitions of the intellectuals. Though the masses, too, sought the superman, they sought in him an extension of themselves. The first of these supermen, concentrating the impulses and contradictions of the masses, was Napoleon III. He was a clever French guess at the future, not the real thing; for France remained too conservative in institutions and social structure to experience the full rule of the masses. The real superman of the masses was Hitler, in whom anonymity was personified; or perhaps even more in the enigmatical *Politbureaus* of the "new democracies," who have put the superman into commission.

In a deeper sense, the true superman, for whom 1848 prepared the way, has turned out to be the masses themselves. The masses have performed labours greater than those of Hercules and have accomplished miracles more wonderful than those of a divine Saviour; more than any individual superman, they have shown themselves to be beyond good and evil. The age which began in 1848 was the age of the masses: the age of mass production, of mass migration and of mass war. In the pursuit of universal happiness everything became universal: universal suffrage, universal education, universal military service, finally universal destruction. The train which Robert Owen signalled has been driven by the masses themselves; the intellectuals have remained passengers, criticizing—or more occasionally—commending the train's progress. The historic task of the intellectuals was to sever mankind from its roots and to launch it on its career of movement. This was the task which was accomplished in 1848.

VI

DE TOCQUEVILLE IN 1848

REVOLUTION is for society what a passionate love is for the individual; those who experience it are marked for ever, separated from their own past and from the rest of mankind. Some writers have captured the ecstasy of love; hardly any have rekindled the soul-purging fires of revolution. The writer of genius lives, for the most part, in a private world; it is not surprising that he deals usually with private passions. There have been some good observers of revolution—the best of them, I would guess, John Reed. Still, they observe from outside; it is like reading about the love-affair of the man next door. Two writers of the highest eminence, Lamartine and Trotsky, played the leading part in a revolution and created works of surpassing literary merit, but though their books tell us much about Lamartine and Trotsky, they do not tell us what revolution is like. The more brilliantly they write, the more the truth eludes them. For revolution calls in question the foundations of social life; it can be grasped only by one who has experienced it and yet possesses the detachment of a political psychologist.

Alexis de Tocqueville was this unique man; and his *Recollections of 1848* is the best book about a revolution ever written by a contemporary. Yet even Tocqueville was overwhelmed by his experience. This book is not a finished work, a complete work of art like his two masterpieces, *Democracy in America* and *The "Ancien Régime" and the Revolution.* He wrote to instruct himself, not to persuade the public. Usually he reined in his brilliance; here, writing only for himself, he was not ashamed to be clever. The *Recollections* were only published thirty years after his death and then only with many omissions, where his pen still seemed too sharp or—more occasionally—where his political judgment ran counter to the illusions of the Third Republic.

Alexis de Tocqueville was a liberal aristocrat: he understood both the world that was dying and the world that was coming. As a historian in politics, he both observed events and tried to shape them. Liberty was his passion; and his life was dominated by the question—how can liberty survive the fall of traditional institutions and of traditional morality? Louis Philippe and the men of the *bourgeois* monarchy thought that society could exist without belief: they pinned their faith to legality and supposed that nothing could happen so long as they observed the terms of the Charter. "They resembled the man who refused to believe that his house was on fire, because he had the key to it in his pocket." The Opposition were in no better case; they evoked the spectre of revolution without ever fearing that it would become a reality. Their sole motive was "a taste for holding office and a desire to live on the public money." Tocqueville describes this as "the secret malady which has undermined all former [French] governments and which will undermine all governments to come." Tocqueville was alone in his doubts. A few weeks before the revolution he asked—how can you expect men to respect private property when all other beliefs and privileges have lost their force? The French revolution of 1848 posed "the social question"; it is still without an answer.

Earlier revolutions had been the work of the middle classes; the masses had been merely cannon-fodder. In 1848 the masses acted independently, without leaders and without a programme. This was symbolized on the morning of February 24, when Tocqueville passed along the deserted boulevard:

> There was hardly a soul to be seen, although it was nearly nine o'clock; but . . . the great trees along the curb came tumbling down into the roadway as though of their own accord. These acts of destruction were the work of isolated individuals, who went about their business silently, regularly and hurriedly, preparing in this way the materials for the barricades which others were to erect.

The political events of February 24 had no connection with this elemental force; they merely echoed the sentiments of previous revolutions—the love-affair expressed the nostalgic regrets of a middle-aged man.

> Men were fruitlessly endeavouring to warm themselves at the fire of our fathers' passions, imitating their gestures and attitudes as they had seen them represented on the stage, but unable to imitate their enthusiasm or to be inflamed with their fury. . . . Although I clearly saw that the catastrophe of the piece would be a terrible one, I was never able to take the actors very seriously, and the whole seemed to me like a bad tragedy performed by provincial actors.

The leaders did not know what to do with the revolution for which they had become responsible: "in a rebellion, as in a novel, the most difficult part to invent is the end." The only novelty was universal suffrage; this "shook the country from top to bottom without bringing to light a single new man worthy of coming to the front."

Universal suffrage revealed an aspect of the social question which had never occurred to the revolutionaries. "In establishing universal suffrage they thought they were summoning the people to the assistance of the Revolution; they were only giving them arms against it." Alexis de Tocqueville was almost the first to realize that once the peasants acquired their land free of landlords and feudal dues they would become the most conservative of all classes. This was not grasped by Marx or by later Marxists, who went on treating "workers and peasants" as a revolutionary combination until the events of 1932 in the Ukraine and the present political situation in eastern Europe revealed that the conflict between town workers and peasants is the most ghastly as it is the most fierce of all civil wars. In 1848 the revolutionaries, faced with a conservative National Assembly, were at a loss how to proceed. They did not attempt to conquer the countryside, or even to seduce it; they supposed that it would be enough to stage a new revolution in Paris. The last of the romantic revolutions occurred on May 15; its only programme was war for the liberation of Poland. It was then that Tocqueville set eyes on the most persistent of revolutionaries:

> He had wan, emaciated cheeks, white lips, a sickly, wicked and repulsive expression, a dirty pallor, the appearance of a mouldy corpse; he wore no visible linen; an old black frock-coat tightly covered his lean, withered limbs; he seemed to have passed his life in a sewer and to have just left it. I was told it was Blanqui.

May 15 brought all the known revolutionaries to prison; and their absence completed the terrible impact of the June Days:

> the most extensive and the most singular insurrection that has occurred in our history and perhaps in any other. . . . The insurgents fought without a war-cry, without leaders, without flags and yet with a marvellous harmony and an amount of military experience that astonished the oldest officers. . . . It was not a political struggle, but a struggle of class against class, a sort of Servile War . . . the revolt of one whole section of the population against another.

The proletariat had appeared on the stage of history; even Marx drew all his teachings of the proletarian revolution from the June Days. Yet Marx saw less deeply than Tocqueville. The revolution of the masses was a revolution of destruction. Marx regarded the proletariat merely as a slave of the lamp, which would carry him to supreme power; Tocqueville recognized that the masses had repudiated all leadership, the leadership of Blanqui and of Barbès as much as the leadership of Lamartine and of Ledru-Rollin. The contrast explains much that happened in his day and more in ours. The Communist revolutions, far from fulfilling the wish of the masses, establish a dictatorship over the masses; they are the last device by which intellectuals bar the way against anarchy. When traditions and beliefs have perished, only force remains; this cannot be concealed by synthetic beliefs and simulated devotions. Yet force cannot provide a lasting answer. One day the masses will knock again at the door—and they will knock more fiercely at the Communist door than at any other.

Tocqueville's revolutionary memories end abruptly with the days of June. The revolution was over. There follows a strange epilogue, out of tone with the rest of the book, yet essential to it—memoirs of the few months when Tocqueville attempted to lead a life of action. Of course he had acted during the revolution. He had been elected a member of the National Assembly, he had kept his courage on May 15 and during the June Days, he had served—though without much effect—on the committee which drafted the Constitution. Still, this was not action of the first order. Twelve months later, in June 1849, Tocqueville suddenly appeared as Foreign

Minister in a cabinet formed "to save the Republic." The great political philosopher proved a signal failure as a practical politician. The lover of liberty became the minister of Louis Napoleon, looking for support to a clericalist majority in the Assembly; and this government of "pure" Republicans first suppressed a radical rising in the streets of Paris and then restored Papal rule in Rome. Had Tocqueville remained longer in power, he would have anticipated the foreign policy of Vichy; for, arguing that France was in decline, he proposed to build up a united Germany as a barrier against Russia. There is some danger in public life from stupid politicians; there is even more from politicians who are too clever. Political understanding of the highest order led Tocqueville into being the associate of Louis Napoleon and of the clericals; it would have been better if he had understood less. He wished to show that Republicans could be conservative in home and foreign policy. This served to suppress the radicals and to destroy the Roman republic; it did not save the republic in France.

Tocqueville knew that somewhere he had gone wrong. When he left office, after some four months, he withdrew for ever from public life; and his apology in this last chapter is laboured, unconvincing even to himself. He had fallen victim to the doctrine of "the lesser evil"—better Louis Napoleon than anarchy, better Falloux and his clerical associates than a new radical revolution. So nowadays we say: better Wall Street than the Kremlin, better de Gaulle than the Communists. Yet Tocqueville himself, in the conclusion of *Democracy in America*, had seen the falsity of this argument; liberty cannot be saved by resistance. He could not apply this teaching when it came to his own country. The social peril threw him off his balance. Hence the malignancy of his picture of Blanqui, who, despite his madness and his pallor (acquired from a lifetime of imprisonment) was also a soldier of liberty—and one who paid a far higher price for it than Tocqueville. No doubt the masses threatened all sorts of "civilized" values; the answer to this danger was to bring the masses within the pale of civilization, not to shoot them down in the June Days. After all, anarchy is a form of liberty, which is more than can be said for dictatorship or clericalism. The greatest invention of 1848, which Tocqueville disowned, was Social Democracy; this was the only way in which civilization could be saved.

Thus Tocqueville's recollections provide an object-lesson as well as a social analysis of the first order. They are a warning against being too clever in politics; in fact, the intellectual more than others should have simple principles and should stick to them. Liberty has to be defended against all comers; all the same, the constant enemies of liberty are on the right, and the lover of liberty must never be shaken from his position on the left. Above all, he who loves liberty must have faith in the people. Otherwise he will, like Tocqueville, withdraw from public life and despair of the future.

VII

CRIMEA: THE WAR THAT WOULD NOT BOIL

John Bright, with ponderous Victorian wit, called the Crimean War 'a crime'; most historians have presented it as a bewildering series of diplomatic and military blunders. With the experience of the last few years to enlighten us, we should do better: we know that the diplomatic tangles since 1945, which may seem bewildering to the future historian, conceal the reality of 'the cold war'. The Crimean War was the cold war in an earlier phase. Two world systems, mutually uncomprehending, lurched against each other, each convinced of its defensive good faith. The struggle between them was fought in a ragged way at the edges. Both sides shrank from the head-on collision which would have produced a war to remake the world—Russia from lack of strength, the Western Powers from lack of conviction. Though the Crimean War seemed indecisive, great decisions followed from it. Without it neither Germany nor Italy could have been united; without it Europe would never have known 'the liberal era', that halcyon age which ended in 1914 and which, for centuries to come, men will regard as 'normal times', just as the barbarians looked back to the peace and security of Augustan Rome.

The Crimean War is often treated in England as a war over the Eastern Question, a war to secure the route to India, and thus a rehearsal for Disraeli's 'peace with honour' campaign in 1878. This is to err both in time and place. The war had little or nothing to do with the security of India. The Suez Canal was not built; the overland route catered for a few travellers in a hurry; for that matter Russia's land-route to India was still in the future. The Crimean War was fought for essentially European considerations—against Russia rather than in favour of Turkey. It was fought for the sake of the Balance of Power and for 'the liberties of Europe'; more positively, it aimed to substitute diplomacy by agreement, the Concert of Europe, for the settlement of affairs at the dictation of a single Great Power. Disraeli was a consistent disciple of Metternich when he criticized the Crimean War and yet opposed Russia in 1878: the Crimean War had general altruistic motives, the crisis of 1878 was caused solely by the defence of Imperial interests. In other words, 1878 was a Tory affair; the Crimean War, with all its muddle, sprang from Whig principles, the last fling of a dying party.

British policy in the Near East had not been consistently anti-Russian before the Crimean War, though it became so afterwards. Canning, for instance, co-operated with Russia throughout the Greek war of independence; and though Palmerston thought of working with France against Russia in the Near East in 1833, he ended up by working with Russia against France in 1839 and 1840. Throughout the eighteen-forties, and indeed until the beginning of 1853, British suspicions were turned against France both at Constantinople and in Egypt; and Great Britain and Russia often made common cause in resisting French encroachment. Nor can there be an easy dividing line in their attitude to the Ottoman Empire, as though Russia wanted to break it up and Great Britain wished to preserve it. Both Powers found it a convenience; and both Powers doubted its capacity to survive. Their difference was in timing, not in judgement of the situation.

The British attitude to Russia was very different when it came to Europe; hence the Crimean War makes sense only with a European background. Ever since 1815 British statesmen had been obsessed with the thought that, if France ceased to dominate Europe, Russia would take her place; as Napoleon had said, in fifty years all Europe would be either Republican or Cossack. Hence Castlereagh's rather absurd alliance with France and Austria in January 1815; hence Canning's calling in of a New World to redress the balance of the Old (though the New World did not respond to his invitation); hence Palmerston's welcome to the July monarchy in France and his Quadruple Alliance with Spain and Portugal as well in 1834. This was one side of British policy: to maintain France as a Great Power and yet to keep her harmless—just strong enough to check Russia's domination without reviving the same taste in herself. The other element in British policy was to develop the independence of Central Europe, so that it could hold its own against both Cossacks and Republicans without constant alarms or war. This was what was meant by the favourite description of Prussia and Austria as Great Britain's 'natural allies': they were serving the purposes of British policy without any effort on the British side. Curiously enough, Metternich and Palmerston, who were supposed to hate each other so much, were pursuing exactly the same aims and served each other's needs. So long as the 'Metternich system' worked, Central Europe was independent of both France and Russia; and the Balance of Power in Europe freed Great Britain from European commitments.

The revolutions of 1848 ended this finely drawn policy. The fall of Metternich was a disaster to the British position; and it was little consolation to make out that he had fallen because of his refusal to take British advice. The revolutions of 1848 seemed to make France more powerful than before; to weaken Prussia; and to threaten Austria with elimination from the ranks of the Great Powers. Europe would become either Republican or Cossack. Though this bitter saying was not at once fulfilled, it seemed at most postponed. On the one side, France emerged from the revolutionary year under the rule of a new Bonaparte, inescapably committed to the overthrow of the treaties of 1815 and almost as much to the restoration of French domination in Europe. On the other, the revolutions in Central Europe—in Germany, in Italy and in Hungary—were defeated only with Russian backing; so far as Hungary went, only with Russian military aid. By 1850, Francis Joseph of Austria and Frederick William IV of Prussia seemed to be Russian dependants, subservient not only from ideological similarity, but from their inability to hold their monarchical power except with Russian support. The Holy Alliance was the Cominform of Kings.

The defeat of the revolutions of 1848 with Russian aid had a profound effect on British public opinion. Before 1848 fear of Russia had been a diplomat's calculation; there had been no 'Russian bogey'. After 1848 British liberals picked up the habit of continental radicals and began to regard Russia as the tyrant of Europe. War against Russia was regarded as the preliminary to any radical success elsewhere. The old diplomatic apprehension of Russia now seemed tepid and half-hearted. In radical circles, for instance, it was common doctrine that Palmerston was in Russian pay; the proof was found in his reluctance to launch the great European 'war of liberation'.

This theory can be found worked out in the essays which Karl Marx wrote on *The Eastern Question*; he learnt it from the pro-Turk lunatic, Urquhart. Except among radicals and exiles, fear of France still predominated in England until the spring of 1853. Indeed, belief that the British were more apprehensive about Belgium than about Turkey was one of the factors which led Tsar Nicholas to act so carelessly and so provocatively in May 1853, when the war-crisis first began to stir.

There was, of course, another and more obvious cause of Russian confidence. A coalition ministry had been formed in England at the end of 1852 under Lord Aberdeen; and Aberdeen, though a free trader, was an old-fashioned Tory. He had no sympathy with radical hostility to Russia; great confidence in the Tsar's good faith; and great distrust of Napoleon III. If Aberdeen had had his way there would have been no Crimean War. Russia would have strengthened her position in Turkey, consolidated her reactionary hold over Europe; and Great Britain would have consoled herself by taking Egypt. This would have been a reasonable, though not an idealistic, solution; hence the later regrets of Lord Salisbury, a reasonable man without ideals, that it was not adopted. It could only have been adopted by a purely Tory cabinet; and from such a cabinet Aberdeen was barred by his free-trade doctrines. Instead, he was saddled with Whig colleagues, Palmerston and Russell, who were both in their way friendly to France and who both, without yet distrusting the Tsar, wished to draw a sharp line against any new Russian advance. Russell had been Prime Minister; Palmerston was going to be. They were both pretty clear that a firm line against Russia would be a winning card in the game for public favour which they were playing against each other. Here too, if Palmerston and Russell had had their way, there would have been no war. The Tsar would have stepped aside from the Eastern Question before his prestige was involved and waited for a more favourable opportunity. Perhaps even, as we go on dreaming nowadays, Russian despotism would have saved everyone the trouble of a war by crumbling from within. It was this mixture of conciliation always too grudging and firmness always too late which, on the British side, produced the Crimean War.

There was, however, another principal in the war, one often forgotten in British and even in Russian accounts. Neither the Tsar nor the British Government wanted war; Napoleon III did. Not necessarily the Crimean War as it worked itself out, but a war which would disrupt the existing structure of Europe. Thus Great Britain became involved in war in order to preserve the Balance of Power and to defend the liberties of Europe; Napoleon III pushed into war in order to overthrow the Balance of Power and to clear the way for French domination. After all, it is a simple calculation that if the allies of a Great War fall out the defeated party will come into his own. In 1853 the calculation was made in Paris; now it is made in every German village. The Crimean War was not a good war from Napoleon III's point of view; a war in Poland, in Italy, or on the Rhine, would have been much better. But it was better than no war at all. On the other hand, Napoleon III had learnt from his uncle's failure—had learnt, that is, in the scrappy, illogical way, in which men use the past to prop up their own prejudices. Napoleon III supposed, though wrongly, that his uncle's great mistake had been to quarrel with England; his key to success was therefore to be the British alliance, and the Crimean War was welcome to him in that it gave him this alliance. In the long run, however, Napoleon III did no better with the British alliance than his uncle had done without it—unless it is better to die in Chislehurst than at St. Helena.

By the summer of 1853 France, Russia and Great Britain were all tugging themselves into war in their different ways. The Tsar, though with no deep-laid plans for encroaching on Turkey, had grown too confident; regarding Prussia and Austria as his satellites, he supposed that he could display his prestige at Constantinople without risk. When this proved mistaken, he—like the Russians generally when they are challenged—felt genuinely threatened with aggression; and in Russian eyes the Crimean War was a defensive war. The British Government, though also without deep-laid plans, would not allow the Tsar's claims and, in their anxiety to win the alliance of France, often acted more firmly than Napoleon III expected or desired. Napoleon, on his side, wanted to shake Russia's prestige and to build up his own; but most of all, he wanted to keep in step with the British, who, with the same motive, constantly quickened the pace until the two fleets tumbled into the Black Sea more to prove mutual good faith and enthusiasm as allies than to oppose Russia. As a matter of fact, when the British and French fleets entered the Black Sea at the end of 1853, the Crimean War, not yet started, had already been won so far as the original causes of war, or excuses for it, were concerned. That is, the Tsar was quite prepared to drop his immediate claims on Turkey, once it became clear that England and France intended to resist them. This did not satisfy the western allies. With their public opinion roused and their resources mobilized, what they wanted was a decision, not merely the withdrawal of the present Russian demands. The problem of the Crimean War, never solved, lay here. The Russians had dropped their demands because the British and French fleets had entered the Black Sea. How could the renewal of these demands be prevented when the British and French fleets went away again?

The problem had two sides, military and diplomatic. The military problem was, how to get at the Russians, in order to inflict on them the defeat which would make them accept the terms needed for Europe's security? The diplomatic problem was, what were the terms which should be imposed on the Russians when they were defeated? The two problems were mixed up throughout the war. Sometimes the allies tried to devise terms which would make a defeat of the Russians unnecessary; sometimes they dreamt of a defeat so decisive as to spare them the trouble of devising terms. At bottom the problem was insoluble. The Western Powers could not alone inflict on Russia a decisive and lasting defeat; nor, even were she defeated, could they devise terms which would ensure against a renewal of her expansion. It would have been a different matter if Austria and Prussia, the states of Central Europe, could have been drawn into the war. Hence the real decision of the Crimean War came from the two Germanic powers when they decided to stay out of it. Austria and Prussia were 'the third force'. Their persistence in this line of policy both caused the Crimean War and led to its being indecisive. Until the beginning of 1854 the Tsar had regarded them as reliable satellite states, dependent on his support. As soon, however, as he depended on their support, they ceased to be satellites. He could no longer keep France out of the Near East by a threat from Prussia on the Rhine and from Austria in Italy.

The Western Powers imagined that 'the third force' had come over to their side and that a full-scale defeat of Russia was in sight. Certainly a coalition of all the Great Powers of Europe against Russia would have excluded her from Europe, might even have destroyed her as a Great Power. Poland would have been restored, Turkey secured; Louis Napoleon would have become master of Europe. This was an outcome more unwelcome to Prussia and Austria even than Russian domination of Turkey. Whereas the Western Powers wanted a decision, the Central Powers wanted no decision; and they got their way. Prussia had the great advantage that she was indifferent to the affairs of the Near East, though concerned with the general European balance. Hence her neutrality was genuinely impartial. Her only aim, which seemed craven enough, was to ensure that no fighting took place on Prussian soil. This no doubt benefited Russia and won her gratitude; but since Prussia did not promise anything to the Western Powers, she did not disappoint them either. When the war ended, Prussia was not at first invited to the Peace Congress at Paris. This seemed a humiliation; later events showed the enormous gains to be won from keeping out of other people's quarrels. Any contemporary statesman who wishes to reap the advantages of the third course should study the policy of Prussia during the Crimean War.

Austrian policy is equally instructive: it shows the disadvantages of a neutrality which offends both sides. Whereas Prussia was neutral from indifference, Austria was neutral from being too deeply committed. She had her own grounds for opposing Russia. Russia's control of the mouth of the Danube, where her troops had established themselves in 1853, cut one of Austria's main economic arteries with the outer world. Thus the practical aim of Austrian policy was to get Russia out of Rumania and to get herself in. But there were complicating factors. If Austria entered the war on the side of the Western Powers, she would bear the brunt of the fighting; worse, an allied victory, expelling Russia from Europe, would make Napoleon III supreme and thus clear the way for the national principle. Austria would win Rumania at too high a price if she lost her Italian lands, the symbol of her Imperial greatness. Yet, apart from her anxiety about Rumania, Austria dared not favour Russia nor even keep a resolute neutrality, for fear that Napoleon III would explode Italy against her. As a result Austria followed the worst of all policies. She offended the Tsar by refusing to promise a secure neutrality; she offended the Western Powers by refusing to go to war. She pressed her alliance on England and France in order to conciliate them; she failed to operate it and left them more estranged then before. Neutrality, like virtue, has its merits if maintained inviolate; it can also be sold for a high price. The one impossible thing is to be up for auction and to remain virtuous at the same time.

The first stage of the Crimean War was the stage when the Western Powers imagined that 'the third force' could be drawn into the war and a real decision thus produced. This stage lasted until the summer of 1854, by which time Prussian neutrality was certain and Austrian belligerence uncertain. The Crimean War, in the strict sense of the term, followed—the war with all its blunders and muddles which perplexed contemporaries and baffled posterity. Yet the confusion had a simple cause—how could the allies get at Russia when the great neutral buffer of Central Europe was interposed between them? The allies had hoped that the Russians would obligingly remain in Rumania in order that they might be defeated there; instead the Russians withdrew from Rumania in July 1854. In their perplexity the allies decided on Sebastopol, the Russian naval base in the Crimea, which was supposed to be vulnerable to an amphibious operation. As a matter of fact, it took nearly a year's fighting and the mobilization of armies on a continental scale for this amphibious operation to succeed.

It takes two to make a war. Russian strength in the Near East lay in her proximity; her strength in the European balance lay in her army. Her naval power in the Black Sea was a secondary affair; and it could always be checked if the British and French fleets, or even the British fleet alone, passed the Straits. If the Russians had abandoned Sebastopol and sealed off the Crimea, the western allies would have scored a success of prestige; but Russia would have been no weaker than before. The allies would have cruised undisturbed in the Black Sea until their position became ridiculous; they would then have retired, and Russia's pressure on Turkey could have been resumed. But autocratic monarchics also have their prestige. The Tsar did not grasp that if the allies failed to defeat him, he had won; whereas, whatever efforts he made at Sebastopol, he could not defeat the allies. Russia's military strength lies in withdrawal; but this has always to be imposed upon her by her enemies, instead of being a conscious choice. Alexander I fought Napoleon at Austerlitz and even wanted to fight on the frontier in 1812; Stalin was only saved from catastrophe on the frontier in 1941 by being caught unprepared. In the Crimean War, the Tsar obligingly provided the maritime powers with the battlefield which they could never have found for themselves. Instead of being withdrawn, the Russian armies in Sebastopol were reinforced; and Russia exhausted herself for the sake of the maritime powers. The allies lamented that they had not taken Sebastopol by a *coup de main* when they landed in 1854; if they had, there would have been no Crimean War and nothing would have been achieved at all. For the essence of war is not to take this point or that, but to destroy, or at least to weaken, the military strength of the enemy. This was accomplished by the year's fighting in front of Sebastopol. The Russian armies were greatly weakened; Russia's military prestige lessened; most of all, Russia's economic resources were intolerably strained. It took Russia a generation to recover from the effort of the Crimean War; and in this generation Europe was remade without Russian interference.

The defeat of the Russian armies, and the weakening of Russian power, were the real result of the Crimean War; but this was a result too vague to satisfy the victorious allies. Their victory had to be translated into a treaty of peace; yet they had no clear idea what this treaty should contain. As on other occasions, the Western Powers knew what they were fighting against, not what they were fighting for. They were fighting against Russia; and their real wish was that Russia should cease to exist or—what amounts to the same thing—become a modest and satisfied member of an Anglo-French world. Napoleon III was prepared to accept the logic of this wish. When Sebastopol fell, he proposed to the British Government a programme which would sweep Russia from Europe and destroy her as a Great Power—the programme of full national reconstruction, especially of Poland, which would incidentally make France supreme in Europe. The British Government had the exactly opposite aim: they had wished to destroy Russian supremacy in Europe without putting French supremacy in its place. Yet on the other hand they were the more eager of the two to continue the war until a 'decision' had been reached. A characteristic compromise followed. Each accepted the other's negative: the war was brought to an end, without any positive war-aims being drawn up.

This is not to say that the Crimean War accomplished nothing, nor even that the Treaty of Paris contained nothing of moment. Apart from the weakening of Russian power, which could not be put into a treaty, the Crimean War had two achievements, one which lasted for nearly eighty years, the other for fifteen years. The more permanent outcome, as things go in international affairs, was the independence of Rumania, freeing the mouths of the Danube from either Russian or Austrian control. The Russian army had withdrawn in July 1854; the Austrian army had taken its place, and the Austrians had hoped to annex Rumania. But they would not pay the French price, which was to give up Italy; therefore they had to withdraw in their turn, and Rumania became a genuinely independent state, a buffer between Russian interests and those of Central Europe, until the time of Stalin and Hitler.

The more prized achievement of the treaty of Paris was the 'neutralization' of the Black Sea. Russia was forbidden to maintain a fleet in the Black Sea, or to rebuild her naval arsenals; it is true that the same restrictions were imposed on Turkey, but since the Turks could maintain a fleet in the Sea of Marmora they could always dominate the Black Sea in time of war. The neutralization clauses of the Treaty of Paris were a rehearsal for the demilitarization of the Rhineland in the Treaty of Versailles, and equally futile. Either Russia accepted them because she feared England and France; in that case she would repudiate them when she ceased to fear England or France. Alternatively Russia accepted them because she had changed her ways and given up aggression against Turkey; in that case they were unnecessary. The British and French would not keep their fleets in the Black Sea indefinitely; they were not even sure that they would remain indefinitely on good terms. Hence they tried to make the Russians promise that they would continue to behave as though the allied fleets were still in the Black Sea when in fact they had been long withdrawn. A treaty of peace can only define the conditions of the present; it cannot bind the future. This the Russians demonstrated fifteen years later, when they repudiated the Black Sea clauses of the Treaty of Paris. The British doctrine of the sanctity of treaties was upheld only by the pious pretence of a conference in London, at which the Powers, to no one's surprise, confirmed what Russia had already done. The neutralization clauses taught a lesson which was ignored in 1919: if you wish to perpetuate a military victory, you must perpetuate the balance of forces which produced that victory.

The Crimean War was, in short, a war that did not come off, a war without a decision. But that was itself the decision. Though Russian strength was not broken, Russian influence in Europe was lessened. Though French prestige was increased, France did not become dominant in Europe. Napoleon III thought he had freed his hands in order to remodel Italy and Germany to his own taste; it turned out that Italy and Germany had freed their own hands to remodel themselves against him. Cavour and Bismarck, not Napoleon III, were the real victors of the Crimean War. If there were a moral to be drawn from the Crimean War which might apply to the present, it would be this: in a war between Russia and the west, it is the Powers which keep out who will be the real gainers. Last time it gave Prussia mastery of Germany.

For the British, the Crimean War, though superficially inconclusive, was less of a disappointment than it was to Napoleon III. They had set out to lessen Russian power; and they had succeeded. Later on, they imagined that they had intended to give Turkey the chance of reforming herself; and were correspondingly embittered when no reform followed. Nevertheless, the Crimean War brought real gains to the British. The Balance of Power in Europe was strengthened, not overthrown; and Great Britain did not need to intervene in a continental war for sixty years thereafter. Two generations of peace are something to be thankful for; it is more than we have had in our lifetime.

VIII

CAVOUR AND GARIBALDI

IT used to be the fashion to contrast the unification of Germany and of Italy. In Italy idealism; in Germany *realpolitik*. In Italy the spread of parliamentary liberalism; in Germany the triumph of the Prussian army. Bismarck appeared always in a general's tunic, ruthless, unscrupulous, a master of force and dishonesty. Cavour was the civilian statesman, relying on parliamentary speeches for his success. The failure of the German radicals was lamented; there were few to regret the failure of Mazzini or Garibaldi. They were impractical dreamers who did not understand the greatness of Cavour; and it was a good thing for Italy when they were shipped off Garibaldi to Caprera, Mazzini back to exile in London. More recently, Cavour has had a bad press. His private correspondence has at last been published (it is now almost complete); and his own words have shown him to be much more like Bismarck, much less like Gladstone, than used to be supposed. He wielded the weapons of traditional diplomacy with incomparable skill, but also with incomparable lack of principle; and Metternich turns out to have been his exemplar as well as his enemy.

Cavour did not care much about the unification of Italy, or at any rate ranked it low in his scale of values. Himself with little national feeling, preferring to speak and write in French, his deepest concern was for moderate liberalism. He wanted a free press, free trade, and a parliament based on limited suffrage, first in Piedmont and then perhaps in northern Italy. But he did not regard the unification of the whole peninsula as a noble idea or believe that it would of itself bring about a moral regeneration. He had nothing but contempt for idealists like Mazzini and could have said with Bismarck: 'The great questions of our day will not be settled by speeches and majority resolutions but by blood and iron.' What he lacked in blood and iron he made up for in deceit. The Italian question was for him a problem in European diplomacy, not a matter of national sentiment. He hardly thought about the Italian people except to fear them. His thoughts were concentrated on Napoleon III. And the later observer must confess that the unification of

Italy might well have been impossible, unless Napoleon III had been brought in to defeat Austria in 1859. After all, the victory of nationalism was not inevitable. Poland had to wait until the twentieth century, despite a much stronger national sentiment; the Ukraine waits to the present day.

We still need a history of Italian unification from the European angle. Professor Valsecchi of Milan is writing it; but so far he has only got to the early days of the Crimean war. Meanwhile, Mr. Mack Smith has given us a new version of the story at a later stage[1]—the stage of 1860, when Lombardy and central Italy had been united to Piedmont, but when the Two Sicilies and the Papal States (to say nothing of Venetia) had still to be liberated. This was the moment of greatest contrast between Cavour's reliance on diplomacy and the faith of the radicals in their own ideals. Cavour still feared the intervention of 'the Holy Alliance', still pinned his calculations to the favour of Napoleon. Garibaldi believed that the entire peninsula could be brought together by a spontaneous outburst of national enthusiasm; and he thought the prize worth any risk. He was determined to act somewhere—against Austria in Venetia, against Rome despite its French garrison, or, when Sicily rebelled, against the Bourbon kingdom of the Two Sicilies. It used to be held that Cavour secretly encouraged Garibaldi and was in alliance with him. The truth is less creditable. He pushed Garibaldi off to Sicily in order to get him out of the way and in the hope that failure would ruin the radicals once and for all. Instead, Garibaldi succeeded beyond his wildest dreams; and Cavour had to sweep up the pieces of a policy in ruins.

Mr. Mack Smith has produced a surprising book to come out of Cambridge. He acknowledges his debt to Professor Butterfield; and one would have expected praise of Cavour and condemnation of Garibaldi from a member of this neo-Machiavellian group. But not at all. With brilliant, though well-founded, perversity, Mr. Mack Smith turns things upside down. It is Garibaldi who was the realist, arriving at the right conclusions by instinct, and Cavour who was the dogmatic muddler. Mr. Mack Smith is perhaps a little unfair to Cavour. As things turned out, Italy in 1860 was able 'to do it herself', as she had mistakenly boasted she would in 1848; and Europe counted for little. But this could not have been foreseen when the Thousand sailed. Napoleon III still seemed to dominate

1. *Cavour and Garibaldi 1860. A Study in Political Conflict.* By D. Mack Smith.

Europe, his decline lay far in the future; and Cavour was not the only man to fear the might of France. Moreover he was right on one essential point, the question of Rome. Rome dominated the Italian problem; and even Garibaldi went to Sicily principally in order to reach Rome by the back door. Yet the French could be got out of Rome only by diplomacy, not by force; and for the sake of Italy Garibaldi had to fail before he reached Rome, unless the Pope had already withdrawn—and the French along with him. Moreover, Mr. Mack Smith underrates the danger that Austria, Prussia and Russia would come together in resistance to 'the revolution'. They nearly did when they met at Warsaw in October 1860; and they were prevented more by the diplomacy of Napoleon III (and hence indirectly of Cavour) than by Garibaldi's success in the south.

Still, by and large, the emphasis is put the right way. Cavour was blinded by his rigid hostility towards the radicals. He saw in them only 'the social peril', and was convinced that anarchy must follow their victory. His primary object was that Garibaldi should fail; only in the second place did he want Italy to be united. This view divided him not only from the radicals, but even from his king, Victor Emanuel, who was ready 'to become simple *monsu Savoia* and clap his hands at Mazzini's success if this sacrifice were necessary for the making of Italy'. Yet Cavour's own policy was more Utopian than that of any radical. He imagined that Italy could be brought into being solely by the moderate liberals—the most useless of all classes in a revolution. Ricasoli's ruthlessness made this policy work in central Italy; but in the south there was nothing between the aristocracy and the masses. The few middle-class lawyers there supported unification only in order to get the courts open again; they would not fight for it, and Garibaldi succeeded by rousing the masses. This was a social revolution against the landowners—a revolution which Garibaldi exploited for the national cause. He had no social programme, despite his emotional sympathy with the peasants and despite Cavour's suspicions; and he allowed them to fall under the rule of a harsher, more rigid Piedmontese bureaucracy without ever understanding how he had betrayed them.

Cavour always suspected Garibaldi; Garibaldi never suspected Cavour. This is the central theme of the whole affair. Of course, Garibaldi disliked Cavour and resented his cession of Nice to Napoleon III; but he thought that, just as he had dropped his republicanism, Cavour would drop his hostility to the radicals for the sake of united Italy. If the radicals united Italy, this would certainly weaken Cavour and perhaps even lead to his fall; but again Garibaldi, being ready to make the greatest personal sacrifices on his side, could not understand that Cavour would not do the same. Cavour, like Bismarck, regarded himself as indispensable; when he proved unyielding on this, everyone had to give way to him in the last resort—and Italy paid the price. Garibaldi put Italy first; Cavour put himself first. Therefore Cavour was bound to win in the end, despite the great advantages which Garibaldi accumulated in Sicily and Naples.

For they were great advantages. The liberation of the Two Sicilies seems easy in retrospect; we almost fail to notice that it needed a leader of genius to accomplish it. European radicalism produced three great dictators—Kossuth in Hungary, Mazzini in Rome, Garibaldi in the Two Sicilies. Garibaldi was the least intellectual of the three, with few ideas and unable to formulate even these clearly. Yet he was easily the most successful. He evoked from the people and even from the politicians a personal devotion almost without parallel in modern history; again and again he chose the right course by instinct; and he showed himself the greatest general that Italy has ever produced. In the late summer of 1860 Sicily was a true radical paradise, radiating the hope—or perhaps the illusion—that every evil legacy of the past had been swept away. Cavour was not the serpent in this garden of Eden; Garibaldi's success had eclipsed him for the time being. The real trouble was that Garibaldi and the people of Sicily were at cross-purposes. They supposed that he had brought them freedom; he looked on Sicily only as the first halt on the road to Rome. Both alike resisted Cavour's plan for an immediate annexation of Sicily to the kingdom of Sardinia. But the Sicilians wanted permanent autonomy for their island; Garibaldi and his radical supporters wished to use Sicily as a base for further successes. Once Garibaldi had crossed to the mainland and carried all before him, he lost interest in Sicily; and it irritated him to have to return in order to settle its internal conflicts. Even in Naples, he listened impatiently to the republican arguments of Mazzini and the federalist schemes of Cataneo. The march on Rome was the only thing that interested him.

The resistance of the Neapolitan army on the Volturno gave

Cavour his chance. He was able to stop Garibaldi just in time. He acted no doubt cynically and basely, discrediting Garibaldi unjustifiably with the king and killing the idealism of the radical movement. But there was something wrong with a radicalism which could think only of further battles. The radicals had an aggressive foreign policy; they improvised casually in home affairs. Mr. Mack Smith is inclined to regret that Sicily and even Naples did not survive as autonomous radical states. Was Cavour alone to blame? After all he had only another six months to live; and the radicals had plenty of chance in the future if they could take it. They never made much of it; and Italy has been kept going (so far as it goes at all) by hard-headed officials of Cavour's stamp. Idealists make revolutions; practical men come afterwards and clear up the mess. Garibaldi was luckier than most revolutionary leaders. He remained an idealist to the end of the chapter. If Cavour had not existed, Garibaldi must either have failed or have ended by playing the part of Cavour himself. Perhaps it was Cavour who made the greatest sacrifice after all. Garibaldi returned to Caprera; Cavour remained in power.

IX

THE MAN OF DECEMBER

SOME historical characters—I would say most—become simpler as you know more about them. The lines get stronger, clearer; you see a whole man, you know how he will behave, how he will face difficulties, how he will respond to success. In the end he will go into one of those two pigeon-holes that are so jeered at and yet are essential for the moral judgement that we finally have to make: he can be docketed as 'a good thing'—or a bad one. But some few escape us and baffle examination. The more we strip off their disguises, the more new disguises appear. Such was Louis Napoleon, the man of mystery. Conspirator and statesman; dreamer and realist; despot and democrat; maker of wars and man of peace; creator and muddler; you can go on indefinitely, until you begin to think that he had no character at all, that at the heart of him was a gigantic nothing. All the greatest political observers of the time tried to penetrate his secret: Tocqueville, Marx, Thiers, Victor Hugo—all failed to make sense of him. Bismarck called him a Sphinx, and added: he was a Sphinx without a riddle. Was it not rather that he had too many riddles, and riddles to which he himself did not know the answer?

Everything about him baffles inquiry. Was he the son of his father? It seems unlikely. Yet if not, then of whom? He was a master of concealment. Whatever his other failings, he left few traces. The letters of Napoleon I fill sixty-four volumes; the letters of Napoleon III, even if they could be brought together, would not fill one. He talked endlessly to a great variety of witnesses, but—like the smoke of the cigarettes that he was one of the first to favour—his talk was vague and intangible; it vanished into the air, leaving only a faint romantic odour, a thin cloud of mystery. He was a creature of the Romantic movement, a Byronic hero gone seedy and rather out-at-elbows. Bulwer Lytton and the young Disraeli had the same touch, both in their writings and in their lives: an articial excitement, a grandeur of ideas and a triviality of performance.

The men who grew up in the thirty years after the battle of Waterloo played out their lives in the shadow of the great Napoleon, Napoleon I. He had done great things; they manufactured great phrases. When Napoleon I called himself Emperor of the French, this was an empire which stretched across Europe to the frontiers of Russia and Turkey. Napoleon III, as Emperor, ruled only over the old Kingdom of France, and all that he added to his empire in nearly twenty years was Savoy and a scrap of Indo-China. This was a typical gesture of the Romantic movement, and its great legacy to our own time: the name on the bottle was more important than the drink inside it; the man who writes the advertisement is more important than the man who makes the goods—as for the goods themselves, they are of no importance at all.

One writer has called Louis Napoleon 'the modern Emperor'; another 'the first mountebank dictator'. Perhaps they are the same thing. The radicals of 1848 had claimed that they were bringing the masses into politics. The response had been disappointing. It was Louis Napoleon who first got the djinn out of the bottle. He said himself: 'Other French governments have ruled with the support of perhaps one million of the educated masses; I have called in the other twenty-nine million.' This determined his policy. Napoleon I did great things and then sought to present them in a striking way; Napoleon III looked for things that would appear striking and only then dressed them up as important. He deceived everyone, including himself. He could be an idealist free trader with Richard Cobden; a respectable sovereign with Queen Victoria; an unscrupulous schemer when he was with Bismarck. But there was also the myth that he had created for himself and which took in even him. He really saw himself as the all-wise dictator, the Cæsar who would reconcile all the classes in France and would remake the map of Europe. 'When a man of my name is in power, he must do great things.' He thrashed about like a lion in a cage, convinced that it ought to be ranging the jungle; always looking for great things to do, never finding them. He was no lion; he would have made an agreeable, though untrustworthy, domestic cat.

Great men in public life love power. That is what stamps them. They fight to get it and they use it ruthlessly when it is in their hands. Louis Napoleon would not pass this test of greatness. He loved conspiracy: the process of intrigue by which he moved towards power or the endless plans for using it. But he hated the action which threatened to follow these plans. For instance, the *coup d'état* of 2 December 1851 had been planned months before and put off at least twice. When it came to the point, Louis Napoleon hesitated again and might have put it off once more, had not the politicians of the assembly forced his hands, by beginning to make plans against him. And that, he thought, was unfair as well as being dangerous: like other conspirators, he claimed a monopoly in dishonesty.

The famous meeting at Plombières was a perfect example of his methods: the secret messages through somebody else's doctor; Cavour's trip to Plombières under a false name; the long discussions which left nothing on paper. The two men redrew the map of Italy in a few bold strokes; war and peace, and the future destinies of a nation, were settled between the puffs of a cigarette. Napoleon was roused only when they turned to discuss the trick with which they could provoke war; the conspirator's device was the thing that won his interest and held it for hour after hour. Cavour displayed all his gifts in devising schemes to lure Austria into the war that was to be her ruin; and Napoleon was delighted. It was very different when the time came to put the plans into action. Then Napoleon was all for delay, as fertile in excuses as he had once been in plans, and resentful when Cavour held him to his bargain. Six weeks before the war for the liberation of Italy broke out, he told Cavour that the war would have to be postponed for at least a year; and then no doubt he would have been for further delay. 'You should know how to wait as I do.' But his waiting had no purpose. He preferred to dream rather than to act; to make great plans, not to carry them out. He was a procrastinating adventurer; more of a scoundrel in his thoughts than in his deeds.

It was the same when Bismarck discussed the future of Germany with him at Biarritz in 1865. Napoleon supplied the keynote of the talks: 'We must not make events; we must let them happen.' Imagine a man who has lived by robbing banks saying: 'We must not blow open the safe; we must wait for it to fall open.' Bismarck is often credited with having tricked Napoleon at Biarritz: he got permission to go ahead with his plans for defeating Austria, yet promised Napoleon nothing in return. There was no trickery in this; it was what Napoleon wanted. But, again, not for the sophisticated reason so often given. He did not avoid formulating his demands for German territory for fear that Bismarck would think them too great and give up war against Austria. It was his old line of waiting. He did not know what to demand; he only knew how to wait, or so he thought. The conversations at Biarritz suited him even better than the bargain at Plombières. With Cavour he had had to commit himself to action, however grudgingly; with Bismarck he committed himself only to inaction, a course of policy which he meant to follow in any case. Bismarck was to provide the action; and Napoleon was somehow to profit from it. He was like a man who haunts the gambling-rooms in the belief that, if he encourages others to bet, he will one day draw a great prize.

The twenty years when Louis Napoleon ruled France were a period of great creative activity in every country of Europe. The steam engine and the railway spread across the Continent. In France, too, the Second Empire promised energy and creation; yet it was in these twenty years that France lost the leadership of Europe in politics, in economics, in culture. The Second Empire claimed to be Wagner and turned out to be Offenbach—a frivolous echo of the past, not an inspiration for the future. It was the bastard of the great Napoleon—in name, in policy, even in men. It was said at the time that, though Louis Napoleon was not the son of his father, everyone else at Court was the son of his mother. Morny was his illegitimate half-brother; Walewski the illegitimate son of Napoleon I. Its emotions were sham, also. This system which claimed to care for the masses was run by the most dishonest politicians who have ever governed France. All of them, even Napoleon himself, were convinced that the Empire would not last; and they plundered France while the opportunity lasted. Under the July monarchy Guizot had said to the French middle classes: 'Get rich.' The statesmen of the Second Empire applied this doctrine.

In foreign affairs there was the same contradiction between the phrases and the reality. Napoleon liked to believe that his empire had sprung from the resentment which every Frenchman felt against the settlement of Europe made at Vienna in 1815 after the defeat of his uncle. In reality, this settlement had given France a position of primacy in Europe and had made her secure: if it was changed, France was bound to suffer. Hence Napoleon was constantly driven forward; and as constantly shrank from the results. In Sorel's words: 'His name was his fortune and his undoing. His origins condemned him to success.' Any other Frenchman might have defended the settlement of 1815; a Napoleon could not. Louis Napoleon believed that nationalism was the winning cause in Europe; and he meant to associate himself with its success. Despite his inaction, he could never support conservatism when it came to the point; and he tried to satisfy German and Italian nationalism without injuring France. In the outcome, he failed on both counts. He estranged Italy by holding on to Rome; he tried to make German unity stop at the Main; and by his very inaction took the decisive steps which ended the career of France as the Great Power of Europe.

Yet, with all his cunning, there was great good will. He really cared for Italy; he sympathized with Germany, or at any rate with German romanticism. He dreamt always of a Europe in which there would be 'a peaceful redress of grievances'; and he was the first European statesman in a responsible position to put forward plans for general disarmament. But, of course, they were plans in which the preponderance of France had to be recognized and made permanent. Disarmament, as always, seemed most attractive to the power that was on the decline.

Though he ruined France as a great power, he made France what she still is—as far as looks go. The Paris which tourists admire, the Paris of the opera and the great boulevards, is the creation of Napoleon III. Like every adventurer who has arrived Napoleon wanted something solid to show, something that would assert his permanence against the facts. And the Paris of Napoleon III has not done badly—better, at any rate, than the Berlin of Hitler or the Rome of Mussolini. Yet even this was a fraud. Its real purpose was to make long, wide streets so that a revolt could be put down easily, hardly a gesture of confidence towards the twenty-nine million. And having tricked others, Napoleon here misled himself. When his empire fell, there was no whiff of grapeshot; not a shot was fired. The boulevards had failed of their purpose.

We imagine nowadays—and even take pride in the thought—that dictators, swindling their way to power and keeping power by a succession of tricks, are a disease peculiar to the twentieth century. But there is nothing new in Hitler or Mussolini: Louis Napoleon had all their cards up his sleeve, except, perhaps, their brutality. He did not need a Nietzsche to put him beyond good and evil; he had arrived at the idea for himself. Certainly he owed his success to the same historic causes. The great French revolution destroyed the history of France before going on to destroy the history of Europe. Destroy tradition; destroy the political values on which a community has been built up, and only class war remains.

Marx did not discover this class war. He observed it in France and then generalized it as a formula for the future. That is the only way of the prophet: to foretell as the future what has already happened. Marx's prophecy has come off better than most, but in one vital point he went wrong. He supposed that the class war would be fought to a finish, that one side would win. And, since the bourgeoisie could not exterminate the proletariat, the proletariat would exterminate the bourgeoisie. There has been a different outcome: someone has slipped in between, played off one class against the other and exploited both. This, not his ragbag of ideas, was the great historical innovation of Louis Napoleon. He appealed to the fears of the middle classes when he made the *coup d'état* and presented himself as 'the Guardian of Order'. But he was also, in his muddled way, a socialist; he did more for the French working classes than any other French government before or since; and when he died a trade-union representative was the only man to come from France to his funeral.

But there was also another France, the France that had been created by the great revolution after what had been destroyed: the France that cared for liberty and the Rights of Man. This made the great difference between Louis Napoleon and his twentieth-century successors. The generals and civil servants and business men of Germany no doubt thought Hitler a barbarian; but once he had gained power, they licked his boots. The writers and political leaders of France never forgave Napoleon for the trickery and violence by which he had come to power. They turned their backs on him and condemned him to rely on his fellow-gangsters. It is not surprising that many Frenchmen supported Napoleon, especially in his hour of success; what is surprising and honourable is that so many Frenchmen opposed him from beginning to end. It was easy to be against Napoleon when he turned out to be the man of Sedan. It was his doom that he was branded from the start, and branded in history, as the man of December.

X

BISMARCK'S MORALITY

Historical reputations are a sort of political barometer; every generation gets the heroes it deserves. Professor Geyl recently gave a brilliant demonstration of this in the case of Napoleon. In English history, Henry VIII, hero of the late Professor Pollard, is going down; and Elizabeth, courted by Professor Neale and Mr. Rouse, is coming up. No doubt, in our era of decline, we prefer subtlety to animal vigour. Bismarck is the German barometer, the test of what German historians think of themselves and of the world. Of course, there are other significant German figures—Luther and Goethe, for example. Luther has gone down with the general decline of religion; unless you take his faith seriously, he was a repellent boor. Goethe is always produced when the Germans are feeling sorry for themselves. He has to act as excuse for the concentration camps and the gas-chambers; after all, a nation which produced Goethe cannot be wholly bad. Goethe was certainly a poet of the highest genius; apart from this, he was a complacent prig, servile and self-satisfied. He won't really do if the Germans are to escape the fate of Sodom and Gomorrah. Bismarck, with all his faults, is a better card for the Germans to play. He has that essential quality of the significant figure: he can be made to sparkle whichever way you look at him.

It is all the more surprising that hitherto there has been no good life of Bismarck. The standard German life by Max Lenx is no more than an enlarged obituary. Grant Robertson's splendid sketch, written during the first German war, gives out in 1871 when Bismarck had nineteen years of high office still ahead of him. During the second German war Erich Eyck, a German living in England, wrote a three-volume life which was published in Switzerland. He has now produced a reduced version in one volume[1] for the English reader. It would be a poor compliment to say that this is the best life of Bismarck;

[1] Erich Eyck, *Bismarck and the German Empire.*

it is the only life of Bismarck and will hold its own for years to come. For one thing, it covers the whole story from beginning to end. Or rather, to be precise, it gives out when Bismarck left office and omits the last eight years when Bismarck conducted a malicious and unscrupulous campaign against William II who had dismissed him. Still, it is more important that Dr. Eyck has read and digested the enormous mass of Bismarck literature. Even more than Napoleon, Bismarck has been the victim of too much scholarship. For the first eight years of Bismarck's time in office alone, there are forty-four volumes of published documents from the Austrian, Prussian, and French archives. No one has really sorted them out till Dr. Eyck faced them. Then there have been endless works of meticulous research, conducted as solemnly as the study of Holy Writ; every scrap of Bismarck's writing, every fragment of his conversation, have been assembled in the fifteen volumes of his Collected Works; and Bismarck added to the confusion in probably the most misleading work of autobiography ever written. Dr. Eyck is the master of his subject. Even though the bibliographical apparatus has been omitted in the English edition, the reader can have confidence that Dr. Eyck has examined all the evidence before passing judgement.

This last sentence suggests one of Dr. Eyck's defects. He is by training a lawyer, by profession a liberal journalist; and he took up history to relieve the tedium of exile. It is not so easy to become a historian as is sometimes supposed. Dr. Eyck gives the impression that he is always out for a verdict; and so far as Bismarck is concerned it is usually a verdict of guilty. Bismarck himself claimed that he kept five balls in the air; Dr. Eyck tends to insist that one ball must have been the decisive one and the others just kept spinning to deceive the audience. Bismarck had political genius of the highest order; certainly therefore he knew what he was doing. Dr. Eyck interprets this as meaning that Bismarck knew where he was going, a very different matter. The nineteenth century was an age of political optimism, and therefore most politicians thought in terms of objective—even though what they accomplished often turned out very differently from what they intended. Dr. Eyck's attitude is all right for them. But Bismarck was not a political optimist. He did not want to go anywhere; quite the reverse, he wished to slow things down. Most of the things that Bismarck accomplished—the war with

Austria, the war with France, the so-called unification of Germany—would have been accomplished anyway. What Bismarck really achieved was to make them less decisive than they would have been otherwise. He propped up the Habsburg monarchy for fifty years after its collapse; he preserved France as a Great Power; he retarded German unification until the days of Hitler; within his own limited Germany he staved off the triumph of plebiscitarian democracy.

This criticism leads to the deeper defect in Dr. Eyck's approach. His judgements are those of a contemporary, not of a historian. Dr. Eyck grew up dreaming of a liberal constitutional monarchy in Germany, associated with the Western Powers and with a liberal German Austria, and pushing Russia far to the east. Bismarck did not share this dream; and therefore Dr. Eyck condemns him. For instance, he condemns Bismarck for not making an alliance with England against Russia in 1879; yet such an alliance would certainly have led to war in the Near East. In fact, Dr. Eyck is not far removed from the conviction now widespread in the Western world—when is war not wicked, not a crime against humanity, not destructive, in fact when is war not war? When it is against Russia. Yet Dr. Eyck expresses a judgement on Austrian politics which is to me much more shocking than anything Bismarck ever did. He condemns Francis Joseph for dismissing his German ministers in 1879 and writes: 'We now know that in fact Francis Joseph brought about the collapse of his dynasty by banishing his faithful German subjects to the wilderness.' In other words Francis Joseph ought to have left power in the hands of the German minority—simply because they were middle-class liberals—and not attempted to conciliate his Slav subjects.

Dr. Eyck's verdict on Bismarck is that, though he was a wicked man, he accomplished a glorious work. He describes his enormous achievement—'the fulfilment of the dream of the German nations, their unification in a powerful and glorious Empire'. Again, 'the critics of his methods and his personality never can, nor will, doubt his singular greatness and his everlasting glory'. Bismarck's reputation for wickedness is a very curious affair. He has become the Old Nick of modern times; yet what did he do that others did not? He treated Austria much more considerately than Lincoln treated the southern states; he used his victory over France with much more moderation than Napoleon III would have used a victory over

Prussia. He bullied Denmark in 1864. Was this worse than the way Palmerston bullied Greece in 1850 or China in 1860? Though he was jealous of political rivals, he was no more jealous than Gladstone was of Chamberlain. It is difficult to discover noble idealists among the European statesmen with whom Bismarck had to deal—Gorchakov? Thiers? Andrássy? Disraeli? Bismarck did not lack morality; what he lacked was uplift. He could not make his voice quaver with unselfish zeal, as Gladstone's voice quavered when he occupied Egypt. Bismarck fought 'necessary' wars and killed thousands; the idealists of the twentieth century fight 'just' wars and kill millions. Bismarck defended national sovereignty, or rather accepted it as a fact; this was no more wicked than to reject the Schuman plan on the same grounds.

Though Bismarck lacked humbug, he did not lack principles. Only they were not liberal principles. They were principles founded in distrust of human nature, principles of doubt and restraint. When men dislike Bismarck for his realism, what they really dislike is reality. Take his most famous sentence: 'The great questions of our time will not be settled by resolutions and majority votes—that was the mistake of the men of 1848 and 1849—but by blood and iron.' Who can deny that this is true as a statement of fact? What settled the question of Nazi domination of Europe—resolutions or the allied armies? What will settle the question of Korea—majority votes at Lake Success or American strength? This is a very different matter from saying that principles and beliefs are ineffective. They can be extremely effective if translated into blood and iron and not simply into resolutions and majority votes. As a matter of fact Bismarck never underrated the importance of principles; rather he erred in taking the principles of others too seriously. He conducted political war first against the Roman Catholics, then against the Social Democrats, because he thought that they meant what they said—the Catholics that they were loyal only to the Pope, the Socialists that they were revolutionaries. The basis of our modern liberal democracies is that men do not mean what they say. This was indeed the justification for our first liberal act—the emancipation of the Roman Catholics from the penal laws. Nowadays, Mr. Attlee does not really believe that Mr. Churchill wishes to exploit the poor; and Mr. Churchill does not really believe that Mr. Attlee would lead the country to ruin. Most of our present troubles with the

Russians spring from the conviction of Roosevelt and his advisers that the Communist leaders did not mean what they had been saying for thirty years—at least no more than Roosevelt meant what he said at election time. Unfortunately the Communists are old-fashioned—like Bismarck.

Bismarck was old-fashioned in a more fundamental sense. He came from a peaceful, stable society; and he valued stability above movement. First inside Germany and then in Europe he achieved a balance of opposing forces, and so created a generation of stability. Men fall easily into the habit of taking security for granted; and the generation which flourished after 1878 soon regarded internal order and European peace as normal. In fact the years between 1878 and 1914—years with no revolutions outside Russia and no wars outside the Balkans—were the most abnormal years in modern history; and whatever the future has in store for us it is pretty certain that we shall never see the like of them again. Instead of dismissing Bismarck as a nasty man, it would be wiser to bear in mind that these years were his doing; that without him the great war of all against all—of class against class, of nation against nation—would have got under way sooner.

Finally, when judging Bismarck as a politician, one has to remember one other thing, which is not obvious to a German writer: Bismarck was dealing with Germans. The personal spite; the raucous evocation of Power; the irritation at opposition—these were qualities which he shared with other German politicians. The restraint; the ability to see into the minds of others; the readiness to risk his own prestige for the sake of peace and moderation; these were the things that Bismarck added. No doubt Germany and German policy in Bismarck's day had many faults; but no German since has done any better. I suspect that Bismarck would have preferred this cool praise to the eternal glory and moral disapproval which Dr. Eyck offers him.

XI

BISMARCK AND EUROPE

LEGENDS of Bismarck sprawl over the history of the later nineteenth century. First, the contemporary legend—the Bismarck who produced calculated effects on diplomats and politicians, wore military uniform and revealed only late in life that he had done it in order to save the wear-and-tear on his more expensive civilian clothes. Then the legend of German historians who saw in Bismarck the maker of German unity and for whom he could do nothing wrong or even mistaken. And, the reverse of this, the legend primarily of French historians, though often accepted in England too, for whom Bismarck could do nothing right—the man who planned the downfall of France as a Great Power and was responsible for three invasions of 'the national territory'. More recently there has grown up a version, to which I myself have contributed a little, of Bismarck as the thwarted conservative, exponent of the doctrine of 'the lesser evil', of whom one might say that everything he did he did unwillingly and only because anyone else could have done more of it. Though his political offspring were illegitimate, they were 'only little ones'. The study of Bismarck has become a modern scholasticism, each act and each saying combed over and elaborated on as though it were Holy Writ or one of those few documents which, surviving by chance, give mediaeval historians the illusion that they are engaged in a more scientific discipline than ours.

I have recently been fortunate enough to start examining Bismarck's diplomacy all over again. It would be foolish to pretend that it is possible to shut out of mind the versions of those who have gone before—Sybel and Ollivier, Friedjung and Matter, Grant Robertson and Marcks, Eyck and Srbik. But all of them had some political axe to grind; they were all concerned to show that he had failed or, more rarely, succeeded. I have clean hands. I really do not care—though this may sound untrue—I do not care about the Germans any more one way or the other. I am prepared to believe that Europe is finished; and I am only curious to know what happened to Europe in the second half of the nineteenth century without worrying any more about the outcome. So much of the diplomatic record has now been published that it is possible to write the story virtually from the archives, at any rate so far as Austria, France, and Prussia are concerned. Some details of British diplomacy could, no doubt, be added from further study of the archives, though I do not think they would be details of much moment. Russian policy is admittedly still obscure; and a documentary study of this between 1863 and 1871 would be one of the most welcome tasks which a Soviet scholar might perform. But even here the broad outline is clearer than it was a few years ago. I would add two points of caution or of apology. First, I am only concerned to look again at Bismarck's diplomacy, not at his work in Germany. I am convinced that his decisive achievement was in domestic politics and that the Bismarckian compromise or contradiction within Germany—it comes to much the same thing—is what mattered most in European history. Second, there can be no doubt that Bismarck was a great man. He ran down his predecessors and exaggerated his own achievement; he made more mistakes than he or his admirers would admit; he knocked sometimes at the wrong door and more often at doors that were already open. All the same, it is impossible to read his most casual utterance without feeling that here was someone outsize. It would be a waste of time to try to prove anything else; and equally unnecessary to be reiterating how great he was.

It is a great mistake to begin the story of German unification with Bismarck's accession to power in 1862, or even to treat the events of 1848 as a preliminary without relevance. Everything, including Bismarck's own work, springs from the revolutionary year. It is now widely held that France or Russia or both of them would have forbidden national unification in 1848. There seems little evidence of this. The French radicals supposed that national Germany would be their ally in liberating Poland; and though Bastide, Foreign Minister from May until December 1848, saw no reason to encourage a national Germany, his only approach to Russia was made to deter the Tsar from reviving the policy of the Holy Alliance. The Tsar's policy in 1848 was simple: he was determined not to move his armies beyond Russia's frontiers. Hence, he refused to intervene even in Slesvig-Holstein, though an important Russian interest—free passage of the Sound—was at stake there. In fact the only Power who threatened action over the Elbe duchies was England, the Power which otherwise favoured German unification. This is what Palmerston meant by his complaint against 'the parcel of children' at Frankfurt. The German liberals, he thought, ought to be creating 'a natural ally' for Great Britain on the continent instead of threatening the security of the Baltic. In any case, whatever the attitude of France and Russia to a hypothetical liberal Germany, neither of them made any objection to the consolidation of north Germany under Prussia. The Erfurt union, which made Prussia supreme north of the Main, was carried through without objection from either Russia or France. It is true that the Tsar's object in intervening in Hungary was, in part, to restore a balance in central Europe between Prussia and Austria; but he held, as the French did, that this balance was improved rather than the reverse by the strengthening of Prussia in northern Germany.

Russia followed the same policy in the crisis of 1850 which ended with the agreement of Olomouc. Certainly the Tsar wished to prevent a war between Prussia and Austria; but he wanted a settlement without either victors or vanquished. His real aim was to consolidate both Prussia and Austria as a neutral conservative buffer between Russia and western Europe. Hence he declared that he would support whichever was attacked; though, in fact, at the crisis Russia promised Austria only moral support. It was not danger from Russia which led the Prussians to give way; nor, for that matter, was it military weakness. Prince William was confident that Prussia could win; and this opinion was shared by the Russian generals who had seen Austrian troops in action in Hungary. Paskievich, the Russian commander-in-chief, even believed that Prussia would be a match for Russia and Austria combined. Prussia's real weakness was that both Frederick William IV and his conservative ministers regarded war with Austria as 'wicked'. They gave way more from conviction than from fear; and after 1850, as before it, Prussia was committed to the policy of reconciling hegemony north of the Main and partnership with Austria. This was also Russia's policy, as was shown in the spring of 1851, when the Tsar forbade Schwarzenberg's programme of uniting Germany under Austria—the Empire of seventy millions.

Though Bismarck welcomed the settlement of Olomouc, no one has contributed more to the version that Prussia thereafter became subservient to Austria. This version cannot be sustained. There was perhaps subservience when Manteuffel, the Prussian foreign minister, made a defensive alliance with Austria for three years in 1851. This certainly implied a Prussian guarantee for Austria's possessions in Italy, which she steadily refused thereafter; but it also barred the way against what seemed more likely in 1851—an Austrian alliance with Napoleonic imperialism. At any rate, there was no subservience in the alliance, when it was renewed on 20 April 1854. Though it, too, seemed to serve an Austrian purpose—by guaranteeing the Danubian principalities (later called Rumania) against Russia—this was in reality only the bait by which Austria was held from making an alliance with England and France. If Austria had joined the Western Powers in war against Russia, Prussia could not have stayed out. Whichever side she joined, she would have had to bear the main brunt of a war fought probably on her own soil—a war from which she could not possibly have gained and in which she might well have lost her Polish lands. As it was, Prussia performed the great service to Russia of keeping Austria neutral at no cost to herself; and, by advocating neutrality at the Diet, won the leadership of the German states as well. Yet this was the time when Bismarck denounced the incompetence of his official superiors. He opposed the alliance with Austria. At the beginning of the war he would seem to have favoured supporting Russia; at the end of it he preached, in one of his most famous compositions, that Prussia should make a third in the coming partnership between Russia and France. His own action in 1879 is the best comment on this policy. As Imperial Chancellor, Bismarck judged Manteuffel to have been right and himself wrong; but he took care not to say so.

Bismarck overrated all along the dynamism of the Franco-Russian entente. He thought that Napoleon III and Alexander II were set on remaking the map of Europe, both east and west, in the immediate future and that Prussia must hasten to play the jackal with them if she were not to be left out of things. Official Prussian policy, whether under Frederick William IV and Manteuffel or under the Prince Regent and the despised Schleinitz, stuck to its old line: support for Austria once she had recognized Prussian hegemony north of the Main. This policy came within sight of success in the Italian war of 1859. If Napoleon had insisted on his original aim of liberating Venetia as well as Lombardy, even more if Alexander II had taken the opportunity to reopen the Eastern Question—in fact, if France and Russia had been as dynamic as Bismarck supposed—Austria would have had to pay Prussia's price. As it was, she lost Lombardy and thus ended the war without Prussia's help. The real turning point came in the following year, 1860. In July Schleinitz and Rechberg, the Austrian foreign minister, met at Teplitz and agreed on a defensive alliance between their two countries—an alliance which Bismarck himself quoted as a precedent in 1879. The awkward question of Prussian hegemony north of the Main was postponed to a military convention that was to be negotiated subsequently. All this was a preliminary to a meeting of the two German rulers with the Tsar at Warsaw in September. They believed that Alexander II had taken fright at Napoleon's revolutionary policy and would now urge joint resistance in Italy. When it came to the point Alexander II could not give up his hopes for revising the settlement of 1856 in the Near East with French help and therefore would do nothing against Italy, Napoleon's satellite. The Holy Alliance turned out to be a mirage; and the Prussians were quick to draw the lesson. They screwed up their terms in the military discussions with Austria; and when these broke down, the alliance vanished with them. If there was a decisive moment in the relations between Prussia and Austria, it was in April 1861, and not after Bismarck became Prime Minister.

Bismarck's predecessors perhaps had different allies in mind. Schleinitz counted on the 'liberal' alliance with England, so far as he counted on anything at all. This policy was ruined by the American civil war, which locked up British military resources in Canada. Moreover, the British were increasingly aware that their navy was out of date. These factors, rather than any ideological swing towards isolationism, made Great Britain ineffective during Europe's years of destiny. Bernstorff who followed Schleinitz looked instead to France; his object was to replace Russia as France's continental ally. When Bismarck arrived in October 1862, he certainly meant to play the role of a Prussian Cavour; but with this difference from Cavour (as from Bernstorff) that he intended to co-operate with Russia as well as with France—a partnership therefore that would be anti-British as well as anti-Austrian. In fact he missed the bus (if there was ever one to catch). He assumed that the Franco-Russian entente was solid; instead it collapsed before he had been in office six months. Almost his first act was to ask in Paris what the French attitude would be 'if things hot up in Germany'. He was too late. Drouyn de Lhuys, enemy of Russia and advocate of alliance with Austria, had just returned to the Quai d'Orsay. Bismarck's query was brushed aside. Three months later the Polish revolt blew the Franco-Russian entente sky-high. Years afterwards Bismarck built up the story that he had pulled off a great stroke of policy by supporting the Russians in Poland and therefore winning their gratitude. This is untrue. The Russians thought they could deal with the Poles alone and much resented Prussian patronage. Moreover Bismarck's step ensured that, if it came to war over Poland, Prussia would have to fight for the sake of Russia's Polish lands; and he had to beg to be excused from the alliance with Russia within six weeks of making it. Even as it was, the quarrel over Poland was disastrous for Prussia. The great hope of Prussian policy had been that the French threat to Venetia and Russian threats in the Near East would so embarrass Austria as to make her surrender the hegemony of northern Germany to Prussia without a war. This hope was now ruined. The Franco-Russian entente had never been a threat to Prussia; rather it gave her security. The entente was directed against Austria; and France would not endanger it by seeking gains on the Rhine. The French threat there, if it ever existed, was created by the estrangement between France and Russia, not by their entente. No doubt Russia was now prepared to tolerate a Prussian war against France; but so she always had been, and this was a very different thing from active support—that the Russians never offered.

The truth is that, once the Franco-Russian entente broke down, Prussia was forced back to friendship with Austria as her only means of security. Here again Bismarck later created a myth—the story that the Slesvig-Holstein affair was a trap for Austria from the beginning. I think rather that, as so often, Bismarck, always impulsive and always exaggeratedly nervous of the aggressive designs of others, rushed himself into a commitment and then had to exercise all his great genius in order to get out of a tangle of his own making. For there is the fact. In January 1864 he made an alliance with Austria which did not include that recognition of Prussian hegemony north of the Main on which his predecessors had always insisted. His motive was fear, not gain; fear that, as in 1848, Prussia would be pushed forward in Slesvig by German feeling and then have to face a coalition of the Powers, reinforced this time by Austria. The Conference of London which tried to settle the Slesvig question showed that these fears were exaggerated. The Russian government was estranged from the Western Powers both by the Crimean War and, more recently, by the Polish affair. Besides, the Russians did not object to Prussia's gaining control of the Sound as long as she did not do it on a basis of nationalist enthusiasm. They objected much more to Austria's getting a foothold there and would have preferred an isolated Prussian action. Thus, curiously enough, the partnership with Austria—which Bismarck had insisted on as essential—was the one thing that worried the Russians and made them hostile. Still they did not mean to act in 1864—as, for that matter, they had refused anything but moral reproofs in regard to Slesvig both in 1848 and 1850. The real opposition in the previous crises had come from England; and the British—estranged from Russia by the Crimean War, suspicious of Napoleon III as a result of his annexation of Savoy, and with their forces tied in Canada—had no means of action. It is inconceivable that there could ever have been an Anglo-Austrian alliance to check Prussia in Slesvig; and, short of this, there was nothing the British could do. They twice took soundings for French support, in February and again in June. Both met with the same response. Napoleon would not act against the 'national' principle; Drouyn, who hated nationalism in general and Prussia in particular, demanded concrete gains on the Rhine—a prospect more unwelcome to the British than the Danish loss of the Duchies.

The three non-German Powers were in fact far more suspicious of each other than concerned about what might happen in Germany. The only thing that alarmed them was Prussia's alliance with Austria—Bismarck's own doing. Had he acted alone against Denmark, he would have had the approval of all the Powers except Austria; but he would have had to act on a liberal basis. Prussia's foreign danger, in short, was increased, if not created, by Bismarck's conflict with the liberals. He made the Austrian alliance, not to trick Austria, but to save himself. This is, I think, the answer to the disputed question whether Bismarck was ever sincere in his conservative partnership with Austria. He was a man of extremes. He could conceive a full return to the system of Metternich; hence in August 1864 he pressed on Austria not only a Prussian guarantee of Venetia, but a campaign for the recovery of Lombardy. He could also conceive of a 'revolutionary' alliance with France, by which Prussia expelled Austria from Germany north of the Main while France gained land on the Rhine. What he never foresaw was the moderate outcome—neither reactionary nor revolutionary—for which he has been so much praised. Moderation is said to be the most difficult of policies; it was certainly difficult for Bismarck.

I make no doubt that the offer of an alliance which he made to Austria in August 1864 was genuine. It seemed to him 'in the logic of the situation'. If Prussia was not to follow a revolutionary course, she must follow a reactionary one. Once more he asked less than his predecessors. In his exaggerated fear of French aggression, he offered Austria alliance against France without demanding Prussian hegemony north of the Main. William I, not Bismarck, insisted on this condition; and the Austrians thought Prussia so dependent on their support that they named Silesia as their price. The deadlock drove Bismarck off on the alternative 'revolutionary' course. He screwed up tension against Austria; and in May 1865 spoke openly of his policy as 'war against Austria in alliance with France'. A new compromise followed in August 1865, the Treaty of Gastein. This compromise came mainly from the side of the Austrians; and Bismarck accepted it merely because it was offered. But he was also bewildered by the failure of his 'revolutionary' policy to explode. When he approached the French for an alliance, they refused to display territorial ambitions. Napoleon went ostentatiously into the country; and left policy to be defined by Drouyn the conservative.

In October 1865 Bismarck visited Napoleon at Biarritz in order to clear up the mystery of French policy. It is often said that he tricked Napoleon by vague talk of future French gains in Germany. This is not so. It is true that the two rogues discussed 'advantages which might offer themselves unsought', advantages, of course, in Germany; but this was a casual theme. Napoleon's overriding interest was Venetia; he was determined to complete the work of 1859 and not leave to his son 'a volcano for a throne'. His price was Venetia; and

Bismarck paid it. He promised that he would not guarantee Venetia to Austria; and in return Napoleon promised that he would not make an alliance with Austria against Prussia—'he would not go and stand beside a target'. This was the essential bargain of Biarritz: Venetia for Italy, and French neutrality in a war between Prussia and Austria. Bismarck gave the bargain a positive shape when he concluded his alliance with Italy in April 1866; this ensured Napoleon that he would get what he wanted, and Bismarck was able to wage a limited war against Austria. Napoleon, not Bismarck, made the moderate programme possible and enabled Prussia to win hegemony north of the Main without a general European upheaval. To the very last Bismarck could not believe in his own success. In May 1866 he offered the Austrians peace if they would share the military headship of Germany. The Austrians would have agreed if they could have had in exchange a Prussian guarantee of Venetia; this, owing to his bargain with Napoleon, was the one thing that Bismarck could not give. Venetia compelled Bismarck to go to war. It also compelled Napoleon to favour war—it was the factor which wrecked his proposal for a European Congress. Most paradoxically of all, it even led the Austrians to want war. By May 1866 they had come to believe that the only way out of their difficulties was to surrender Venetia and gain Silesia in exchange. This would win Napoleon as an ally against both Prussia and Russia; it would free their southern frontier; and it would restore their prestige in Germany. But it was only possible by means of war against Prussia. Therefore, in the last resort, it was the Austrians who were eager to bring the war on. It is a curious fact that every European war between 1815 and 1914 was exploded by the Power standing on the defensive: England and France insisted on the Crimean War; Austria on the wars of 1859, 1866, and 1914; and France on the war of 1870. It is also a curiosity how little military considerations weighed in the decision to provoke war or to avoid it. Thus, the Prussians accepted the compromise of August 1865, although they were confident of victory. There is little foundation for the later story that they put off war until they could clinch their military superiority by making an alliance with Italy. And this alliance, when it was made in April 1866, was concluded for its political effect on Napoleon, rather than to divide the Austrian armies—this again was an advantage which the Prussians only discovered after it happened. On the other side, the Austrians did not provoke war in June 1866 because their military position had improved, but because it had got worse; they could bear the tension no longer. Finally, the French decision not to intervene after the Prussian victory at Sadova sprang purely from considerations of policy; the question whether the French army was capable of intervention was hardly raised. I am not sure whether any conclusion can be drawn from this odd ignoring of the basic facts.

There is another oddity. The war between Austria and Prussia had been on the horizon for sixteen years. Yet it had great difficulty in getting itself declared. Austria tried to provoke Bismarck by placing the question of the Duchies before the Diet on 1 June. Bismarck retaliated by occupying Holstein. He hoped that the Austrian troops there would resist, but they got away before he could catch them. On 14 June the Austrian motion for federal mobilization against Prussia was carried in the Diet. Prussia declared the confederation at an end; and on 15 June invaded Saxony. On 21 June, when Prussian troops reached the Austrian frontier, the Crown Prince, who was in command, merely notified the nearest Austrian officer that 'a state of war' existed. That was all. The Italians did a little better. La Marmora sent a declaration of war to Albrecht, the Austrian commander-in-chief, before taking the offensive. Both Italy and Prussia were committed to programmes which could not be justified in international law, and were bound to appear as aggressors if they put their claims on paper. They would, in fact, have been hard put to it to start the war if Austria had not done the job for them.

The war of 1866 was not the revolutionary war which had been preached by Bismarck until his visit to Biarritz; it was the moderate war as always envisaged by the Prussian statesmen whom Bismarck had despised. It is often regarded as something of a miracle that Bismarck carried it through without intervention from either France or Russia; but in truth neither of them had any objection to a Prussian hegemony in northern Germany which is all that was accomplished. The Russians, in any case, were in no state to intervene. For fifteen years after the Crimean War they almost ceased to be a military power so far as Europe was concerned. Between 1856 and 1863 the annual call-up for the army was not enforced; and the Polish revolt in 1863, itself caused by an attempted call-up, further delayed their recovery. They owed their security during this period of neglect to the Prussian buffer; and were therefore glad to see it strengthened. No doubt they would have expostulated if Bismarck had annexed the states of southern Germany or dismembered the Austrian Empire, but this was never on the programme. His moderation against Austria in 1866 has been much vaunted. Yet even he put up his terms. He excluded Austria from Germany, instead of dividing it with her at the Main. The King and the generals, who grumbled at his moderation, merely wanted some satisfactions of prestige—annexation of some Austrian territory in Silesia or a victory-march through Vienna. They certainly had no thought of destroying the Habsburg Empire. Nor is it true that Austria was reconciled by Bismarck's moderation. The Austrians had burnt their fingers in 1866 and meant to take less risks next time; but they still hoped for a next time. The war of 1866 was a milestone, not a turning-point, in Austro-Prussian relations.

The real turning-point, for all Europe, was, no doubt, that France did not intervene; but even the dramatic nature of this has been exaggerated owing to the fact that history has been written by those who opposed or regretted the decision, while Napoleon, the man who made it, remained silent. He had made up his mind all along; he was on the side of 'the revolution', on the side, that is, of Prussia in Germany, as he had been on the side of Sardinia in Italy. There was no real crisis of decision in Paris between 4 July and 10 July. It was simply that Napoleon, having deceived his ministers from the first, had now to override them. He thought—and perhaps rightly—that the European situation had changed in his favour; Prussia stronger than before and therefore less dependent on Russia; Austria excluded from Germany and therefore freer to balance Russia in the Near East; Italy contented with the acquisition of Venetia; and southern Germany 'internationally independent'. Even if he had known of the Prussian treaties of alliance with the southern States, he would have regarded this as an improvement on the German confederation. Then southern Germany had been guaranteed by both Prussia and Austria; now by Prussia alone, and with her Napoleon had no quarrel. Indeed he took Bismarck's breath away by insisting on Prussia's annexing the whole of north Germany—a victory for the revolution over moderation.

In the summer of 1866 Napoleon supposed that he had at last achieved the revolutionary coalition with Prussia and Italy; and he meant to complete it by resurrecting his entente with Russia. He was of course misled by the analogy with Italy. He supposed that, since the Italians continued to need protection against Austria, Prussia needed it also; and his half-hearted demands for compensation, which culminated in the attempted annexation of Luxembourg in March 1867, were all designed to make an alliance with Prussia acceptable to French public opinion. It is common to speak of these negotiations, and especially the Luxembourg affair, as a trap which Bismarck laid for the French. If it was a trap, why did he not spring it? The truth is simpler. The affair was not of Bismarck's seeking; it was thrust on him by the French and, though no doubt he had to consider German feeling, he would have welcomed an alliance with France, if Russia had been included in it. There, it seems to me, is the real explanation. The key to European diplomacy between 1866 and 1870 is to be found in the Near East, and not on the Rhine or even in Poland. So long as Russia and France were at loggerheads in the Near East, Bismarck could not let Luxembourg go to France without implicitly taking her side against Russia. But equally he refused a Russian offer to keep Austria neutral, because this also involved paying a price in the Near East. In April 1867 at the height of the Luxembourg crisis, he first suggested the solution that was his ultimate favourite: the revival of the Holy Alliance. It was contemptuously refused by both the other parties. Austria would not join without concessions in Germany, Russia would not guarantee the integrity of Austria nor allow her gains in the Balkans. The Eastern Question dictated a peaceful outcome of the Luxembourg affair. France would not allow Russia a free hand against Turkey; Prussia would not allow her a free hand against Austria. Therefore both botched up the Luxembourg question as best they could. The great turning-point had been reached without design and before anyone noticed it. Both French and German public opinion had taken a hand in diplomacy; and henceforth they were not to be reconciled—perhaps not even to the present day.

There is not much to be said of Bismarck's diplomacy between 1867 and 1870. As always when the Near East took the centre of the stage, he had none except to keep out of the way; or, at most, to act as honest broker when the conflicts of the other Powers threatened to involve Prussia. When the Franco-Russian entente seemed to be working in the Near East during the autumn of 1867, he played in with it; and, with Italy joining in too, this was the last display of the 'revolutionary coalition'. Bismarck backed out of the Near East as soon as the entente broke down, so as not to be left alone on the Russian side. In March 1868 he refused a direct Russian demand for an alliance against Austria-Hungary, though 'of course neither Power could afford to allow the destruction of the other'. In the autumn of 1868 he used the Hohenzollern family influence to damp down irredentist agitation in Rumania, so as to avoid having to choose between Russia and Austria-Hungary; and in 1869 he helped Russia and France to wind up the Cretan affair. He never took seriously the talk of an alliance between Austria-Hungary and France; it was, he said, 'conjectural rubbish', as indeed it turned out to be. He calculated quite rightly that the Habsburg government would never dare to offend Hungarian and Austrian-German feeling by supporting French interference in southern Germany; and equally that Napoleon would not break with Russia for the sake of Austria-Hungary. This disposes of the defence put up for Bismarck by some of his admirers that he had to provoke war against France in order to anticipate either an Austro-French or a Franco-Russian agreement. There was never any serious chance of the first; and the second offered Prussia advantages, not dangers.

There is a simpler defence of Bismarck's policy in 1870, that is, if he needs one: he did not provoke the war at all, except in the narrowest sense of exploding it at the last moment. Later on, when the war had become a national legend, Bismarck tried to take the credit for it; but it was unearned. Of course the Hohenzollern candidature for the throne of Spain was of his making. Its object was to act as a check on France, not to provoke her into war. His encouragement of or indifference towards the Spanish affair varied inversely with the Franco-Russian entente. When France and Russia were on good terms, this gave Prussia security, both against Austria-Hungary and against being involved in an eastern war; whenever they quarrelled, he looked round for other means of distracting French attention from the Rhine. He first took up the Hohenzollern candidature in February 1869, when Russia and France were in dispute over Crete. He dropped it as soon as they settled the question; and left it alone so long as their entente seemed within sight of renewal. He revived it once more, in the spring of 1870, when the Franco-Russian approach broke down. But the Hohenzollern candidature was primarily not a move in foreign policy at all. Bismarck's overriding concern was with southern Germany; and a Hohenzollern on the Spanish throne—like the project of declaring William I German Emperor which he aired at the same time—was designed to raise Prussian prestige south of the Main. In June 1870 Alexander II met Bismarck and William I at Ems—one of the many legendary meetings at which a war was supposed to have been plotted. In fact war against France was never mentioned. Bismarck expressed disapproval of Habsburg policy in the Near East; and he tried to persuade the Tsar that the south German princes would make a better bargain with William I than if they waited to be swept away by a more democratic wave in favour of his liberal successor. There could hardly be clearer evidence that Bismarck was not expecting the Franco-Prussian war at that time.

Of the actual war-crisis in July 1870 two things seem to me clear beyond all doubt, if one can escape from the layers of myth and prejudice. First, no one could have expected it to explode in the way that it did. According to all rational calculation, Leopold of Hohenzollern ought to have been on the throne of Spain before the French, or anyone else, knew what was happening. The actual leakage was due to the blunder of a cipher-clerk in the German legation at Madrid—an unpredictable event. Second, no one could have expected the French to turn the crisis into a war. Bismarck thought the affair would end in a humiliation for Prussia. That is why he stayed in the country and left William I to do the negotiating. The course of events was a setback for Bismarck, though he quickly made the best of things. So far as he had a settled policy, it was to incorporate southern Germany with Russian and even French approval—a decisive stroke against Austria and back to the dynamic coalition with France and Russia that he had always favoured. After all, he believed, rightly, that the Empire was the form of French government most favourable to Prussian interests; and he went on trying to restore Napoleon III even at the beginning of 1871. He had sometimes thought that a French revolution would lead to war; it was quite against his intentions that war led to a French revolution.

It is a further myth that Bismarck's diplomacy secured the neutrality of Russia and Austria-Hungary. Neither Power ever had any intention or inclination to go to war. Bismarck made no promises to the Russians of support in the Near East; and they made no promises to him. The Russians did not mobilize any troops in Galicia—they had, in fact, none to mobilize. They did not threaten Austria-Hungary. They promised the Austrians to stay neutral, if Austria-Hungary did the same; but in view of their military weakness, they would have stayed neutral in any case. For that matter, they did not believe that their interests would be injured by a French victory over Prussia—nor by a Prussian victory over France. The Austrians remained neutral solely from consideration of their own interests also. Beust wished to mobilize in order to intervene after the decisive battles had been fought; and, since he expected France to win that battle, his intention was to protect southern Germany against her. Andrássy, too, favoured mobilization; only he insisted on a declaration of neutrality so that, after the French victory which he also expected, both France and Prussia could be persuaded to join a crusade against Russia. This was as crazy as most of Andrássy's schemes. Gorchakov, the Russian chancellor, passed the correct verdict on the French dreams for an Austrian alliance when he said: 'Russia did not paralyse a support which had no chance of being realized.' Neither Russia or Austria-Hungary cared which way the war went in western Europe. So far as there was any element of calculation in their policy, it was simply that, once France was out of the way, Germany would no longer be able to follow a neutral line in the Near East—the only topic that interested them.

From Bismarck's point of view, the war of 1870 was a senseless affair; and he admitted as much in his many later apologies to the French. So far as he had any responsibility for it (and he did not have much), this sprang from his desire to weaken German liberalism by making France the national enemy instead of Russia. Whatever the responsibilities, the consequences of dividing Germany with Austria and of quarrelling with France were all that Bismarck had foreseen in his days at Frankfurt. Vienna took Berlin prisoner. In the Crimean War Prussian statesmen had worked to prevent Austria's going to the assistance of the western Powers; in the Bulgarian crisis of 1887 Bismarck had to implore the British to go to the assistance of Austria-Hungary; and a generation later his successors had to go to her assistance themselves. In 1879 Bismarck, and none other, tied 'the trim Prussian frigate to the worm-eaten Austrian galleon'—tied them together for good, although the galleon was now more worm-eaten by a generation. Was this really a triumph for his diplomacy?

To my mind, the younger Bismarck was the greater one—the Bismarck who modelled himself on Cavour rather than the Bismarck who modelled himself on Metternich, the 'mad Junker' rather than the sane one. He saw clearly that a national reconstruction of central Europe in co-operation with Russia and France was the wisest course for Prussia. But, when it came to the point, he himself prevented this. He overrated, no doubt, Russian and French dynamism; and when this failed swung away on the opposite tack. But his rejection of his own earlier policy had a deeper cause. The national principle in Europe only made sense on a liberal basis, as Cavour appreciated. Both Bismarck and Napoleon III hated the liberalism which was essential to the success of their foreign policy. Napoleon pretended to accept it; Bismarck hardly troubled to make the pretence. Germany and France could not work together except on a liberal basis; hence Napoleon III and Bismarck between them ensured that they would not work together at all. Everything sprang from this failure. Without French co-operation, Germany could not risk a national remaking of eastern Europe by Russia; therefore she had to prop up Austria-Hungary. The diplomacy of Bismarck's later years was simply an elaborate jugglery to conceal the fact that he had abandoned his earlier visions and had been forced to repeat, or even to outdo, the mistakes of his predecessors. It is curious, and more than a coincidence, that in the very weeks when Bismarck was founding his so-called 'league of peace' by means of the Austro-German alliance, Gladstone was formulating his principles of international co-operation in the Midlothian campaign. Nor is it, I think, an accident that in every subsequent world-conflict, Bismarck's heirs, the boasted real-politikers, have always been defeated by the heirs of Gladstone, those who hope to make the world anew. Once Bismarck had been one of these. He set out to remake central Europe. Instead he tied himself to the Habsburgs, and, like everyone who follows this path, ended up by believing that peace could be kept by tricks.

XII

(1)

THE RULER IN BERLIN

On July 31, 1914, Berchtold, Austro-Hungarian Foreign Minister, was dismayed by advice from Bethmann, the German Chancellor, to act with restraint and not to give the signal for war. His distraction was interrupted by Conrad, Chief of the Austrian General Staff. Conrad showed him a telegram from Moltke, Chief of the German General Staff, which urged that Austria-Hungary should at once mobilize against Russia and so launch a European war. Berchtold, with his irresponsible giggle, exclaimed: "That beats everything. Who rules then in Berlin?" This flippant remark was a profound judgment on the Germany of William II, and for that matter on the work of Bismarck. The question baffled contemporaries and has baffled later observers.

Between 1871 and 1890 it had seemed possible to answer the question. Bismarck ruled in Berlin. He devised legislation, determined policy, controlled even the military leaders; his decisions settled Germany's course. Yet Bismarck himself did not give this answer. He always insisted that Germany was ruled by the King of Prussia; and claimed that this was the core of his achievement. Bismarck's answer was not a mere pretence; even he, the greatest of political Germans, shrank from ultimate responsibility and shouldered it on to a "King by the Grace of God." All the same, the version was nonsense in practice, and largely even in theory. Germany could not be ruled by the King-Emperor, as Prussia had been ruled by Frederick the Great or even by Frederick William IV. Men may obey their king, even in a period when monarchical sentiment is declining; they will not obey someone else's king, and the King of Prussia was the king of others for the majority of Germans. The King of Prussia was German Emperor by conquest, by invitation of the German princes, by political intrigue, by constitutional arrangement, by everything except "the Grace of God." The German Emperor had no coronation—hence no religious sanction. Right still counted for much in Germany; and the Emperor's right rested on national sentiment, not on divine appointment.

Bismarck's creation deserved its name of "the second Empire"; its spirit was, in truth, nearer to the demagogy of Napoleon III than to the mystic tradition of "the Holy Roman Empire of the German Nation." After 1806, when the Holy Roman Empire ended, German authority could rest only on the masses. Bismarck had concealed this fact, as the titanic figure of Napoleon I had concealed it in France in similar circumstances. With the fall of Bismarck it could be concealed no longer. The question, "Who rules in Berlin?" was stated with ever-increasing urgency, until it found an answer in 1933.

William II had perhaps supposed in 1890 that he himself would rule in Berlin. This view was held later by those who wished "to hang the Kaiser." The fault of William was his failure to rule, not that he ruled wrongly. Dr. Eyck, his latest historian,[1] is nearer the truth when he draws a parallel with the system of English government in the reign of George III. George III, too, used to be accused of personal rule; this is a myth no longer believed by anyone. On the personal side it is unfair to compare William II with George III. William had considerable political gifts, to say nothing of his gift for phrase-making. Theodore Roosevelt said to him in 1910: "In America you would have your ward behind you and would lead your delegation at your party's national convention." In fact, William was a first-rate "key-note" speaker. On the great issues of politics he often saw farther than his professional advisers. In 1890 he was right to reject Bismarck's programme of a *coup d'état* in favour of reconciling the working-classes to the Reich; in 1905 he was right in opposing Holstein's policy of the Tangier visit; he was right (from the German point of view) in promoting the Baghdad railway; he was right in distrusting the moribund Habsburg monarchy and, at the end, in advocating concessions to Rumania as the one way of staving off disaster; even his advances to both Russia and

[1] *Das Persönliche Regiment Wilhelms II.* Politische Geschichte des deutschen Kaiserreiches von 1890 bis 1914. By Erich Eyck.

England did more good than harm—without such a gesture, for example, as his visit to the deathbed of Queen Victoria, estrangement between England and Germany would have come even sooner than it did. While the German Foreign Office was confidently snubbing all the Great Powers in turn, William II saw the dangers of "the free hand" and never ceased, though by erratic impulses, to seek for some great political combination.

His immediate reactions, no doubt, were often as wild as his longer vision was sound. He would scribble, "We must mobilize at once" on the news of some colonial dispute; and even proposed to arrest the transference of the British Fleet to the North Sea by an ultimatum. He exploded repeatedly against Austrian failure to destroy Serbia; yet he realized more clearly than any German diplomatist that this was a futile programme and, in his serious moments, urged reconciliation. His marginal notes, which made so much stir when published, were written for pleasure, not for action; and no action ever followed from them. They were the outbreaks of a man knowing himself, and known to be, irresponsible. The Kruger telegram is a case in point. This was certainly a watering-down of William's original idea of landing marines at Delagoa Bay. All the same, it would never have been sent, had it not suited Holstein's scheme of frightening England with the shadow of a Continental League. When this scheme failed, Marschall and Holstein shifted the blame to William, though the policy underlying it was theirs. So later, in the great crisis of the reign, Germans of all classes, from Bülow downwards, used the *Daily Telegraph* affair as a means for shifting on to William II all the consequences of German arrogance and power.

William II was not a ruler; he was a medium. He reflected the political mind of Germany and expressed it with genius. Contemporary observers were much at fault when they attributed the great German Navy to a personal whim of William II. The Navy was a demagogic cause, promoted by Liberal professors and popular even among Socialist and Roman Catholic voters. Had William surrendered altogether to his demagogic impulses, he would have anticipated Hitler's undisputed power. As it was, his upbringing and conscience reined him in; the King of Prussia restrained the German Emperor, as Prussia, in Bismarck's conception, restrained Germany. These negations were not a solution; and since William failed to lead, the problem was returned to the Chancellors. Here, indeed, is the profound political interest of the reign of William II—the search for a principle of authority and responsibility when this could no longer be provided by the Crown. To return to the analogy with George III: Dr. Eyck supposes that George III was defeated by "the opposition of Charles Fox," and blames the Germans for not producing a Liberal figure of similar eminence. This does that charming gambler too much honour. Growth of a sense of responsibility, not of an opposition, transformed the British Constitution; and this responsibility rested on a governing class which was truly representative of "the political nation." In Bismarckian Germany the governing classes, military and civil, were not merely out of touch with the masses who had now become the nation: they were actively and consciously opposed to everything that was dearest to national ambition. Bismarck's greatest achievement was his defeat of Greater Germany: he preserved the Habsburg monarchy and insisted that his truncated Germany was a "satiated State." This flew in the face of national sentiment. The only binding force in the governing classes was resistance to the popular will. Liberal observers, misled by Western analogies, thought that this implied principally resistance to a constitutional system; but the national masses demanded most of all a truly united Germany.

The reign of William II saw two attempts to break the deadlock between the governing classes and the nation; in different ways both Caprivi and Bülow aspired "to rule in Berlin." Caprivi took the way of Liberalism; Bülow attempted to wield the bow of Bismarck and to create a new Bismarckian compromise by agility and intrigue. Caprivi, who followed Bismarck as Chancellor, has been neglected by historians; yet he was the most significant of Bismarck's successors, for he conducted the experiment in Liberalism which later writers often suggested as the "solution" of the German problem. In fact Caprivi was the only parliamentary Chancellor of Imperial Germany. Though appointed by the Emperor, he thought in terms of a parliamentary majority, and this could be created only by means of a "national" programme. Hence Caprivi gave up Bismarck's negative foreign policy and supported the German cause in south-eastern Europe: domestic and foreign demagogy went hand in hand. Caprivi justified the imperial military programme by reference to Russia, instead of to France; and the climax of his policy came in 1893 when he carried the increased Army grant with the votes of Roman Catholics, Poles and some Progressives. As Dr. Eyck rightly says, the split in the Progressive party which followed this vote marked the end of Liberalism as a political force in Germany. Dr. Eyck calls it suicide; suicide is sometimes the only solution. Liberalism had no future if it failed to support Caprivi; equally it had no future if it supported him. For Caprivi himself had no future. In 1894 he ran into conflict with Botho Eulenburg, Prime Minister of Prussia. Caprivi wanted a democratic reform of the Prussian suffrage, Eulenburg a revival of the anti-Socialist laws. William II took the only course and dismissed them both. The decisive answer was given: no one could rule in Berlin.

This answer was accepted by Hohenlohe, the next Chancellor. Dr. Eyck speaks contemptuously of his age and feebleness; these were the necessary conditions of his existence. As a Bavarian, he would not restrain Germany for the sake of Prussia; as a Conservative, he would not break Prussia for the sake of Germany. With little power over events and no influence in the Reichstag, he tolerated all the decisive lurches in German policy: the Baghdad railway, the great Navy, the establishment in China were all Hohenlohe's doing, or rather consequences of his lack of doing. He deliberately avoided asking the great question, let alone attempting to answer it. Yet it was a question which demanded an answer. The man who attempted to answer it in the reign of William II was Bülow, Chancellor from 1900 to 1909. Bülow's name is weighed down by his *Memoirs*, the most trivial record ever left by a man who has occupied high position. Nevertheless he dominated the history of Wilhelmine Germany. Bülow was the only Imperial Chancellor after Bismarck to count in

German politics—the only one who made effective speeches and to whom men looked for a "policy." Still more, "the Bülow *bloc*" of 1906 was the first stable parliamentary combination behind the Chancellor since Bismarck broke with the National Liberals in 1879, and it was a more reliable coalition than any created under the Weimar republic. Finally, in 1908, Bülow—whether deliberately or not—used the *Daily Telegraph* affair to eject William II from politics and to impose upon him the limitations of a constitutional monarch. William II never recovered from this blow; it ended whatever fragments of "personal rule" remained.

Bülow's success was barren. It served only to reveal that the problem of German government lay deeper than in William's character; it was rooted in the foundations of Bismarck's Reich. The humiliation of William II left Bülow face to face with the Prussian Conservatives; and once more, as with Caprivi, it became clear that the twin causes of "world policy" and internal democracy could be achieved only after the defeat of the classes which Bismarck had preserved, the forces of old Prussia. Bülow declared to the Conservatives who brought him down: "We shall meet again at Philippi." The engagement was not fought in Bülow's lifetime; it was won by his demagogic heir in 1933 and completed by the massacres which followed July 20, 1944. Bülow's fall led to another, more fateful, interregnum, the Chancellorship of Bethmann Hollweg. Hohenlohe had allowed policy to be made without him; Bethmann Hollweg had it made against him. It was a grotesque, though inevitable, conclusion to Bismarck's work that the Chancellor should be helpless both in the Reichstag and in the Prussian Landtag; universal suffrage and privileged class-franchise alike rejected him. Yet for this very reason he was the only possible Chancellor. As in Metternich's Austria, "administration had taken the place of government."

A solution of a sort was found, perhaps against Bethmann Hollweg's will: a solution of foreign policy. German foreign policy of the 1890's had been "cabinet diplomacy," even though it made an occasional demagogic gesture. The last display of this "cabinet diplomacy" was the first Moroccan crisis of 1905, a crisis deliberately engineered by Holstein without any preparation of public opinion and hence ending in failure for Germany. Once more, in the Bosnian crisis, Bülow was the man of the transition: demagogue enough to back the German cause in south-eastern Europe, Bismarckian enough to regret having done so. In 1911 national opinion came into its own: the Agadir crisis was fought with public backing from start to finish. Nevertheless, Agadir was a false start, a red herring: it was deliberately designed by Kiderlen, last of the Bismarckians, to distract German chauvinism from eastern Europe and so from the mortal conflict with Russia. Until Agadir, Germany had remained a Power which, if not "satiated," could still be satisfied with colonial gains; after Agadir, Germany had to bid for the mastery of Europe. This inescapable fate determined the diplomacy of 1913 and 1914, which Dr. Eyck describes in full detail: German policy sought in vain to avoid the mission of conquest which was being thrust upon it. Few historians will quarrel with Dr. Eyck's verdict that the German statesmen and generals did not deliberately plan the outbreak of world war in July 1914; yet a war of conquest was the only possible outcome of German history. Bethmann Hollweg had been the only Imperial Chancellor to be censured by the Reichstag; he was also the only Chancellor to receive from the Reichstag a unanimous vote of confidence. Certainly in August 1914 Bethmann Hollweg did not "rule in Berlin"; what ruled at last in Berlin was the will of the German people for power.

The German problem, past and present, is the problem of German unity. Though this does not exist now, we are tempted to think that it existed in some Golden Age of the past. Dr. Eyck's book is a reminder that this Golden Age cannot be found in the age of William II. Imperial Germany was never a united national State, in the sense that France was united and made a nation by the great revolution. In Imperial Germany, almost as much as in the Holy Roman Empire, there was a balance of authorities and classes; instead of authoritarian rule there was "organized anarchy." Germany had, in some sort, a "governing class"—the Prussian army officers and Prussian administrators. Though this class held

Germany together, it was even more concerned to hold Germany back; while offering Germany a corset, it strapped on a strait-jacket. The first German war weakened this class; the Hitler revolution completed its destruction. There are now no forces within Germany to resist the full programme of German unification, and the present partition rests solely on the occupying armies. This gives it a unique and precarious character. A Germany free from foreign control will seek to restore the united Greater Germany which Hitler achieved in 1938; nor will democracy provide an automatic safeguard against a new German aggression. In the reign of William II every step towards democracy was a step towards general war. The Navy was popular, "world policy" was popular, support for the German cause in eastern Europe was popular. Attempts at reconciliation with others were unpopular; and William's prestige was ruined in 1908 when it became known that he favoured friendship with England.

The harsh truth of German history is that the solution of the German question cannot be found within Germany. Partition cannot be maintained as a permanent policy; yet a united Germany will keep Europe in apprehension, and would be tolerable only in a world of United Nations. Wilhelmine Germany overshadowed her neighbours by playing off East and West; any future Germany will seek to do the same. If the Great Powers were on friendly terms, there would even now be no German problem; so long as they remain estranged, Germany will offer the occasion, and may be the originator of future wars. "Who rules in Berlin?" The question once dominated German history; now it torments all the world. In our impatience and anxiety we are led to hope that one day the German people may rule in Berlin. That outcome is, in the long run, unavoidable; it will be tolerable only if there also rules in Berlin awareness of a community of nations. It is for the Germans to seek unity on a democratic and pacific basis; the Great Powers must ensure that the Germans do not promote unity by a programme of foreign aggression. At the present time, both the Germans and the Great Powers are failing in their task; and the question, "Who rules in Berlin?" has lost nothing of its menacing character.

XII

(2)

FRANCIS JOSEPH: THE LAST AGE OF THE HABSBURGS

ON December 2, 1848, Francis Joseph became Emperor of Austria. He was to reign for almost sixty-eight years, the longest effective reign of modern times. His life spanned the epochs of history. Metternich had ceased to be Imperial Chancellor less than nine months before his accession; two years after his death Austria-Hungary disintegrated into national States. When he was born, Napoleon's son, the King of Rome, was living in Vienna as an Austrian archduke; when he died Adolf Hitler, still an Austrian subject, was serving in the German Army. His reign opened in revolution and closed in war.

Francis Joseph himself fought two wars: in the first he lost his Italian territories; in the second he lost the hegemony of Germany. He started a third war and did not live to see its end; this end was the loss of everything. He won no wars; he lost more territory than he gained. His success was in surviving at all. He was a symbol of rigidity and of resistance, if not of life, in an Imperial organization which, while it had lost creative power, refused to break in pieces. He called himself "the last monarch of the old school" and imagined himself at one with Charles V or Louis XIV. Their pride rested on unquestioning self-confidence; his was always conscious of the challenge of "the revolution." He represented traditional beliefs and institutions, when these had been forced on to the defensive; like them he lacked faith even in himself. He always expected failure and disappointment, and he always got them.

The manner of his accession set the pattern for his reign. The Court was at the little Moravian town of Olomouc, in refuge from the Vienna Revolution of October 1848. The revolution had been crushed, and the counter-revolutionary

Prime Minister, Felix Schwarzenberg, wanted to show by a striking gesture that a new era of ruthless power had opened. The mild, half-witted Emperor Ferdinand was therefore pushed aside in favour of his nephew Francis Joseph, the young pupil of clericalist soldiers. The actual abdication was hurried through in a room of the archbishop's palace before a few Court officials. No one had had time or opportunity to look up the precedents, and the only ceremony was a blessing of Ferdinand on his nephew. Thus Francis Joseph, the personification of monarchical right, ascended his throne in a hole-and-corner manner; this august "crowned head" reigned for nineteen years without any kind of coronation—and was then only crowned King of Hungary. For though the House of Habsburg could rightly claim to be the most historic dynasty in Europe, Hungary was the only part of the Habsburg Empire with a living tradition; yet this tradition was largely of resistance against the Habsburg rulers.

When Francis Joseph took over the throne he exclaimed: "Farewell, my youth!" It was his only human remark. From the first he turned himself into an institution. He sacrificed everything for the sake of the dynasty, and he expected others to sacrifice everything too. Though he had a sincere love for his wife, Elizabeth, the most beautiful woman of her age, he would not extenuate the harsh ritual of Court life even for her. Elizabeth's spirit would not be stifled, and she left him, after providing Catherine Schratt, the Emperor's mistress for more than thirty years and the only human being who came into contact with him and remained human. Elizabeth wandered restlessly across Europe from Corfu to Ireland until she was assassinated by an anarchist on a Lake of Geneva steamer. Rudolph, Francis Joseph's only son, was also driven into wild courses by the repressive Court life and committed suicide at the end of a somewhat sordid romance. Francis Ferdinand, the Emperor's nephew and next heir, married morganatically outside the permitted degrees of royalty. When he and his wife were assassinated at Sarajevo in 1914 the first thought of Francis Joseph was that dynastic purity had been saved: "A higher power has reasserted the rules that I was unable to maintain."

Francis Joseph had no tastes and no friends. Though Vienna was largely built in his reign he set no mark on it; the Imperial buildings are heavy and lifeless. He did nothing to encourage the arts, not even the art of Johann Strauss or of Lehar. Viennese culture, real though frivolous, had no contact with this conscientious worker at his bureaucratic task. His Ministers experienced even more than the usual "thanks of the House of Habsburg." He used them, thrust them forward into conflict, and then, on an impulse or a rumour of failure, would fling them aside. Taaffe, Prime Minister of Austria for fourteen years and the Emperor's boyhood companion, was thus dismissed without explanation or thanks in 1893, and so, in 1906, was Beck, Chief of Staff for thirty years. Francis Joseph ruled without imagination and without winning the hearts of men. After he had been reconciled with the Hungarians and presumably wished to conciliate them he decorated the royal palace at Budapest with scenes of his victories over the Hungarians in 1849. His only thought was of dynastic power. Yet, though rigid in his dynastic aims, he was ready to try any means of sustaining his Empire. He began with military dictatorship and sometimes reverted to it. Taught by defeat, he made concessions to all in turn; the Compromise of 1867 gave Hungary internal independence, and in the same year Austria received a liberal Constitution. Later he sought to win over the Czechs, and finally, in 1907, forced universal suffrage through the Austrian Parliament in order to be able to play off the masses against the middle-class politicians in a vast game of *rouge et noir*. His greatest hatred was for "liberalism" —the attempt to limit the prerogatives of the Crown. Against this liberalism he would call on any ally and would even invoke the rival nationalisms which were tearing his Empire to pieces.

Clever writers in Vienna tried for more than a century to invent an Austrian "mission." This "mission" was supposed to be the security which the Empire gave to fifty million people, in which they could prosper and develop their cultural life. In the twentieth century this "mission" took on a predominantly economic tone, and Austria was praised as a great

"Free Trade area." In truth, the mission was a device by which Hungarian landowners and German capitalists grew rich from the labour of the lesser peoples. It was these two groups whom Francis Joseph took unwillingly into partnership. In his own mind Francis Joseph cared for none of these "missions." He did not regard the dynasty as the servant of the Austrian peoples; it was for them to be the servants of the dynasty and to sustain its military greatness. Viennese intellectuals complained that Francis Joseph did not follow the example of Joseph II, the "people's Emperor." To do this he would have had to lead peasants against their lords and subject peoples, Slav and Rumanian, against the Germans and Magyars, the two privileged nationalities. Such a course was outside dynastic imagining. Francis Joseph was fated to end his reign as a German auxiliary; the only "mission" he left to his successor was to be a German agent—or to disappear.

XIII

THE FAILURE OF THE HABSBURG MONARCHY

THE HABSBURG MONARCHY was the toughest organization in the history of modern Europe; no other has stood up so long to such battering from so many sides. The Habsburgs rode out the storm of the Reformation; withstood the impact of the Turks; challenged Louis XIV; and survived the French revolution. The age of nationalism was their doom. This reason alone would justify a new analysis of the national problem in the Habsburg Empire. And there are others. In 1919, after the First World War, the national State seemed to be the pattern for the future. Now we are not so sure. Even the old-established national States of western Europe are drawing together in terms of incipient federalism; how much less likely is it that the national States of eastern Europe will survive in undiminished sovereignty. Thirty years ago writers tended to regard the great Habsburg Empire as the 'normal' civilized order from which the national States were an unfortunate decline; then, for a short time, men regarded the national States as something equally 'normal' and yet more final. Now we are coming to recognize that both were transitory like all else in history; Francis Joseph could not live for ever nor could the world stand still in 1919. The present system in eastern Europe has elements of federalism, mixed up in its communist dictatorship; and it is almost certain that no future swing of events will bring back either the Habsburgs or the national States with unrestricted sovereignty. Thus it is rewarding, at any rate as a preliminary exercise, to analyse not only the national problem in the Habsburg Monarchy, but also the attempts to reconcile nationalism with a supranational structure.[1]

This is what Professor Kann has attempted to do in his two

[1] Robert A. Kann, *The Multinational Empire*. Nationalism and National Reform in the Habsburg Monarchy, 1848–1918. Vol. i, Empire and Nationalities. Vol. ii, Empire Reform.

formidable volumes. They provide more material for a study of the problem than has hitherto existed in any single book in English. His work, it must be admitted, is rather uncritical. It is an anatomy in Burton's sense, not an analysis. Material is accumulated; quotations are piled one on top of another without discrimination. Altogether his book illustrates the modern delusion that if only we know enough facts we shall arrive at the answer. This is particularly true of his first volume, which sets out to present the national problem. Kann recognizes, of course, that nationalism is tangled up with history; and he elaborates two principles that are common to all discussions of the Habsburg Monarchy. One is the division between the nations with a history—the Germans, the Magyars, and even the Czechs—and the nations whose cultural tradition had been completely broken, such as the Slovaks or the Ruthenes. The other is the doctrine of the 'historico-political individualities', by which historical units, such as Hungary or Bohemia, were identified with national claims (Magyar or Czech) which did not in fact correspond with them. Thus history bedevilled the national problem in a twofold way. The nations with a history despised the nations without a history; moreover, they tried to enforce against them, or even against other nations with a history, claims based on history, not on national right. The Magyars insisted on the unity of Hungary against the subject races; the Czechs insisted on the unity of Bohemia against the Germans; the Germans, for that matter, tried to maintain the unity of a German-controlled empire against all comers.

Kann further recognizes that there were in the Habsburg Monarchy two sorts of nationalism; the nationalism of landowners and the nationalism of professors—the one traditional, the other academic. But he does not push this analysis far enough. Like most liberal writers, he dismisses Magyar nationalism as 'feudal' and never makes the vital point that its real standard-bearers were the petty gentry, not the great aristocrats. If Hungary had had to depend solely on the Andrássys and Apponyis, its nationalism would have been as artificial as was the Czech movement in the days when it looked to the Thuns and Clam-Martinics. When we come to academic or cultural nationalism, the distinctions are more complicated and more essential. The first age of national awakening is strictly academic. It is led by university professors and is concerned with such things as the study of mediaeval manuscripts, the evolution of a national language from a peasant dialect, and the rewriting of history on national lines. The second stage comes when the pupils of the professors get out into the world. Then it is a question of the language used first in secondary, finally in elementary schools; the battle is fought over popular newspapers, not over learned works of research. Finally, the elementary school-teachers themselves have pupils: men of some education, who remain peasants or factory workers. We have arrived at mass-nationalism; what Kann calls, without analysing it, the integral nationalism of the twentieth century.

Each of these nationalisms is different in character, in its demands, in the weight of its support. Incredible as it may seem, Kann does not attempt these distinctions; he does not even attempt to estimate the numbers of supporters that any national movement had at any particular moment. Yet there can never be a time at which, say, the equation 'German equals German nationalist' is true. Kann accepts the consequences of this without understanding the reasons for it. He discusses the two non-national movements of the Social Democrats and the Christian Socials; but the point is lost. Yet it is a simple one. Only when nationalism becomes a mass movement do the mass movements become important. On the other hand, at this very time, they begin to lose their non-national character. In the last decade of the Habsburg Monarchy both international socialism and international clericalism were beginning to disintegrate under the impact of nationalism; and the process was carried further in the inter-war years. Nowadays even communism is shaken by the nationalist heresy.

The second volume of Kann's book deals with the attempts at reform. But, since there has been no real diagnosis, the reader is constantly puzzled by the question: 'What is it they were trying to solve?' Of course, the men of the time were equally puzzled by this question; hence perhaps their failure. It was commonly believed that the national question was a question of administration. If men could have officials, teachers, and judges using the national language, they would be satisfied. The example of Hungary was decisive and misleading. There can be no dispute that autonomous local administration in the *comitats* was the secret of Hungary's success both in surviving as a nation and then in defeating Habsburg encroachments. But it did not follow from this that, if other nationalities got autonomous local government, they too would automatically repeat Hungary's success. In fact, under dualism, Hungary became a centralized modern State and the *comitats* an empty form, at the very time when centralization was being weakened in the rest of the Empire for the sake of local autonomy. The explanation was simple. Local autonomy was a vital weapon so long as it was a question of resisting the central government; as soon as this battle had been won, it became useless and even an embarrassment. If the *comitats* had remained genuinely autonomous they would have been captured by the nationalities; and Hungary would have ceased to be a Magyar State.

In the last resort the national question is not a question of schools or of government officials—these are mere preliminaries. It is a question of power. Men wish to decide their own destinies. In a national State this leads them to resist kings and emperors and to demand democracy. In a multinational State they resist the rule of other nationalities as well. The Czechs or Rumanians or Ruthenians did not wish merely to use their own languages in school or in the courts; they were determined not to be involved in wars for the sake of German supremacy or for Magyar and Polish causes. The most extraordinary thing in all the discussions about the 'Austrian problem' is the question always left out: who was to rule? Or rather, the omission was deliberate. Every so-called solution assumed that the Habsburgs would remain in supreme control in Vienna; hence the only problem to be solved was that of local administration. Anybody can think of satisfactory schemes for chopping up the Empire into national units or historical units or a mixture of both, which would have done quite well if they had settled the essential problem; in reality they were remote from it. The more perfectly the central parliament represented the different nationalities of the Empire the more futile it became; for the more it was divided. The basic misunderstanding can be seen in the very title of Kann's book. The Habsburg Monarchy was not a multinational empire; it was a supranational empire. Nations can perhaps co-operate if they have a common loyalty to bind them together; they cannot co-operate, at any rate within a single State, merely for the sake of co-operating. The Habsburgs had once provided the common loyalty; in the nineteenth century they failed to do so any longer, and it was this Habsburg failure, not the rise of the nationalities, which doomed their Empire.

The Habsburgs are missing from Kann's book—missing that is as a principle and a cause. Francis Joseph appears merely as ruler, playing the same role as, say, a President of the United States. But Americans are not loyal to President Truman as such; they are loyal to the constitution, to the American 'idea'. The Habsburgs failed to find 'an idea'. How could they be expected to find one? For them, as much as for the nationalities, politics was a question of power; and, so far as they were concerned, it was a question of foreign power. One of the great blunders of modern political thinking is to invent an abstract entity called the State. Many States can be organizations for welfare or internal order, or whatever else suits the theorist. But some half-dozen States, called the Great Powers, are organizations primarily for power—that is, for fighting wars or for preventing them. Hence all analogies between the Habsburg Monarchy and, say, Switzerland break down. The Habsburg Monarchy was a Great Power or it was nothing. If it could have survived in war against other Great Powers it would not have undergone national disintegration.

The practical historian is thus driven back to analysing the failures of Habsburg power—failure in its armaments, failure in its system of communications, failure in its food supplies, above all failure in its foreign policy. The Habsburgs were fond of finding their doom in a 'Piedmont'; first in the original Piedmont, which nearly brought disaster to them in 1859; then in Serbia, which was the 'Piedmont of the South Slavs'. This analysis, correct enough in its way, has been much misunderstood. The essence of a 'Piedmont' was not that it represented a national challenge; the Habsburgs could deal with such. A 'Piedmont' rejected any need for the Habsburgs at all; it was a rival Power. Both Italy and the South Slav State wished to destroy the Habsburg Monarchy, not to reform it; both would have turned with a smile from the elegant plans of reform catalogued by Kann. It is ironical that they should now be the two States which feel most acutely the consequences of the Monarchy's disappearance: both have Russia on their borders. In the last resort the Habsburg Monarchy was not a device for enabling a number of nationalities to live together. It was an attempt to find a 'third way' in central Europe which should be neither German nor Russian. Once the Habsburgs became Germany's satellites in war they had failed in their mission. Their doom was of their own making.

XIV

FASHODA

On September 19, 1898, Kitchener—fresh from his destruction of Dervish power at Omdurman a fortnight before—encountered a small French force at Fashoda, on the Upper Nile. Kitchener had behind him a victorious army; Marchand, the French commander, a handful of men. France was at the worst moment of the Dreyfus case; her Army was distrusted and confused; her Navy had declined after a period of reform in the previous decade. Russia, her ally, was absorbed in China and indifferent to the affairs of the Near East. In England, Imperialism was at its height. The British Government rested on a compact majority: Chamberlain, as always, was for resolute action, and Salisbury had long planned to restore in Egypt his waning fame. British naval preponderance was greater than ever in our history: the Navy was able to hold the seas against France without special precautions, and the total extra cost of the Fashoda crisis over peace-time estimates was £13,600. For this sum England gained undisputed mastery in the Near East from her only traditional rival. No empire has ever been won so cheaply. Yet the abiding importance of the Fashoda affair was in the affairs of Europe; and the fate of Marchand ultimately turned the scales in the balance of power.

In regard to Egypt and the Sudan, Fashoda was an epilogue, the inevitable conclusion of an old theme. The issue was not whether France or England should control Egypt (and so the Near East). That issue had been decided against France in 1798 when Nelson destroyed Bonaparte's ships at the Battle of the Nile; it had been decided in favour of England in 1882 when the British occupied Egypt without French co-operation. The sole issue was whether France was to receive compensation for renouncing the legacy which Bonaparte had failed to bequeath to her. Unable to challenge the British directly in Egypt, the French had planned to disturb them from the rear by arriving unexpectedly in the Sudan. The basis of this plan was the assumption that it would be easy to dam the Upper Nile and so to dominate Egypt.

This assumption was wrong; and the discovery that even if Marchand stayed in Fashoda he could not carry out this threat was the last blow to French plans. The French assumed, too, that the dispute would always be conducted on a diplomatic and legal plane—a game of chess, as it were, with strict rules. The legal issue was simple (except that the disputants changed sides during the dispute). Since the Egyptian withdrawal from the Sudan in 1885 the British had treated former Egyptian territory as without an owner, *res nullius*. They took part of it for themselves and claimed more; they gave some to the Italians and proposed to lease a large section to Leopold II, king of the Belgians. Against this the French maintained the rights of the Khedive and even of the Sultan, his overlord. Once the French arrived on the Nile they abandoned this argument and, in their turn, insisted that Fashoda was ownerless. The British had reconquered the Sudan in the name of Egypt and in their own as well. At Fashoda they were doubtful of their own rights, since in 1894 they had attempted to lease it to Leopold II (as a barrier against France). For this reason Kitchener hoisted only the Egyptian flag at Fashoda, and not the Union Jack as well, as at Khartum. Still, the legal issue was irrelevant; the British had abandoned it in favour of a decision by force. As Salisbury said: "We claim the Sudan by right of conquest, because that is the simplest and most effective." The French could not compete with this right; Marchand withdrew in November 1898, and the French renounced all access to the Nile Valley in March 1899. The British had far more trouble with Leopold II, who would not renounce his lease (anti-French and so now purposeless) until 1906.

Fashoda completed British security in Egypt and so revolutionized British Near Eastern policy. Once established at Alexandria, the British no longer feared Russian control of Constantinople. The greatest obstacle to better relations between England and Russia was removed; and therewith England severed the last link of interest which held her to the Central Powers. It was the end of the system of associations which had sprung from the Congress of Berlin in 1878.

Fashoda and its outcome also modified French policy towards Russia. Until 1898 it had been possible to dream of a grandiose Franco-Russian action which would give Constantinople to Russia and Egypt to France. This dream was without substance. The French, patrons and creditors of Turkey, would pay too high a price for Egypt if they handed over control of Turkey to Russia; and, in any case, the Russians were not interested—Chinese ambitions eclipsed the Near East. Thus Fashoda emptied the Franco-Russian alliance of the anti-British purpose which it had originally possessed; thereafter it could only be anti-German.

Here, in Franco-German relations, was the true significance of the Fashoda crisis. France had always been torn between continental and overseas interests; and so had missed success in both. Conflict with England had deprived Napoleon of empire in Europe; danger from across the Rhine had kept the French out of Egypt in 1798, in 1840 and in 1882. Had there been no war of 1870 and no question of Alsace and Lorraine, France would certainly have bid again for Egypt; the Suez Canal was purely a French enterprise, and Napoleon III had presided at its opening in 1869. In 1884 Bismarck had reproached the French that they would not play *le grand jeu* in Egypt; they would not engage in a struggle for existence against England in the Near East. The supreme German blunder was to suppose that there was for France any "great game" other than the maintenance of French independence and the redress of the national wrong. The French expeditions to the Upper Nile were designed to wind up the Egyptian affair on honourable terms, not to open "the great game"; and Delcassé, maker of the Anglo-French entente in 1904, was consistent when as Minister of the Colonies he launched the French explorers in 1894. Admittedly Delcassé put out feelers for German support at the height of the Fashoda crisis; the condition for accepting this support was autonomy for Alsace and Lorraine.

Even without this, German diplomatic backing for France would have had immeasurable effect on French public opinion; it was the last, and greatest, opportunity at which the Germans might have established a peaceful hegemony of Europe. Instead, the Germans encouraged both sides to war and believed that the European situation was turning ever more in their favour. In reality, Fashoda and its outcome made the Anglo-French entente inevitable; hence Delcassé insisted from the beginning that France had received fair treatment. Ultimately, in 1904, France got better terms than she could have expected in 1898; this was partly the result of the Boer War, partly of local circumstances in Morocco. The basic terms had been settled in 1898 and remained unaltered. France renounced the Near East in order to maintain her independence in Europe; equally, though less obviously, England, by accepting the French renunciation, became the guarantor of French independence. More than any other single event, Fashoda fixed the pattern of the Triple Entente and so of the war of 1914.

XV

THE ENTENTE CORDIALE

THE agreements which gave formal expression to the Anglo-French entente were published on April 8, 1904. British opinion welcomed the agreements enthusiastically, but saw in them colonial arrangements and nothing more. "We have settled our differences with France" was the common phrase. England had made a good bargain: apart from the sorting out of many minor disputes she had made her control of the two ends of the Mediterranean secure from French interference for ever. At the one end France recognized British predominance in Egypt and finally renounced her own claims; at the other end France gave new guarantees for the invulnerability of Gibraltar, for she agreed, as the condition of her bringing Morocco into the French Empire, that the Moorish coastline opposite Gibraltar should pass to Spain and should be preserved unfortified by the three Powers.

No wonder the British welcomed the agreements: in cheering the French they were, in characteristic British fashion, cheering a good loser. The heirs of Napoleon were acknowledging finally the victory of Nelson. There was on the British side hardly a shade of precaution against Germany. The British were, of course, glad to escape from the attitude of dependence on Germany into which the danger of conflict with France had sometimes led them. But they did not fear Germany, nor had they any cause of conflict with her: the trivial colonial disputes were long ended, and although the building of the German fleet was a nuisance the British were confident that they could always hold their own at sea unaided —after all, in 1905 the British Navy attained a superiority over the combined naval forces of all other Powers unparalleled in our history.

Still less was there on the British side any great principle, any idea of co-operation between the Western democracies against German militarism. Lord Lansdowne, the Foreign Secretary, had worked as hard in 1901 for an alliance with Germany as in 1903 and 1904 for an entente with France. It would be difficult to see in the Irish landowner who resigned from Gladstone's Government in 1880 rather than acquiesce in Irish land reform and the Tory die-hard who defended the House of Lords in 1910 a champion of democracy; and the author of the Lansdowne peace letter, who in 1916 advocated a *status quo* peace (for the sake of social order) and even then saw no need for Germany to atone for her crimes, detected no threat to civilization in the Germany of 1904.

With the French it was far otherwise: there the advocates of the entente knew what they were doing, knew that they were staking the future of France for the sake of Western democratic civilization. For more than two hundred years the French had carried on colonial conflicts with England, and for more than two hundred years French ambitions in Europe had made her the loser in these colonial conflicts. French domination in Europe was ended at Leipzig and Waterloo, and its last echoes were silenced at Sedan. After 1871 necessity left France free as never before to pursue colonial aims and to find a substitute for lost European glory in the Mediterranean empire which was the legacy of Bonaparte's expedition to Egypt in 1798. Germany, as Bismarck was constantly urging, was eager for reconciliation, and if France had been reconciled with Germany as Austria-Hungary had been after 1866 she could have had German support against England in Egypt as Austria-Hungary had it against Russia in the Near East.

Reconciliation was the logical, easy course, but it was not taken. Only a small unpopular minority advocated revenge. The great majority recognized that France had been irretrievably defeated, yet they would not accept German patronage. For almost thirty years France refused to acknowledge the inevitable; she tried to oust the British from Egypt without German support. The Fashoda crisis of 1898 showed that the attempt was impossible, and Delcassé, then newly Foreign Minister, determined the future destinies of France when, without appealing for German assistance, he ordered Marchand to withdraw.

For the English the entente had no anti-German point, but the French knew that in making the entente they were becoming the hostage of democracy on the continent of Europe. They had no hope of winning British assistance for a war of revenge. Indeed, in the then state of the British Army they did not even value British assistance for a defensive war; the Army of their Russian ally remained their sole military support. But the French were determined not to become partners in the German order. To renounce Egypt was a crime against the memory of Bonaparte; to renounce Alsace and Lorraine would be a crime against the national principle, an infringement of the Rights of Man.

The French hesitated for thirty years, but at the crisis of their destiny they remained faithful to the ideas of the Revolution. Relinquishing material gain and Mediterranean empire, they chose to remain independent and to remain democratic; they continued to be the standard-bearers of Western civilization against militarism and autocracy. They chose with their eyes open; they knew that if they held out against German temptation it was on them that the German blow would fall. By making the Anglo-French entente the French brought on themselves the sufferings of 1914–18 and of 1940–44, but in 1904 the prospect of a German hegemony of Europe achieved by peaceful means vanished for ever.

Small wonder that the French hesitated. Small wonder that the entente was not received on the French side with the easy popularity which it evoked in England. Small wonder that at first the nerve of the French almost failed and that, fifteen months after the conclusion of the entente, Delcassé, its author, was driven from office on German orders. Yet the work of Delcassé was not undone. France looked the dangers in the face and, when the time came, accepted them. Many Frenchmen contributed to this decision. Yet Delcassé was more than their spokesman. He was not a great man; indeed, in some ways he was foolish and hot-headed. He offended his own colleagues and injured his own cause. But he had in him the flame of loyalty to the ideas of 1789, to the principles of national independence and of human equality. He was determined to keep France free, both at home and abroad. The entente was perhaps no more than a new expression of the unity of Western democratic civilization, but Delcassé gave it that expression. Forty years after, all those Englishmen who recognize the difference between French civilization and German order may well say: "Homage to Theophile Delcassé!"

XVI

THE SECRET OF THE THIRD REPUBLIC

THE Third Republic puzzled contemporary observers; now it baffles the historian. The Revolution, the Empire or the Monarchy of July can be reduced to a formula; the Third Republic defies definition. It is much easier to describe the forces which threatened it than to discover those which preserved it; hence French historians have written brilliantly on Boulangism, on Royalism or on the revolutionary Syndicalists. It is even possible to explain the origins of the Third Republic; but its founders, whether Thiers or Gambetta, would have been astonished at its development. Inaugurated with radical phrases, it gave France the most conservative system of government in Europe; established by the massacre of Parisian workers, it was the first Great Power to have Socialist ministers, and at the beginning of the twentieth century the leader of the Socialist party was its greatest parliamentarian; repudiating the Empire that had preceded it, it made France the second Imperial Power in the world; born of defeat, it recovered for France the Rhine frontier which two Emperors had lost. Despite its feeble origins, it gave France within fifty years the highest position she had held in Europe since the days of Louis XIV. Twenty years after this achievement, it brought France lower than she had ever been in modern times. The Third Republic went from the greatest success to the worst defeat; yet it had no other aim than compromise and a quiet life.

The most baffling period in this baffling story is that of the national revival between 1912 and 1914. Within these two years France abandoned the policy of conciliation towards Germany and claimed again the position of a Great Power; thus she acquired the vitality which enabled her to withstand not only the first shock of the German attack, but still more the shock of Verdun and of the failure of Nivelle; to survive, despite many alarms, until at last the elderly Clémenceau seemed to give her at last a new youth. Clémenceau became war-dictator; all the same Clémenceau was not a characteristic figure of the Third Republic, and the study of his career throws no light upon it. Rather he was the enemy of all that the Third Republic represented and passed his life attacking its ministers. When he was criticized for this, he replied: "Bah! I have always overthrown the same ministry." The antagonism was clear to him, though not always to his opponents.

It is Caillaux, not Clémenceau, the "traitor," not the dictator, who should be studied; it is Agadir, not the victories of 1918, which express the spirit of the Third Republic. Its secret, if it is to be found anywhere, will be found in Caillaux's *Memoirs*,[1] the two first volumes of which were published during the occupation and the third in July 1947. This is not an impartial contribution. It is a subtly delayed revenge against the men who brought Caillaux to ruin, above all, against Poincaré and Clémenceau who, according to Caillaux, by asking too much of France ruined the Third Republic. Caillaux promises revelations; all he gives is the warmed-up gossip of the Palais Bourbon. The reader, half-recollecting Caillaux's story, opens the book full of sympathy for its author; by the end he has almost been convinced that the charges made against Caillaux must have some foundation.

Caillaux, however, does not present himself as a topic of controversy; rather, caught in the storm, he has tried to brave it. The first volume is the story of the days of easy success, when nothing seemed to threaten the stability of the Third Republic. Caillaux was not a Republican by family origin or by education, and still less a Radical Socialist. His father had been a minister in Broglie's government of "May 16" (1877); Caillaux himself began in the Inspectorate of Finance. He was essentially a man of order, hating excess and violence, whether Bonapartist or Republican; he became a Radical, when he saw that the lower middle class and the peasants

[1] *Mes Memoires.* I. Ma Jeunesse orgeuilleuse, 1863–1909. II. Mes audaces. Agadir 1909–12. III. Clairvoyance et force d'âme dans les Épreuves, 1912–30. By Joseph Caillaux.

had become the governing classes. His father approved this step: "One must go with the governing forces of one's country." The same argument would have made Caillaux a loyal servant of the Bourbons or of the Directory. Caillaux entered politics as a "government man"; he had the good luck to become, almost at once, Minister of Finance under Waldeck-Rousseau. Caillaux perhaps exaggerates the work and character of this parliamentarian whom he presents as a great man. He hints at an apostolic succession of Radical leaders: Waldeck-Rousseau, Rouvier, Caillaux, patriots though pacific, whose work was destroyed by ambitious "warmongers." Certainly if Caillaux is to be judged by his own account of the years between 1898 and 1909, he must be recognized as the best Minister of Finance in the Third Republic. There is one surprising point: from 1906 to 1909 Caillaux was a minister in the government of Clémenceau. He supposed that Clémenceau had been tamed by the bitter years which followed the Panama scandal; he thought that Clémenceau had become, like the others, a good Republican. Despite this, Caillaux strikes a false note. He cannot refrain from anticipating later events and from producing in advance the stories that he had accumulated over the years. He claims that in 1928 Briand told him that the faults of the Treaty of Versailles were due to the fact that "Clémenceau was not free in relation to England." It is difficult to decide whether this story reflects more discredit on Briand or on Caillaux; and it is typical of the "proofs" which Caillaux claims to furnish.

One episode disturbed the quiet of the first decade of the century: the Moroccan crisis of 1905. Caillaux passes rapidly over this topic, attributing the dispute entirely to Delcassé's failure to inform Germany of his Moroccan plans. This is essential to his later argument. If he once admitted that the German object in 1905 was to reduce France to a position of dependence, the policy of Agadir would be condemned in advance. Agadir is the subject of Volume II, the least interesting of the three volumes. The revelations, for what they are worth, have already appeared in Caillaux's earlier book on this subject; they are merely repeated here with more bitterness. Caillaux was at least consistent: having once taken up a line of defence, he neither changed nor added to it, even in a book to be published after his death. Thus there is nothing new concerning the unofficial approach which he made to Germany; nothing on the projects of economic collaboration between Germany and France to which he aspired; and very little on his schemes for acquiring Spanish Morocco with German assistance. His attitude towards England is the strangest feature in his account of Agadir. The English statesmen aimed to show their firm determination to support France; Caillaux represents himself as abandoned by England and extracting from the English statesmen only a reluctant acquiescence. The Agadir crisis was certainly a turning-point in British foreign policy: the moment at which British opinion in general became convinced that it was Germany's ambition to dominate Europe. Caillaux cannot admit this ambition; therefore in his defence he talks only of Morocco, which he justly claims to have won for France without a war. This was not as great an achievement as he makes out. France could have had Morocco whenever she liked on Germany's terms; and Caillaux seemed to have accepted those terms.

This should have been his real defence, except that it was impossible to use it after all that followed. It was the logical development of the beginnings of the Third Republic that France did not challenge the position of Germany in Europe, but contented herself with empire in Africa; this was the policy of Gambetta and of Ferry, the one policy that could combine glory and peace. Caillaux is in the right when he presents his Agadir policy as that of a good Republican in the old sense; even his secret negotiations had their precedents in Gambetta's advances to Bismarck. But times had changed. Instead of being hailed as a great Republican statesman, Caillaux was driven from power, never again to be Prime Minister. French history reached its most dramatic and unexpected turning-point since the Revolution. Caillaux explains his defeat by intrigue and corruption. These played their part, but far more decisive was the unconscious refusal of French sentiment to accept a subordinate place in Europe.

This was shown by the sequel. Caillaux never realized that his chance had passed. In 1914, he was still dreaming of a pacific coalition between Radicals and Socialists, the coalition of Jaurès and Caillaux; this, he claims, would have refused to support Russia in the Balkans and so prepared the way for a Franco-German co-operation to impose peace on Russia and Austria-Hungary. Jaurès was blinded by his preoccupation with electoral reform. Nevertheless, Caillaux insists, the coalition would have been made, had it not been for the calumnies of Calmette and his assassination by Mme. Caillaux. It is typical of Caillaux's vanity that he should find in his private affairs the cause of the first German war, typical also of that lack of a sense of reality which finally brought the Third Republic to disaster. The story of Calmette is told in detail, the most surprising element being the affirmation that the press campaign was inspired by Poincaré, Barthou and Klotz (the last name being added to make the first two seem less improbable). Certainly Poincaré and Barthou were glad to see Caillaux excluded from public life. In May 1913 Poincaré said to Paléologue: "Clémenceau detests me. . . . Yet despite his great faults of pride and jealousy, of resentment and hate, he has one quality which earns him forgiveness, a quality which Caillaux lacks: he has, in the highest degree, national fibre, he is a patriot like the Jacobins of 1793." Caillaux never understood that between 1912 and 1914 France transcended the Third Republic and rejected for ever his policy of conciliation towards Germany.

Curiously enough his energy and self-confidence flag when he comes to talk of the period of the war. Yet it was in 1916 and not in 1914 that Caillaux offered a terrible alternative to the policy of making war. In 1914 all France was determined to resist German domination; by the end of 1916 her effort seemed exhausted. A party of peace came into existence with Caillaux at its head. If Poincaré had appointed Caillaux instead of Clémenceau, a compromise peace would have been attempted. It is inconceivable that Caillaux did nothing, that he attempted no peace propaganda, that he made no contact, however indirect, with the Germans. There is not a word of it in his *Memoirs*. Even stranger, Clémenceau, though still hated, becomes in Volume III a great figure beyond the reach of insults and, almost, the saviour of his country. It is as though Caillaux acknowledged the greatness of his adversary and admitted defeat. Henceforth he reserves his spite for Poincaré, certainly a figure of less importance, but who also had his moment of greatness when he determined to place Clémenceau in power. The story of the peace that failed, the negotiations of 1917, has still to be written; when it is written Caillaux will fill a larger place in it than he claims for himself in his *Memoirs*. This was the last chance of the old Europe and of the historic Great Powers, of Austria-Hungary and France. To succeed, Caillaux would have had to be very different from what he was: less intelligent and less subtle, but also more honest and more patriotic.

Where Caillaux failed after Agadir, Briand succeeded at Locarno and Bonnet at Munich—both attempts to save the continent of Europe by a reconciliation between France and Germany. Caillaux could have claimed to be the John the Baptist of these two strokes and even of the policy of Montoire, which was their last version. Yet though a "government man," Caillaux had in him a strange streak of obstinacy and contradiction. A financier from the upper middle class, he had turned against his origin and, becoming a Radical, had represented a peasant constituency; he had preached reconciliation with Germany at the moment of national revival; he had intrigued for peace during the first German war. Towards the end of his life, he refused to believe in the policy of collaboration with the Germany of Hitler, although this was the official policy of the governing class. Certainly he had no faith in French resistance or in the return of past glory. Like many others, he accepted the government of Vichy and hoped that France, once liberated by her great allies, would then be reconciled with a more civilized Germany. Thus he remained to the end faithful to the policy of Agadir; and to the end he saw in his opponents only warmongers bent on the ruin of Europe.

Only a Franco-German reconciliation could have given Europe peace and stability; this was the core of truth in the policy of Agadir. The mistake was to suppose this reconciliation possible. The Third Republic was Radical though pacific, and its leaders, whether Ferry, Caillaux or Bonnet, believed that in Germany too the policy of war was supported only by a few militarists and by the Kaiser. In reality expansion, if not war, was essential to the German system, and every step towards the rule of the masses increased German violence. A peaceful collaboration was possible only with the German Conservatives, as between Ferry and Bismarck or Caillaux and Kiderlen. This class was losing ground, and there was no Conservative with whom Bonnet could collaborate: he had to pretend to find an aristocrat in Ribbentrop and Bismarckian moderation in Goering. The Third Republic had to choose between Radicalism and Pacifism. In 1914 and 1917, in the strange atmosphere of the national revival, it gave up Pacifism, and Caillaux represented the defeated party. In 1940 it gave up Radicalism and, in fact, ceased to exist for the sake of reconciliation with Germany. This sacrifice only served to show that the policy of Agadir could not have saved the Third Republic and its contradictions. If France had followed Caillaux in 1911, in 1914, or in 1917, she would have been cut off from England and Russia and would have given Germany the mastery of Europe without a struggle. It needed two German wars to repudiate the policy of Agadir, wars which brought the ruin of France, but which ruined Germany as well. The stability of the Continent was and remains possible only at the price of German hegemony. This price France refused to pay, whatever the consequences to herself. The French decision saved Europe from German domination. It was the last great service which France performed for European civilization before herself ceasing to be a Great Power.

XVII

THE CONFERENCE AT ALGEÇIRAS

THE conference of Algeçiras was a decisive moment in European diplomacy. With uncanny foreboding, it anticipated the course of policy which the Great Powers would follow even when diplomacy gave place to war. It was the first great demonstration of the Triple Entente; it was the first demonstration, too, that Italy was drifting away from the Triple Alliance and that the United States were drifting into sympathy with the *Entente Cordiale*. The conference was more than a demonstration of alliances and friendships; it helped to create them. When the delegates went to Algeçiras, relationships between the Powers still seemed fluid; when the conference ended, a pattern of European affairs was laid down which lasted until the peace of Brest-Litovsk and the armistices of November 1918.

It is now possible to study in detail every episode of this decisive diplomatic engagement. The German[1] and British[2] documents have long been in print, though the British documents are a rather slight selection and miss a few points. A selection from the Russian documents was published in *Berliner Monatshefte* for April 1931; and American policy can be followed in the life of Henry White,[3] the principal American delegate. The French documents[4] complete the picture. No doubt there is a little to be learnt from the Italian and Austro-Hungarian archives; but Italian policy can be followed from the British and French documents, and Austro-Hungarian from the German. Already we have the most complete case-history of an international conference, which should be studied in detail by every diplomatic historian and by every intending diplomat. The French volume contains, as well, the journal kept by Révoil, the principal French delegate, from 12 January to 9 April. This journal comes from his private papers. It would be interesting to know for what purpose he kept it. Though very precise, it is also extremely discreet; it is, for the most part, a

1. *Die Grosse Politik der Eüropäischen Cabinette*. Vol. XXI.
2. *British Documents on the Origins of the War*. Vol. III.
3. *Henry White*. By Allan Nevins.
4. *Documents diplomatiques français 1871–1914*, 2e Serie (1901–11), Tome IX. 1re partie (16 janvier–1 mars 1906); 2e partie (2 mars–7 avril 1906). Paris, 1946.

summary of his official telegrams. Perhaps Révoil was one of those men who can think clearly only when they summarize their thoughts and acts on paper. There is no indication that the journal served any official purpose. There is no copy in the archives of the Quai d'Orsay and presumably it was not shown to the Foreign Minister. Was it perhaps kept for the benefit of André Tardieu? Tardieu's remarkable book, *La Conférence d'Algéçiras*, the first great essay in contemporary history, is accurate almost in every detail. Once or twice he is a day wrong in his dates; but he has far more information than could have been learnt in the ordinary way, and often he seems to be quoting Révoil. On the other hand, there is no evidence in the documents or the journal that Révoil and Tardieu actually collaborated during the conference; and on at least one occasion (the article in *Le Temps* on 20 March) Tardieu seems to have acted on his own—to Révoil's annoyance. Probably this problem will never be solved unless there is material in Tardieu's private papers.

When the delegates met at Algeçiras on 16 January 1906, they had no idea that their actions would shape international relations for years to come. It had been many years since a conference of such importance had been held; and both sides had forgotten the lesson of the Congress of Berlin: that great international gatherings succeed only when the broad decisions have been made beforehand. Révoil had been told to secure the general mandate of the Moorish police for France;[1] Radowitz, the German delegate, had been instructed to resist a general mandate.[2] Both had been told not to allow their country to be isolated; but little had been done to build up support. Révoil had a plan by which, at the right moment, the Russian delegate would put forward the French proposals as his own; but this plan was never operated—it would have turned all the German hostility on to Russia. The British were so ill prepared by the French that Nicolson did not at first realize the importance of the police question and as late as 21 January wrote to Grey: 'My own opinion is that if I were French I would be quite ready to surrender the police duties to anyone for a limited period provided I had predominant control over the Bank.'[3] The Germans, on their side, had communicated their

1. Rouvier to Révoil, 12 January 1906. D.D.F. VIII, No. 395.
2. Bülow to Radowitz, 3 January 1906. G.P. XXI, No. 6922.
3. Nicolson to Grey, 21 January 1906. B.D. III, No. 251.

general intentions to their allies[1] and had received a vague promise of support from Vienna. The German ambassador in Rome gave repeated warnings that Italy was not to be relied upon;[2] but these warnings were disregarded in Berlin, and in any case the Germans thought they had a trump-card in the United States, which would be brought on to the German side by the blessed word 'Internationalization'. This reliance on the United States was perhaps the fundamental blunder of German policy at Algeçiras. The Germans overlooked the fact that the Americans, in so far as they were indifferent, would not estrange France for the sake of something that did not matter to them; and in so far as they were concerned (either with Morocco or with the relations of the Great Powers) they would prefer the side of the Anglo-French entente. The only method by which the Germans might have persuaded Roosevelt to play an active part (as he had done between Russia and Japan) would have been to threaten war with France; and this threat, though it might have made Roosevelt act, would not have made him act on the German side.

The tactical question at the conference was simple, and it never changed. Whichever side submitted a plan for the police would expose itself to attack; therefore the side which held out longest without proposing anything would win. Patience, and strong nerves, would decide the issue. The Germans, who had begun the Moroccan conflict solely as a question of prestige, asked only to get out without disgrace; the French were determined to control the police, since this would give them victory both in Morocco and in 'la grande politique'. This concrete objective gave France a great advantage. The French knew what they wanted; the Germans only what they did not want. Still, the nerves of both sides were severely tested before the Germans finally gave way.

After the formal opening on 16 January, the deadlock showed itself at once. Révoil waited for the Germans to approach him. He was warned both by the Italians and by White, the American delegate, that Germany would not agree to a general mandate for France; but Nicolson, despite secret doubts, encouraged him to be firm, and on 19 January Révoil noted: 'Sir Arthur and I have complete faith in each other.'[3] A false alarm followed. The French

1. Bülow to Monts, telegram, 22 December 1905. G.P. XXI, No. 6912.

2. E. G. Monts to Bülow, 2 January 1906. G.P. XXI, No. 6921; 6 January 1906. G.P. XXI, No. 6928.

3. *Journal*, VIII, 19 January 1906.

Senator d'Estournelles de Constant visited Berlin in an effort at unofficial mediation. All he got from Bülow was the suggestion that the question of the police should be postponed: 'Wait some years, three years, perhaps two, then we'll see. Appearances will be saved.' Estournelles de Constant summed up his impression to Rouvier, the French Premier: 'They don't want war, but also they don't want peace. The truth is they don't know what they want.'[1] By some misunderstanding, it was at first supposed that Bülow had proposed direct discussions between Paris and Berlin.[2] Jules Cambon at once sent urgent advice from Madrid against such a course;[3] and inquiry at Berlin showed that Bülow had not in fact proposed it. The episode served only as an illustration of the control exercised over Rouvier by his ambassadors. On 23 January Revoil noted: 'We are in agreement that a waiting attitude is still necessary.'[4] Meanwhile the first German approach to Roosevelt,[5] made on 20 January, had miscarried. The Americans did not like the idea of partitioning Morocco even for police purposes;[6] on the other hand they would not support French claims—in fact they were determined not to be pushed into the position of arbitrators,[7] yet unless someone would arbitrate there was no purpose in an international conference.

The British did not yet understand that they had lost their freedom of action in the Moroccan question; they still supposed that they could mediate between France and Germany. On 24 January Nicolson described the deadlock at Algeçiras;[8] this led Grey to urge private talks on France and Germany. Bülow replied that he had no objection 'to the intervention of any third Power';[9] the French rejected the approach—since the Germans had appealed to the conference, they must abide by the appeal.[10] As a matter of fact Radowitz had already approached Révoil for a private

1. Estournelles de Constant to Rouvier, 21 January 1906. D.D.F., No. 22.
2. Bihourd to Rouvier, telegram, 21 January; Rouvier to Bihourd, telegram, 21 January; Bihourd to Rouvier, telegram, 22 January 1906. D.D.F. IX, Nos. 27, 28, 32.
3. Jules Cambon to Rouvier, telegram, 22 January 1906. D.D.F. IX, No. 33.
4. Révoil, *Journal*, XII, 23 January 1906.
5. Bülow to Sternburg, telegram, 20 January 1906. G.P. XXI, No. 6956.
6. Sternburg to Bülow, telegram, 23 January 1906. G.P. XXI, No. 6958.
7. Jusserand to Rouvier, telegram, 23 January 1906. D.D.F. IX, No. 41.
8. Nicolson to Grey, telegram, 24 January 1906. B.D. III, No. 254.
9. Lascelles to Grey, telegram, 25 January 1906. B.D. III, No. 255.
10. Rouvier to Paul Cambon and others, telegram, 26 January 1906. D.D.F., No. 60. This British approach to France, and its rejection, is not recorded in B.D.; a curious omission.

discussion on 24 January. Radowitz, though rather in disgrace since the fall of Bismarck, was an experienced diplomatist and no doubt wished to score a personal success. The meeting between Radowitz and Révoil on 25 January proved barren: Révoil would reveal nothing, and Radowitz had nothing to reveal.[1] The Germans were, in fact, still waiting for American support; and they did not lose hope even when the Americans again rejected the German advances on 29 January.[2]

On 27 January Rouvier showed the first sign of giving way. He telegraphed to Révoil that, if no agreement could be reached, 'Perhaps it would be wise to find out whether we could not get it accepted that the *question*, and not merely the *mandate for a general organisation*, should be formally *put off* for agreement later';[3] this would have given the Germans all they asked. This proposal by Rouvier was strongly opposed by his diplomatic associates. On 27 January Paul Cambon urged from London a policy of delay with the German Government: 'It must be drawn into making proposals to us one after another without our putting up counter-proposals. . . . So when the Russian proposal is brought out and we support it after a brief hesitation, it will look as though we were making a sacrifice.'[4] From Rome Barrère telegraphed against any weakening.[5] Révoil ignored Rouvier's telegram; or rather answered indirectly, by showing that Russia, Italy and the United States were becoming increasingly sympathetic to the French case.[6] Finally, on 31 January, Rouvier himself warned Révoil against any private concessions to the Germans. Since this telegram was drafted and signed by Georges Louis, it may well represent a victory of the professional diplomats over Rouvier—a last display of the pressure exercised on him after the fall of Delcassé.[7] Certainly Rouvier's telegram of 27 January was a sign of retreat on the French side.

1. Radowitz to Foreign Office, telegram, 25 January 1906. G.P. XXI, No. 6964; Révoil to Rouvier, telegram, 26 January 1906. D.D.F. IX, No. 56; *Journal*, XIV. This meeting is one of the few occasions when Tardieu is wrong in his dates. He gives Radowitz's approach as 25 January and the conversation as 26 January. Tardieu, *La Conférence d'Algéçiras*, p. 139.

2. Bülow to Sternburg, telegram, 27 January; Sternburg to Bülow, telegram, 29 January 1906. G.P. XXI, Nos. 6968, 6971.

3. Rouvier to Révoil, telegram, 27 January 1906. D.D.F. IX, No. 74.

4. Paul Cambon to Rouvier, 27 January 1906. D.D.F. No. 76.

5. Barrère to Rouvier, telegram, 30 January 1906. D.D.F. IX, No. 93.

6. Révoil to Rouvier, telegram, 30 January 1906. D.D.F. IX, No. 92.

7. Rouvier to Révoil, telegram, 31 January 1906. D.D.F. IX, No. 100.

On 31 January Grey and Paul Cambon discussed the question of British aid to France in case of German aggression. This conversation, which defined Anglo-French relations at least until the sharper crisis of 1911, is already well known from the British documents. It had, however, little immediate importance for the course of diplomacy at Algeçiras. Rouvier's outlook was determined by a conviction that British help would be of little use to France; and any hope which he received from Cambon's report must have been more than offset by a gloomy account of Russia's military situation which came in at about the same time.[1]

February had now been reached without any break in the deadlock. Rouvier had weakened for a moment, but had been checked by his associates. Radowitz was the next to try his hand at compromise. On 3 February he had another interview with Révoil and hinted at German willingness to place the police in the hands of France and Spain, if only some cover could be found—such as an inspector from another Power or an assertion of the sovereignty of the Sultan—which would keep up a pretence of international authority.[2] While Radowitz was discussing with Révoil, Tattenbach, the second German delegate, met Nicolson and made a crude attempt to detach him from the French side. This attempt offended Nicolson deeply, the more so as Tattenbach's reminder that Nicolson had previously been violently anti-French ('My present warm support of the French differed considerably from the attitude which I had assumed a few years ago at Tangier') was a shot that went home.[3] Révoil surmised that Tattenbach's approach to Nicolson had been designed in order to prove to his superiors in Berlin the hopelessness of their intransigent policy and the necessity of compromise.[4] There is no means of checking this surmise, since the editors of the *Grosse Politik* suppress all mention of Tattenbach's manœuvre; this is their usual method when a clumsy German move does not succeed.

Certainly Radowitz made no secret of his desire to accept the

1. Moulin to Étienne, Minister of War, 27 January 1906. D.D.F. IX, No. 77.

2. Révoil to Rouvier, telegram, 4 February 1906. D.D.F. IX, No. 117; *Journal*, XXIII, 3 February. Radowitz to Foreign Office, 3 February 1906. G.P. XXI, No. 6980. Radowitz's report is unreliable, since he was anxious to be conciliatory without revealing his initiative to Berlin.

3. Nicolson to Grey, telegram, 4 February 1906. B.D. III, No. 267. Révoil to Rouvier, telegram, 4 February; Bertie to Rouvier (enclosing British correspondence), 15 February 1906. D.D.F. IX, Nos. 118, 203.

4. Révoil to Rouvier, telegram, 4 February 1906. D.D.F. IX, No. 120.

compromise at which he had hinted on 3 February. The Russians had held back so long as there was a danger of open conflict between Germany and France. Now that Germany seemed in retreat, they wished to get the advantage of having acted as mediators and on 7 February appealed to the Germans to be conciliatory.[1] The Russians had counted without Holstein at the German Foreign Office. On 6 February Radowitz appealed to the Foreign Office to accept the French terms.[2] Holstein, however, was convinced that neither the Kaiser nor Bülow would give way.[3] A reply was therefore sent to Radowitz on 8 February, rejecting the French proposal and instructing him to work with the American and Austro-Hungarian delegates in order to defeat French ambitions.[4] Radowitz was now in an embarrassing position. He could not tell his government how much he had offered to concede; neither did he wish to confess in Algeçiras that his government had overruled him. He therefore resorted to the manœuvre of a 'leak' to the press; and on 10 February the German telegraph agency Wolff released a misleading account of the private discussions which had been taking place. This is another piece of German diplomacy which is passed over by the editors of the *Grosse Politik*.

Holstein not only assumed that the Kaiser and Bülow would stand firm; he also hoped that Rouvier might give way, as he had done the previous June. Radolin was therefore instructed to see him and to renew the vague offers of Franco-German friendship which had played their part at the time of the fall of Delcassé. But Rouvier had learnt a bitter lesson from the negotiations of July and September 1905; though still anxious to compromise, he was determined not to be drawn into direct discussions and therefore rejected Radolin's advance on 13 February.[5] But, on the same day, he telegraphed to Révoil, agreeing to an international control over the Franco-Spanish police;[6] Rouvier was, in fact, once more in retreat. On 13 February, too, Radowitz tried again. At a meeting with Révoil, he suggested abandoning the idea of an international

1. Bompard to Rouvier, telegram, 7 February 1906. D.D.F. IX, No. 140. Spring-Rice to Grey, 7 February; telegram, 8 February 1906. B.D. III, Nos. 272, 273.

2. Radowitz to Foreign Office, telegrams, 5 February; 6 February 1906. G.P. XXI, Nos. 6984, 6985.

3. Holstein to Radolin, telegram, 10 February 1906. G.P. XXI, No. 6994.

4. Bülow to Radowitz, 7 February (sent 8 February) 1906. G.P. XXI, No. 6987.

5. Note du Département, 13 February 1906. D.D.F. IX, No. 176. Radolin to Foreign Office, telegram, 13 February 1906. G.P. XXI, No. 7001.

6. Rouvier to Révoil, telegram, 13 February 1906. D.D.F. IX, No. 172.

mandate for the police and instead entrusting the organization of the police to the Sultan. Révoil thought that this would be an acceptable compromise, if the Sultan were instructed that he could only appoint Frenchmen and Spaniards.[1] German honour would be satisfied; and Franco-Spanish interests in Morocco would be satisfied at the same time. Révoil therefore drafted a compromise on these lines and gave it to Radowitz on 16 February.[2] He had little hope of a successful outcome, or so he told Nicolson; no doubt he exaggerated his depression in order to hold Nicolson's sympathy. Nicolson tried to cheer him by saying that, if the conference failed, 'it might be possible for direct negotiations to lead to a more satisfactory result'. Révoil replied: 'Every point in a direct agreement would be directed against Great Britain and inspired by a desire to disturb or overthrow the existing Anglo-French understanding.'[3] Nicolson needed no convincing of this; Révoil's remarks were rather directed to Grey, who was beginning to grow anxious at the prolonged deadlock.

The compromise proposed by Révoil—that the Sultan should be allowed to appoint the police so long as he appointed only French and Spanish—was approved by both Austria-Hungary and the United States, the two countries on whom Holstein had been counting.[4] In fact, Goluchowski, Austrian Foreign Minister, had made the same suggestion independently just before it had been put forward by Révoil.[5] Both Austria-Hungary and the United States asked nothing of the conference except to be out of it without offending either side. Also, the Austrians knew, from their experiences in Macedonia, the impossibility of an international police. All this was ignored by the Germans. Révoil's suggestion was at once rejected by Berlin;[6] and this rejection was repeated sharply to Vienna,[7] and in a more conciliatory tone to Washington.[8] Deadlock was once more complete. It was now 19 February. A

1. Révoil to Rouvier, telegram, 13 February 1906. D.D.F. IX, No. 174. Radowitz to Foreign Office, telegram, 13 February 1906. G.P. XXI, No. 7004.
2. Révoil to Rouvier, telegram, 15 February 1906. D.D.F. IX, No. 193.
3. Nicolson to Grey, 15 February 1906. B.D. III, No. 287.
4. Austrian approval: Radowitz to Foreign Office, telegram, 17 February 1906. G.P. XXI, No. 7022. American approval: Sternburg to Foreign Office, 19 February 1906. G.P. XXI, No. 7019.
5. Wedel to Foreign Office, telegram, 14 February 1906. G.P. XXI, No. 7007.
6. Bülow to Radowitz, telegram, 18 February 1906. G.P. XXI, No. 7013.
7. Memorandum by Kriege, 16 February 1906. G.P. XXI, No. 7009.
8. Bülow to Sternburg, telegram, 21 February 1906. G.P. XXI, No. 7020.

month had passed since the opening of the conference. Nothing had been achieved. Apart from Radowitz in his exposed position, German nerve seemed unshaken. The entente position was the reverse. Nicolson and Révoil had kept their courage; Rouvier, and to a lesser extent, Grey, found it difficult to stand the strain. As for the Russians, the approach of the crisis at Algeçiras made their position increasingly embarrassing. They dared not offend France for the sake of the loan which was so urgent to them; they dared not offend Germany for even more obvious reasons.

After the deadlock of 19 February, Russian appeals to Germany for a compromise became desperate. Lamsdorff urged compromise on the German ambassador; and Witte—the great advocate of a 'Continental league'—was enlisted by Bompard[1] to write a letter appealing to William II.[2] Bompard also appealed directly to the Tsar and got from him the promise of 'his entire personal support',[3] but not a promise to write to William II. The Russian appeals to Germany were unavailing; Bülow refused to leave the police to France and Spain. Grey had much the same experience. On 19 February he did his best to shake Metternich, the German ambassador, with the argument that Anglo-German relations would be much better if the Moroccan question was out of the way.[4] The conversation achieved nothing; and Grey was now convinced that Germany would not yield. The only solution seemed to him to attempt to bribe Germany with the offer of a Moorish port. He recognized that the French might feel that they were being deserted; but he hoped they would realize that 'in a war with Germany our liabilities would be much less than theirs'. He added, as an afterthought, that if there had to be a conflict with Germany it would be better to wait until Russia had recovered and an Anglo-Russian entente made.[5] It was this argument of a Triple Entente, revising the question of Moroco in favour of France, which Grey used to Cambon on 22 February: 'Once France, England and Russia were on good terms, they could reopen the question of the police in Morocco. . . . Therefore we must play for time.'[6]

1. Bompard to Rouvier, telegram, 20 February 1906. D.D.F. IX, No. 231.
2. *Grosse Politik*, XXI, Nos. 7027–30.
3. Bompard to Rouvier, telegram, 22 February 1906. D.D.F. IX, No. 263; Bompard to Rouvier, 24 February 1906. D.D.F. IX, No. 292.
4. Grey to Lascelles, 19 February 1906. B.D. III, No. 296.
5. Grey, memorandum, 20 February 1906. B.D. III, No. 299.
6. Paul Cambon to Rouvier, telegram, 23 February 1906. D.D.F. IX, No. 274.

Pressure to compromise was also brought on Rouvier from another quarter. French policy (and Rouvier's position in particular) had been weakened from the beginning by the unofficial French 'experts' on Germany who had thrust themselves forward in the belief that they knew the Germans and would bring them to a reasonable settlement. In every case, these 'mediators' had strengthened German confidence. Courcel, former ambassador at Berlin and London, was the last of them. He took advantage of a visit to Berlin to see William II, Bülow and Holstein. All three gave him friendly words; on the question at issue they remained unshakable. Bülow told him frankly: 'What matters to us is, as they say, to save our faces', and held out the prospect that after four or five years (not two or three as he told Estournelles de Constant) France would be free to act in Morocco. At present Germany would allow the French to control the police in *one* Moorish port; all the rest must be organized on an international basis, even including German officers. Courcel of course tried to emphasize that he had no official position; all the same he did not conceal his agreement with the German proposals and even said that he would support them, when the occasion arose, in the Senate. It is not surprising that the Germans thought the French on the point of giving way; and themselves became more confident. Bülow, indeed, was so confident that he counted on the Italians, as well as on Austria-Hungary and the United States. He told Courcel: 'I know the Italians. . . . Italy will not desert us.'[1]

Rouvier, summarizing Courcel's report, concluded on 24 February: 'He has brought back from his conversations in Berlin the very clear impression that Germany will not accept an arrangement on terms favourable to us.'[2] Rouvier therefore prepared to retreat. Late in the evening of 23 February, he telegraphed to Révoil that there was no hope of agreement on the basis of the present French plan and that he was being urged even from London to compromise. 'It may be then that we shall have to think of new solutions.'[3] This telegram was the nearest point to victory ever reached by the Germans.

For, just as Rouvier began to weaken, the Austrians began to

1. Courcel to Rouvier, 24 February 1906. D.D.F. IX, No. 291. Memoranda by Holstein, 22 February 1906. G.P. XXI, Nos. 7034, 7035.

2. Rouvier to Révoil, Jules Cambon, Paul Cambon, telegram, 24 February 1906. D.D.F. IX, No. 276.

3. Rouvier to Révoil, telegram, 23 February 1906. D.D.F. IX, No. 272.

weaken also. On 23 February Francis Joseph himself warned the German ambassador that German policy was driving Russia into the arms of England and France;[1] and on 21 February Goluchowski had made it clear to the French ambassador that he, too, disapproved of German policy.[2] The best the Austrians could do to save the situation was to propose that the conference should adjourn without making any decisions. The Austrian suggestion was the signal for the professional French diplomats to go into action. Here, at last, was a proposal (of a negative kind) from the side of the Central Powers; France, by defeating it, could show Germany's isolation. On 24 February both Paul Cambon and Jules Cambon telegraphed to Rouvier, urging that France should not allow the conference to separate without a vote having been taken on the question of the police;[3] and Paul Cambon sent a further telegram denouncing the plan which Courcel had brought back from Berlin: 'The suggestion about the police is the least acceptable of any that have been made to us.'[4] Jules Cambon sent a similar attack on Courcel's plan the following day.[5] Révoil dismissed Courcel's plan with equal firmness: 'The proposals that M. de Courcel regards as offering the basis for agreement are absolutely contrary to the principles which we have defended up till now and which we cannot give up.'[6]

In face of this firm attitude, Rouvier—as on previous occasions—recovered his nerve and allowed the professionals to have their way. Révoil was asked if he could obtain a vote 'which would provide us with a certain moral strength'; and on 27 February Courcel told the German ambassador sadly that Rouvier 'much against his inner conviction was being dragged along by shortsighted hostile forces which were growing stronger every day'.[7] Révoil now had a free hand. Policy had been decided; and the problem was now technical—how to mobilize the strongest voting strength. Révoil at first thought it would be impossible to devise a formula for which the 'neutrals' would vote; and abstention would not be effective.

1. Memorandum by Bülow, 24 February 1906. G.P. XXI, No. 7039.
2. Reverseaux to Rouvier, telegram, 21 February 1906. D.D.F. IX, No. 252.
3. Paul Cambon to Rouvier, telegram, 24 February; Jules Cambon to Rouvier, telegram, 24 February 1906. D.D.F. IX, Nos. 279, 281.
4. Paul Cambon to Rouvier, telegram, 24 February 1906. D.D.F. IX, No. 284.
5. Jules Cambon to Rouvier, telegram, 25 February 1906. D.D.F. IX, No. 299.
6. Révoil to Rouvier, telegram, 24 February 1906. D.D.F. IX, No. 289.
7. Radolin to Foreign Office, 27 February 1906. G.P. XXI, No. 7047.

White, the American delegate, was especially insistent that he could not vote on a question of general principle, however much he agreed with the French case; and the Italians were almost as difficult. It is not clear how, as a result of a week's thought, it was decided that the vote should be forced, not on any actual proposal, but simply on a motion that the question of the police should be considered. Révoil at first planned that the Russians should force a decision by submitting the scheme for the police which they had held in reserve since the opening of the conference; but on 27 February the Russians grew timid—'The Russian delegation does not want to get the blame for producing the storm.'[1] Révoil gives no further indication how the vote of 3 March was prepared. It may be that Nicolson, as his biographer implies,[2] made up his own mind to force a decision and acted without warning his colleague. His tactic certainly succeeded. When on 3 March he proposed that the question of the police should be taken at their next meeting, all voted for his motion, except the delegates of Germany, Austria-Hungary, and Morocco. Bülow commented on the meeting: 'Wenig erfreulich!'[3]

The vote of 3 March at last shook the confidence of Berlin. They could no longer suppose that they were supported by all the neutral powers. Holstein had nothing to propose except a new intrigue with Rouvier through Courcel; and this threadbare expedient was actually tried out. Rouvier rejected the approach firmly. Perhaps he had at last learnt from experience; more probably, as he was on the point of leaving office, he wished to retire with a clean record behind him.[4] The only effect, at any rate, of this manœuvre was to convince the French that the Germans were losing their nerve. Jules Cambon telegraphed: 'Confidence is beginning to be shaken at Berlin and we have only to stand fast.'[5] The episode would hardly be worth remark, except that it proved to be the last diplomatic act of Holstein. The German delegates at Algeçiras understood the position better. They realized that it was they who must give way. On 5 March Tattenbach devised a new

1. *Journal*, XLVII, 27 February 1906. 2. Harold Nicolson, *Lord Carnock*, p. 189.
3. Radowitz to Foreign Office, telegram, 3 March 1906. G.P. XXI, No. 7051.
4. Holstein to Radolin, telegram, 4 March; Radolin to Foreign Office, telegrams, 5 March, 6 March 1906. G.P. XXI, Nos. 7055, 7059, 7067. Rouvier to Révoil, telegram, 5 March; Rouvier, circular telegram, 7 March 1906. D.D.F. IX, Nos. 358, 375.
5. Jules Cambon to Rouvier, telegram, 7 March 1906. D.D.F., No. 382.

proposal on the police virtually conceding all the French wishes, except that there should be a neutral inspector, who should also be in command at Casablanca.[1] This proposal was accepted by Bülow, and the Austrians were asked to put it forward as mediators; a neutral commander at one port was to be a *sine qua non*.[2]

This proposal was an adroit move; and its reception showed that, if the Germans had been more conciliatory from the beginning, the results of the conference might well have been very different. In practice, the new proposal gave the French the footing in Morocco that they wanted; in theory, it preserved the principle of internationalization and so saved the face of the Germans. Sentiment at Algeçiras swung round to the German side. The delegates were, above all, anxious not to commit themselves if it could be avoided; and the German offer seemed to be designed to save them. They waited impatiently for the French to compromise in their turn. The French could not explain that, quite apart from their objections to the principle, Casablanca was the port on which they proposed to base their penetration of Morocco; they had therefore to give the appearance of harsh obstinacy. It was serious enough that the Russian delegate should welcome the German move; it was even more serious that Nicolson regarded it as a genuine compromise. From 8 March to 14 March Nicolson persistently urged Révoil to give way on the question of Casablanca.[3] Grey in London was even more emphatic. On 8 March he told Cambon that the proposal 'represented a real concession on the part of Germany' and quoted Nicolson's opinion in its favour;[4] Cambon's report does its best to weaken the force of Grey's remarks and even implies that Grey was persuaded to co-operate in resistance.[5] Cambon, no doubt, hoped to encourage Rouvier to take a firm line, as he had done with his somewhat selective reporting the previous June. On 12 March Grey repeated his arguments more strongly than before: 'Casablanca is of no importance.' This time Cambon recorded Grey's remarks with reasonable fairness.[6]

1. Radowitz to Foreign Office, telegram, 5 March 1906. G.P. XXI, No. 7060.

2. Bülow to Wedel, telegram, 6 March; Bülow, memorandum, 7 March 1906. G.P. XXI, Nos. 7065, 7069.

3. Nicolson to Grey, telegram, 9 March; telegram, 14 March 1906. B.D. III, Nos. 332, 349. Révoil, *Journal*, LVI, 8 March; LVIII, 10 March 1906.

4. Grey to Bertie, telegram, 9 March 1906. B.D. III, No. 333.

5. Paul Cambon to Rouvier, 9 March 1906. D.D.F. IX, No. 414.

6. Grey to Nicolson, telegram, 12 March 1906. B.D. III, No. 344. Paul Cambon to Rouvier, telegram, 12 March 1906. D.D.F. IX, No. 429.

The general feeling at Algeçiras, and above all the attitude of Nicolson, caused Révoil to retreat. On 10 March Nicolson sounded Radowitz on the possibility of compromise and came away convinced that the Germans would insist on neutral control of Casablanca.[1] Révoil then suggested that a neutral officer might be acceptable if he was instead allotted Tangier (which the French had never hoped to control).[2] On 12 March Radowitz, in conversation with Nicolson, rejected this proposal.[3] On 13 March Révoil therefore decided to give way and recommended the French Government to agree to Swiss control of Casablanca with certain safeguards. 'We must choose between breaking off and agreeing to entrusting the Casablanca police to a neutral Power. After careful reflection, I think that we must not break off.'[4] Once more the Germans, though they did not know it, were in sight of victory. Once more victory escaped them at the last moment.

The German setback had two causes. In the first place the Germans overplayed their hand. On 11 March Radowitz telegraphed: 'It is said to me by all my colleagues, including the English, that after our attitude in the full session they would regard the French insistence on the points described as definitely unacceptable by us as no longer justifiable and that they have told Révoil so.'[5] In view of Nicolson's opinion, expressed to Révoil and to Grey, Radowitz's report was well-founded, though unwise. No doubt, after so many failures, he wished to boast of a success. On 13 March Metternich repeated Radowitz's remark to Grey; and Grey re-replied: 'I did not think that Sir A. Nicolson had said the French ought to accept the Austrian proposal unconditionally.'[6] Grey also telegraphed to Nicolson: 'I replied that you could not have said that France ought to accept the Austrian proposal unconditionally.'[7] Nicolson was now anxious to cover himself with Révoil. He therefore told him of the conversation between Grey and Metternich

1. Nicolson to Grey, telegram, 11 March; 11 March 1906. B.D. III, No. 339.
2. Révoil to Rouvier, telegram, 11 March 1906. D.D.F. IX, No. 422.
3. Révoil, *Journal*, LX, 12 March 1906. Nicolson to Grey, telegram, 13 March 1906. B.D. III, No. 345. Radowitz seems to have rejected the offer of Tangier without referring to Berlin.
4. Révoil to Rouvier, telegram, 13 March 1906. D.D.F. IX, No. 437.
5. Radowitz to Foreign Office, telegram, 11 March 1906. G.P. XXI, No. 7089.
6. Grey to Lascelles, 13 March 1906. B.D. III, No. 348. Metternich does not record Grey's denial. Metternich to Foreign Office, telegram, 13 March 1906. G.P. XXI, No. 7100.
7. Grey to Nicolson, telegram, 14 March 1906. B.D. III, No. 351.

and repeated Grey's sentence in a more emphatic form: 'It is impossible that Sir Arthur has come out for the Austrian proposal.'[1] Révoil, transmitting the story to Paris, made it more emphatic still: 'What you tell me is impossible.'[2] The French Government was thus led to believe that Grey had given Metternich the lie direct; and Nicolson, to cover his indiscretion, had henceforth to appear as a violent opponent of the German plan for Casablanca.

The second cause of Germany's failure was the change of government in France, which was accompanied by a journalistic manœuvre conducted by Tardieu and perhaps assisted by Bertie, the British ambassador. On 7 March Rouvier's government fell on a domestic issue; a new government, with Bourgeois as Foreign Minister, was not formed until 13 March. The new ministers had heard the rumours of Nicolson's endorsement of the Casablanca plan and came into office convinced that England was about to desert them. But on 13 March *le Temps* published the instructions which, it claimed, Rouvier had confirmed to Révoil before leaving office. As a matter of fact, Rouvier had merely telegraphed to Revoil on 8 March: 'The debate which took place in the Chamber yesterday did not touch on anything concerning foreign policy and therefore your instructions remain unchanged';[3] and the article in *le Temps* was a concoction summarizing Rouvier's previous instructions, though not in diplomatic language. Bourgeois denied, no doubt correctly, that Rouvier was responsible for the 'leak'.[4] Révoil, however, was probably less innocent, to judge from the complacent way in which he refers to the publication 'of the last instructions that I received'.[5] Probably the manœuvre was arranged between Révoil and Tardieu to stiffen the new government.

The *Temps* article was, however, unexpectedly effective with the British Government. Bertie telegraphed extracts from it to Grey; and his telegram must have been in emphatic form,[6] for it convinced Grey that the French would not yield over Casablanca. He

1. Révoil, *Journal*, LXII, 14 March 1906.

2. Révoil to Bourgeois, telegram, 15 March 1906. D.D.F. IX, No. 450. It is in this form that the phrase appears in Tardieu, p. 329.

3. Rouvier to Révoil, telegram, 8 March 1906. D.D.F. IX, No. 388.

4. Bourgeois, circular, 15 March 1906. D.D.F. IX, No. 452.

5. Révoil to Bourgeois, telegram, 15 March 1906. D.D.F. IX, No. 450.

6. Unfortunately Bertie's telegram is not printed in B.D. It is referred to in Bertie o Grey, 17 March 1906. Grey, *Twenty-five Years*, I, 105–10.

therefore withdrew his earlier promptings of compromise and instructed Bertie to promise British support to the French.[1] Bertie made the most of these instructions. On 14 March he saw Georges Louis, the *directeur politique*; on 15 March he sent a message to Bourgeois through Crozier, French Minister at Copenhagen, and saw Bourgeois, Étienne, Minister of War, and Clémenceau, Minister of the Interior; on 16 March he saw Étienne, Clémenceau, and Bourgeois again. The French ministers had meant to complain that Great Britain was not supporting them; instead they were met with 'spontaneous' offers of support from Bertie and with strong urging not to give way. Of course Bertie, in his reports to Grey, made out that the French ministers had taken the initiative; but reading between the lines and judging from his conduct on other occasions (such as the Haldane mission in 1912), it is reasonable to assume that he made his own contribution to policy. He exaggerated the doubts of the French ministers to Grey; he exaggerated Grey's firmness to the French ministers.[2] The manœuvre succeeded. On 13 March Grey had still wanted the French to give way, and Révoil had made up his mind to do so. Three days later the British were committed to supporting a firm French line—though much against their will;[3] and the French ministers would not compromise for fear of British disapproval.

Rouvier's fall had not affected German plans. Tardieu is wrong when he argues that the Germans had been prepared to give way on 7 March and renewed their obstinacy on 11 March because of the change of government in France;[4] it is the one major error in his narrative. The Germans remained resolute about Casablanca until 12 March. On that day Bülow lost his nerve and took over the conduct of affairs from Holstein; German policy became ingratiating and conciliatory, instead of being obstinate and harsh. This policy might have produced a response from Rouvier, who in his heart had always desired a compromise; Bourgeois, reinforced

1. Grey to Bertie, telegram, 14 March 1906. B.D. III, No. 350.

2. Bertie to Grey, telegrams, 15 March; telegram, 16 March; 17 March 1906. B.D. III, Nos. 355, 356, 358. Grey, *Twenty-five Years*, pp. 105–10. Bourgeois to Révoil, telegram, 14 March; to Paul Cambon, telegram, 15 March 1906. D.D.F. IX, Nos. 440, 448.

3. Grey to Bertie, 15 March; Hardinge to Nicolson, 15 March 1906. B.D. III, Nos. 353, 354.

4. Tardieu, pp. 313–15.

by Bertie, reacted quite differently. On 15 March he rejected the Casablanca proposal in a conversation with the Austrian ambassador;[1] and he repeated this rejection in another conversation on 17 March.[2] The Austrians were weary of the battle; they urged Bülow to be content with a neutral inspector who would not command at Casablanca.[3] Bülow was weary too; his only concern was to be finished with the question of Morocco, and he accepted the Austrian advice. By 19 March France had won. The police of Morocco would be controlled by France and Spain alone.

During this time Russia and America had been left aside. When it looked as though France would give way, Bülow had urged Lamsdorff to join in urging conciliation on France.[4] This put Lamsdorff in a difficult position. If France gave way, he wanted to have the credit for it; if France remained obstinate, he did not want to be blamed for having taken the German side. On 14 March he sounded Bompard as to the intentions of the new government and hinted that the Germans expected it to be more conciliatory than the previous one; Lamsdorff seems also to have revealed his suspicion that the new government might revert to Rouvier's old plan of buying Germany off in Morocco by offering French participation in the Bagdad railway.[5] When Bourgeois rejected the Austrian compromise, it was necessary for Lamsdorff to show that he, too, had never been out of step; and on 19 March he telegraphed to the Russian ambassador at Berlin, supporting the French position. This was enough in itself to annoy the Germans; but Nelidov, Russian ambassador at Paris, made matters worse. In his anxiety to prove that Russia had never wavered, he showed a copy of Lamsdorff's telegram to Tardieu; and the message appeared in *le Temps*, two hours before it was shown to Bourgeois and a day before it was delivered to the German Foreign Office.[6] Russia paid the penalty for this, when Germany refused to participate in the great Russian loan.

The United States provided a curious, almost absurd, epilogue. Roosevelt had refused to express an opinion when his action could still have been of some use to the Germans; he acted now when it

1. Bourgeois, circular, 15 March 1906. D.D.F. IX, No. 452.
2. Bourgeois to Révoil, telegram, 17 March 1906. D.D.F. IX, No. 466.
3. Bülow to Radowitz, telegram, 19 March 1906. G.P. XXI, No. 7117.
4. Bülow, Directive, 12 March 1906. G.P. XXI, No. 7091.
5. Bompard to Bourgeois, telegram, 14 March 1906. D.D.F. IX, No. 442.
6. Bourgeois to Bompard, telegram, 26 March 1906. D.D.F. IX, No. 557.

was too late. Without warning he turned violently against the Austrian scheme. He discovered in it an implicit partition of Morocco and even suspected that Casablanca was being set aside as Germany's share. He proposed instead a joint Franco-Spanish police in all the ports. This plan was unwelcome to all parties. It offended the French by barring the way against partition;[1] it offended the Spanish by putting them under French supervision; it offended the British by putting French police in Mediterranean ports[2]—it had been one of the principal objects of the Entente agreement to prevent this. It even offended the Germans; for it called upon them to begin the diplomatic struggle all over again. Had Roosevelt's proposal been made at the opening of the conference, Germany and the United States might have worked together and secured the backing of the wavering Powers, Austria-Hungary and Italy, perhaps even of Russia. Now it was too late. The Germans stood aside and allowed the French to argue Roosevelt out of his tardy inspiration. Jusserand, the French ambassador, insisted to the Quai d'Orsay that he could get Roosevelt to withdraw more easily if he were not supported by his British colleague —an odd ending to this story of Anglo-French co-operation.[3]

Agreement was reached on 23 March; the Franco-Spanish plan for the police was formally accepted on 27 March, and the final act of the conference was signed on 7 April. It remained to settle French relations with her friends. Both Jules Cambon[4] and Paul Cambon[5] would have liked to surrender Tangier to Spain; this would both please the Spaniards and burden them with the difficulties with England which were bound to be the lot of whoever controlled Tangier. Révoil and his departmental colleagues refused to be moved by these arguments of *la haute politique*; and Tangier was to remain in dispute, or at any rate in suspense, forty years after the conference of Algeçiras. Paul Cambon also urged that France should reward the British for their support by co-operating with them in the question of the Bagdad railway. Though the Quai d'Orsay was ready to assist in reconciling England and Russia, it

1. Révoil to Bourgeois, telegram, 21 March 1906. D.D.F. IX, No. 502.
2. Grey to Bunsen, 21 March; to Durand, telegram, 22 March 1906. B.D. III, Nos. 372, 374.
3. Jusserand to Bourgeois, telegram, 23 March; 2 April 1906. D.D.F. IX, Nos. 528, 598.
4. Jules Cambon to Bourgeois, telegram, 27 March 1906. D.D.F. IX, No. 563.
5. Paul Cambon to Bourgeois, 29 March 1906. D.D.F. IX, No. 577.

shrank from becoming involved in an Anglo-German conflict: 'Immediately after the conflict over Morocco, France has something better to do than to renew in the Near East the struggle begun so unsuccessfully at Tangier by the Emperor William.'[1]

After the conference a report on the effects of Algeçiras on the relations of the Great Powers was drawn up by de Billy, secretary of the French delegation; it is the last document in the present volume. The Triple Alliance, de Billy wrote, was changing its character. Formed to restrain an aggressive France, it had acted to restrain an aggressive Germany. Austria-Hungary had asserted her independence of Germany and had acted as a mediator instead of as an ally; Italy had resisted German pressure. 'Formerly co-operating with England and Spain to prevent any French activity in Morocco, Italy has now agreed with England to keep Germany out of the western Mediterranean.' The Triple Alliance was based on jealousy between Italy and Austria-Hungary; it should be the object of French diplomacy to reconcile them. As to Russia, the conference had shown that Germany was the principal danger to the peace of Europe and, since Russia needed peace, this had destroyed the plans for a Russo-German reconciliation. Algeçiras had also brought England and Russia together; and Nicolson had used the conference to prepare for his *ambassade* at St. Petersburg. According to de Billy, England had hesitated between a policy of war against Germany and a policy of European alliances which would render Germany harmless without war; Algeçiras had convinced her of the possibility of the second course. Spain had been shown that she could attain her aims in Morocco in co-operation with England and France; but she would listen to German temptations if there was ever division between them. The United States had emerged from isolation; she had discovered that she had no quarrel with England and France, but that Germany threatened her future prosperity. 'The Washington government dislikes the brutal and realistic policy of the Berlin government and answers it by a policy equally realistic, but pacific, because peace and time are working for the United States and against Germany.'

Thus de Billy, revealing no doubt the judgement of French diplomatists, saw in the conference of Algeçiras more than a French success over Germany. He believed that the conference had brought into being a coalition of pacific Powers which would resist

1. Paul Cambon to Bourgeois, 7 April 1906. D.D.F. IX, No. 625.

any Power 'seeking to overturn the Balance of Power for its own advantage'. This coalition was indeed to become a reality in the First World War. At Algeçiras most of the Powers had been concerned only to discharge their obligations without too much embarrassment. None of them, except the two principals, worried about the Balance of Power; and the French succeeded largely by creating the impression that nothing beyond the policing of Morocco was at stake. All the same it had been touch-and-go. On more than one occasion, the chance of a few hours could have altered the entire pattern of negotiations; and then 'the inevitable course of history' would, no doubt, have proceeded in quite a different direction.

XVIII

THE OUTBREAK OF THE FIRST WORLD WAR

ON 4 August 1914, this country declared war on Germany. The European war had already started. Austria-Hungary declared war on Serbia on 28 July. Germany declared war on Russia on 1 August, and on France on 3 August. The Austrians, late as usual, declared war on Russia only on 6 August; Great Britain and France answered by declaring war on Austria-Hungary on 12 August. This delay was significant. Though the Austrians had wanted a war against Serbia, a general European war was not part of their plan, and their empire became its principal victim. Their little Balkan war was swamped in a struggle of the European Great Powers; and there began a general upheaval in Europe which destroyed its stable civilization—an upheaval which has lasted to the present day. The First World War caused vast destruction and the slaughter of more human beings than anything since the barbarian invasions. But its moral impact—the thing which made it difficult for men to think rationally about it—was that it came after a longer period of peace than any known in the recorded history of Europe.

Great Britain had not been involved in a general war since the battle of Waterloo in 1815. The last war between two European Powers had been the war between France and Germany which ended in 1871. There had been colonial wars; and there had been Balkan wars—the last in 1912 and 1913. But these had all been a long way from what was regarded as civilized Europe. Men went on talking about war; there were diplomatic crises; and every Great Power had vast armaments by the standards of the time. The British Navy had never been so powerful; and every Continental country had millions of men trained to enter the field. All the same, the reality of war was remote from men's minds. Everyone assumed that the system, or lack of it, would go on working, as it had worked for so long. There would be alarms and even mobilizations; but somehow peace would come out of it. War, in the phrase of the time, was unthinkable.

So, when war came everyone demanded an explanation; and the search for this has been going on ever since. Special institutes were set up for the study of war-origins; periodicals devoted solely to it were published. Every Great Power published thousands of diplomatic documents. A full bibliography, if one were ever made, of war-origins would run into thousands of volumes. We know what happened between 28 June and 4 August 1914 in more detail than we know of any other five weeks in history. Indeed, if we cannot understand these events and agree about them, we shall never understand or agree about anything. The problem was not merely historical. It went on being of burning political importance. The victorious allies insisted on Germany's war-guilt. The Germans challenged this; and the evidence which they produced shook many scholars, particularly in England and America. Germany, it was felt, had been harshly treated, hastily condemned; and these feelings made many people sympathize with German grievances even when they were voiced by Adolf Hitler. In fact the controversies over the origins of the First World War helped to bring about the second.

These controversies centred at first on the events which followed the murder of Archduke Franz Ferdinand of Austria at Sarajevo on 28 June. Soon men went much further back. The Germans blamed the Franco-Russian alliance which had been concluded in 1894; the French blamed the policy of Bismarck, although he left office in 1890. Others blamed things in general—the structure of alliances or the armaments of the Great Powers. Some blamed more specifically the armament manufacturers. Lenin and other Marxists after him blamed capitalist imperialism. Psychologists blamed the pugnacity of human nature. The worst of such general theories is that they will explain almost anything. The very things that are blamed for the war of 1914—secret diplomacy, the Balance of Power, the great Continental armies—also gave Europe a period of unparalleled peace; and now we are often inclined to think that, if only we could get back to them, we should have peace again. If we are going to probe far back into history, it is no good asking, 'What factors caused the outbreak of war?' The question is rather, 'Why did the factors that had long preserved the peace of Europe fail to do so in 1914?' Perhaps then we should conclude that diplomacy was not secret enough; that the balance did not balance properly; that the expenditure on armaments was too small.

I would point to one factor which has not perhaps been sufficiently explored. Men's minds seem to have been on edge in the last two or three years before the war in a way they had not been before, as though they had become unconsciously weary of peace and security. You can see it in things remote from international politics—in the artistic movement called Futurism, in the militant suffragettes of this country, in the working-class trend towards Syndicalism. Men wanted violence for its own sake; they welcomed war as a relief from materialism. European civilization was, in fact, breaking down even before war destroyed it. All the same, we have tended to look too much for the deeper causes of war and neglected its immediate outbreak. Despite these deeper causes, individual men took the decisions and sent the declarations of war. You may say that they should not bear all the responsibility, but they had some. If two or three men had acted differently, war would not have occurred at that particular moment. And we have a new guide. A famous Italian publisher, Luigi Albertini, when Mussolini excluded him from politics, turned to the study of war-origins. For nearly twenty years he studied the documents and interviewed the surviving statesmen. Two massive volumes of his work have been translated into English; with a third to come. It is unlikely that we shall ever know more of the political and diplomatic events which preceded the war of 1914. We might learn something more from the military records, particularly in Germany and Austria-Hungary, but not, I think, much.

Let me take the events as we know them. The starting-point was the assassination of Archduke Franz Ferdinand at Sarajevo. Why was he there at all? As a gesture of defiance against Serb nationalism; as a demonstration that Bosnia, though inhabited by Serbs and Croats, was going to remain part of the Austrian empire. That explains, too, why Princip and his friends set out to assassinate the Archduke. They were Bosnian Serbs who wanted their national freedom; and far from being encouraged by Serbia, still less acting under Serb orders, their activities were most unwelcome to the Serb Government. Serbia was just recovering from the Balkan wars of the previous year; she had not absorbed her new lands; and war with Austria-Hungary was the very last thing that the Serb Government wanted. No one has ever managed to show that the Serb Government had any connection with the plot, though they may have had some vague knowledge. Indeed it was easy to guess that an Austrian Archduke would be shot at if he visited Sarajevo on 28 June, Serbia's national day. One Serb knew all about it—

Colonel Dimitrevic, or Apis, as he was called, the head of a secret national society. But though he approved the plans, he did not initiate them, or give much serious help. The plot was the work of six young high-minded national idealists. Two of them are still alive. One is a professor at Belgrade University; the other curator of the museum at Sarajevo.

The plans of such young men are not very skilful. In fact all six of them missed their mark. Princip, the strongest character among them, was standing disconsolately on the pavement about to go home when an open car, with Franz Ferdinand in it, stopped right in front of him. The driver had taken a wrong turning and was now about to back. Princip stepped on to the running-board, killed Franz Ferdinand with one shot and, mistakenly, the Archduke's wife with the other—he had hoped to kill the governor of Bosnia. This was the crime of Sarajevo. The Austrian Government were not much concerned to punish it. They wanted to punish a different crime—the crime that Serbia committed by existing as a free national state. The Austrians wanted to prove that they were still a Great Power and somehow to destroy Serbia. They decided to go to war with Serbia, whatever her excuses and apologies. This was the first decision which brought about the world war. The man who made it was Count Berchtold, a frivolous aristocrat, but the Foreign Minister of Austria-Hungary.

He needed the approval of his German ally; and on 5 July he got it. William II, the German Emperor, agreed over the lunch table: Austria-Hungary, he said, must act against Serbia, even at the risk of war with Russia. Bethmann Hollweg, the Chancellor, turned up during the afternoon: and he approved also. There was no formal council, no weighty consideration of the issues. Of course the Germans were bluffing. They thought that Russia would let Serbia be destroyed. But, if not, they were ready for war. The German army was at the height of its strength; the French army was being reorganized; the Russian army would not be properly equipped until 1917. The German line was: if there is to be war, better now than later. William II often talked violently, though he usually repented soon afterwards. The new factor was that Bethmann also supported a policy leading to war. Hence this worthy, pacific man must bear more responsibility than any other individual for what followed. He alone could have stopped the war; and instead he let it happen.

After 5 July, nothing followed for nearly three weeks. The Austrians prepared an ultimatum to Serbia in their usual dilatory way. The other Powers were helpless; they could do nothing until the Austrian demands were known. All sorts of wild guesses have been made about French and Russian activities. But there is not a scrap of evidence that Russia promised to support Serbia or that France promised to support Russia. In fact Serbia agreed to nearly all the Austrian demands. It was no use. The Austrians broke off relations and on 28 July declared war. They did this deliberately, to make a peaceful outcome impossible. Now Russia had to do something. The Russians had no aggressive plans in Europe. In fact they had no interest in Europe except to be left alone. But they could not allow the Balkans, and so Constantinople and the Straits, to fall under the control of the Central Powers. If they did, their economic life, which in those days depended on the outer world, would be strangled—as indeed it was during the war. They tried to warn Austria-Hungary off Serbia. When that failed, they announced their mobilization, first against Austria-Hungary alone, then on 30 July a general mobilization. This was not an act of war—the Russian armies could not be ready for at least six weeks. It was a further gesture of diplomacy—a warning that Russia would not stand aside.

But it was also the last act of diplomacy. The German plans depended on getting in their blow first. If war came, whatever its cause, they must knock out France in the first six weeks and then turn with all their strength against Russia. The plan had been made by Schlieffen, who died in 1913. It made certain that any war in Europe must be a general war—it could not be localized; and it also made certain that, once Germany began to mobilize, war was inevitable. People everywhere had the habit of saying 'Mobilization means war'. This was only true of Germany; other countries had mobilized in the past without war: the British navy in 1911, the Austro-Hungarian army in October 1913. And it was true of Germany only because Schlieffen had said it must be true. In this sense a dead man had the deepest responsibility of all for the European war. On 31 July Germany began to mobilize. With this step effective diplomacy ceased. The diplomatists, and even the kings and emperors, went on trying; but there was nothing they could do. Once the German armies mobilized, war had to be brought on, not averted; and the German diplomatists had to do what they were told by the German soldiers. They were not being consciously more wicked than other diplomatists; they had been told for years that only the Schlieffen plan could save Germany, and they believed what they were told.

Russia was asked to stop mobilizing. When she refused, Germany declared war on her on 1 August. France was asked to promise to stay neutral and to surrender her principal fortresses as security. The French evaded this demand; and on 3 August the Germans declared war on them also. It is often said that the alliances caused the war; but the alliances were not observed in 1914. Germany had promised to aid Austria-Hungary if she were attacked by Russia; but in fact Germany declared war on Russia without this happening. France had promised to aid Russia if she were attacked by Germany. But in fact the French were attacked by Germany before they had made a decision of any kind. No doubt they would have decided to aid Russia; and maybe Russia would have attacked Austria-Hungary. As it was, neither of these things happened. The German rulers launched a preventive war.

As to Great Britain, the German generals never gave her a thought. She had no army on a Continental scale; and they never considered the British Navy. The German armies had to go through Belgium as part of the Schlieffen plan in order to knock out France; and it was the German invasion of Belgium which brought Great Britain into the war. People then and since said that this was not the real reason—that we were pledged to France or that we had encouraged Russia. The fact remains that, but for the invasion of Belgium, British policy would have been much more confused and hesitant, the British people certainly not united. As it was, the British action was not much more than a moral gesture. Their army contributed little: it was the French, not the British, who won the battle of the Marne.

Could the war of 1914 have been averted? You can make all kinds of conditions: if Austria-Hungary had given her peoples more national freedom; if nationalism had never been thought of; if Germany had relied more on her economic, and less on her military power. But in the circumstances of 1914, Great Britain could have kept out of war only if she had been prepared to let Germany defeat France and Russia. France could have kept out of war only if she had surrendered her independence as a Great Power. Russia could have kept out of war only if she had been willing to be strangled at the Straits. In short, they could have avoided war only by agreeing that Germany should become the dominant power of the Continent. None of these Powers decided on war. The three men who made the decisions—even if they too were the victims of circumstances—were Berchtold, Bethmann Hollweg, and the dead man Schlieffen.

XIX
THOMAS GARRIGUE MASARYK

T. G. MASARYK, the Founder-President of Czechoslovakia, was born on 7 March 1850. Though the centenary of his birth will now pass unnoticed in the country he created, nothing can weaken his position as one of the great men of our century; even if his work prove barren, he demonstrated the nobility of the human race. His political career began in earnest when he had already been superannuated as a university professor. If he had died at the age of sixty-five, he would have been remembered only as a sociological writer who exposed some judicial scandals in Austria-Hungary.

His extra years turned him into a maker of history. Between 1915 and 1918 Masaryk brought nations into being and drew the lines for a new map of Europe. Yet Masaryk was not an extreme nationalist. He incurred the hostility of the Czechs by exposing their most famous mediaeval manuscripts as forgeries; and before 1914 he was one of the few Czechs who strove sincerely to transform the Habsburg Monarchy into a democratic federation of peoples.

Unlike most nationalist leaders, Masaryk understood power. He called himself a realist and practised 'Realpolitik' in the Bismarckian manner. Indeed he was more of a realist than Bismarck, for he knew how to use the force of ideals. He said late in life: 'Democracy is the rule of the people, but there can be no government without obedience and discipline.' His predecessors had demanded obedience from hereditary right; he claimed it from force of character. For Masaryk was a man born to rule.

Fear of Pan-Germanism, and the determination to be rid of it, was the motive of his political actions. Certainly he desired freedom for his people; but he would have been less uncompromising in his resistance to Pan-Germanism if he had not believed that it rejected the values of European civilization. He did not hate Germany; he wished 'to force Germany to be human' by preventing her rule over others. The events of 1914 convinced him that the Habsburg Monarchy had lost all independent existence; it had become merely an instrument by which Slav peoples were forced to fight for the German domination of Europe. Thus he sought an alternative to Austria-Hungary, something which would perform the Habsburg 'mission' more successfully. He found this more effective barrier to German mastery in the small nations of Central and Eastern Europe; and claimed that national freedom was the only way of organizing this great middle zone.

Masaryk tuned his arguments to his audience when he set out to convince the statesmen of the Western Powers: spoke of the rights of nationalities, of the cause of democratic freedom, and of great moral principles. These, though genuine convictions, represented only part of his realistic approach. He was well aware that the small nations of East-Central Europe could not hold their own unaided against German power; and his aim was to combine national freedom with security, not to let nationalism run riot.

Masaryk sought to overcome the weakness of German's neighbours by national amalgamation. He did not merely voice national claims; he invented nations. Arguing from the case of partitioned Poland, he represented the Czechs and Slovaks as a single people who would come together as Czechoslovaks when partition was ended; and he had the same programme for the Serbs and the Croats. Himself a Slovak, though born in Moravia, he genuinely believed that the Slovaks would gladly accept Czech history as a substitute for that which they lacked themselves and would regard Hus and Comenius as Slovak heroes. Similarly, he expected the Serbs and Croats to overlook the religious and historical differences which had lasted for a thousand years. It is curious that a professor even of sociology should have been so contemptuous of history; but for Masaryk culture was humanistic, not historical. He admired Hus and Comenius because of what they stood for, not because they were figures in Czech history; and he expected others to do the same.

He thought that nations could be remade at will, if the will were sufficiently noble; and his will was so noble that he partly succeeded. Though Yugoslavia could never be more than a federation of nations, Czechoslovakia became in some sort a genuine national State bound together by common loyalties. But this ideal of a humanistic nationalism was confined to the 'humane' classes; it lost its hold when the agrarian and urban masses came to determine the shape of politics.

Masaryk never supposed that the national amalgams could face out the German threat without assistance. Czechoslovakia and the other succession States were to give the middle zone internal peace; but their existence was to be underwritten by the support of the victorious Allies. In 1914 opinion in Western Europe had only a vague sentiment in favour of national freedom; Masaryk turned this sentiment towards concrete reality. With some justice, though with less than was supposed, he represented the Czechoslovaks as 'peoples struggling to be free'. But his plans were not based solely on support from France and the Anglo-Saxon Powers. He wrote in March 1917:

> Will Great Britain join forces with Russia, or does she consider Germany to be less dangerous to her world empire than Russia? This is the question which Great Britain has to decide, and on her decision will depend the future of the Old and the New World.

It was a disaster for Masaryk when West and East were estranged by the Bolshevik revolution; and he never gave up trying to bring Russia back into European affairs—sometimes by seeking to be reconciled with the Bolsheviks, sometimes by preparing their overthrow. For though always a man of Western culture and never sympathetic to Pan-Slavism, Masaryk was realist enough to know that Germany and Russia would partition Eastern Europe unless Russia was on good terms with the Western Powers.

Except for the name of Czechoslovakia little now seems to remain of Masaryk's work. The national amalgams have not held: Czechs and Slovaks, Croats and Serbs are separate peoples; federalism in Yugoslavia, not national union in Czechoslovakia, has been successful; and all Eastern Europe, except for Yugoslavia, has escaped from German tyranny only to fall under Russian control. For this Russia is not alone to blame. If Western countries saw the peril of Pan-Germanism as clearly as Masaryk did we should not be in our present position. The essential condition which Masaryk laid down, though perhaps now unattainable, remains true: only co-operation between Russia and the Anglo-Saxon Powers can give Europe peace and security. And in spite of the failures of the present there is in Masaryk's life a deeper lesson: nationalism without humanism is harsh and destructive; humanism without nationalism is academic and barren. If there ever is a federation of Europe or of the world it can be based only on free national States, not on the domination of a single Great Power.

XX

MARX AND LENIN

UNIVERSITIES nowadays have Professors of almost everything—Brewing at one, Race Relations at another, Town Planning at a third. Yet there is still room for a pious benefactor. No university has a Professor of Marxism; and the theoretical background of the only religion which is still making converts on a grand scale remains neglected. Mr. Plamenatz will be a strong candidate for this Chair when it is created. It may seem unlikley that anyone should write at this time of day a book about Marxism which is both new and sensible; but Mr. Plamenatz has done it.[1] The existing books are special pleading, almost without exception. They start by assuming either that Marx was right or that he was wrong; and they go on developing one or other of these assumptions at interminable length. Mr. Plamenatz has merely assumed that Marx was a political thinker of the first rank, who should be taken seriously; and he has then examined Marxist doctrine with detached common sense. He treats Lenin as a master of practical politics, not as a serious thinker, and shows how Bolshevism transformed Marxism, somewhat as Paul is said to have done with the teachings of Christ.

Though this is a good book, it is not the book that Mr. Plamenatz set out to write, if his title is any guide. The first and more important part is about Marx, not about German Marxism. But Marx cannot be treated as a purely German thinker even in his methods. He himself claimed to have combined German philosophy, English economics, and French politics; and this is a good deal nearer the truth, though it would be still truer to say that he rode three separate horses and never got them teamed together. The only German quality in Marx was the 'dialectic' framework which he learnt from Hegel; and, as Mr. Plamenatz shows, this was a gigantic nuisance which Marx increasingly abandoned when he wrote on serious questions. Marx's economics derived solely from English writers, principally from Ricardo; and the practical basis of them—made into a generalization of universal application

1. *German Marxism and Russian Communism*. By John Plamenatz.

—was capitalist England of the textile age. His political outlook was that of an extreme French radical; and the only political events on which he made any valuable observations were the French revolution of 1848 and the Paris Commune of 1871. The English Labour party has come nearer than any other to applying the economic part of Marx's programme; just as the French and those who have learned from them are the only ones to have a genuinely revolutionary proletariat.

Neither Marxist economics nor Marxist politics suited German conditions; and the German Marxists had to adapt these doctrines to quite different conditions, a process in which Engels himself led the way. How they did this would make a fascinating study, never yet attempted. It is not enough to mention Bernstein's revisionism or to assert that the German Social Democrats wanted a welfare state, not social revolution. Such a study would have reinforced the argument of Mr. Plamenatz's book; for it would then have appeared that the Germans set the example which the Russians followed. Kautsky first built up a Marxist orthodoxy devised for German conditions; and Lenin learnt the trick from him. Both were forcing a given theory to fit into existing conditions, instead of deriving their theory from these conditions—a confusing, but very usual, process. Mr. Plamenatz sees this clearly enough with the Bolsheviks. They made a revolution, established themselves in power, and then asked: 'how can Marxism be used to justify what we have done?' But the Germans had done exactly the same; and if Mr. Plamenatz had brought this out, he would then have realized that it applied to Marx also. Marx wanted certain things; and he therefore devised theories which proved that they would happen. Principles and actions came before theory in Marx's case, as in everyone else's.

Of course Mr. Plamenatz goes some way to recognizing this. Indeed much of his book is given over to a careful logical demonstration that Marx's theories were dogmas, which could not be justified by the facts. For instance, Marx insisted that the number of labourers increased faster than the machines which employed them; therefore 'the reserve army of the unemployed' would grow ever larger. He expressed this by a mathematical formula which is made more telling by being repeated again and again. But the formula could be proved true only by statistics which Marx did not possess and which indeed do not exist. As a matter of fact scientists often proceed in this way. It is a great mistake to suppose that they generalize only from a random body of experience. More usually they first formulate a theory and then collect the evidence to prove that it is true. The great scientist is not distinguished by guessing less, but by guessing better. The process is much more difficult to apply in history. The natural scientist can make his laboratory produce the necessary evidence to justify his theory. The historian can only turn to the records; and these were never kept to answer the questions which he had in mind. Hence it has been plausibly maintained that no serious history can be attempted before about 1850, when accurate statistics begin; and even these are so faulty that some dismiss the possibility of rigorous history before the outbreak of the Second World War. All historians before then, including Marx, were literary artists—a description which most historians of the present day certainly do their best to avoid.

Marx's generalizations about history can never be shown to be either true or false. They are merely curious. It would be more rewarding to explain how he came by them and what results he expected from them. In fact what we want is a Marxist analysis of Marx. Mr. Plamenatz has a mastery of Marx's writings which would enable him to do it. Unfortunately, like most political theorists, he will not condescend to the routine task of learning history. He treats Marx in detachment without much reference to the intellectual climate of the time. He has therefore missed a discovery of the first importance, though he is constantly on the edge of it. For though Marx was the greatest of Socialist writers and the founder of modern Socialism, he was as a thinker the last flower of Individualism. He achieved Socialism simply by taking *laissez-faire* economics and rationalist psychology and standing them on their heads; but despite this inversion they remained individualist theories. Take, for instance, the class struggle, which is the central point of his doctrine. This is true only if we accept the principle—universally assumed in the middle of the nineteenth century—that every man recognizes his economic interest and pursues it. Every proletarian fights his employer and co-operates with every other proletarian; every peasant or shopkeeper knows that he belongs to a dying class and therefore joins the rising one. If rationalist individualism is true, then Socialism must follow from it. It is not true; and that is why we have not got Socialism.

In exactly the same way, Marxist economics are individualist economics. They assume the working of 'economic laws' and project them into the future. Mr. Plamenatz finds it puzzling why Marx thought that a capitalist should pursue higher profit when he had plenty already. But, given the contemporary assumption that capitalists were capitalists all the time, it must necessarily follow. If a man stopped behaving as a capitalist even for a minute of the day, economic laws would break down, as they always do in practice. Again, it seems an extraordinary thing that Marx had no theory of foreign trade; and the lack of it has handicapped Socialists from then until now. But in the era of Free Trade, no theory of foreign trade was necessary; or rather it was there already. Marx merely assumed that Socialist communities would go on trading with each other according to the best principles of the division of labour. Indeed he even assumed that Socialism would work without planning or conscious forethought; and so it would, if every man followed his own economic interest logically.

Similarly, when Marx came to politics, he shared the individualist radicalism of his time. He, too, assumed that it was highly desirable to strangle the last king with the bowels of the last priest; and he believed that inestimable benefit would follow from this. His only novelty was to show that the last capitalists (and by Marxist laws these would be few) should be strangled at the same time. Mr. Plamenatz keeps asking impatiently: 'but why should Utopia arrive merely because this curious operation has been carried out?' Marx would have answered: 'Because every serious political thinker of my time from Bentham to Mazzini says so.' Marx was superior to his contemporaries in seeing that democracy could not work without a social revolution; but, living in the age of rationalism, he could not be expected to see that it needed a psychological revolution also.

This surely explains Lenin's creation of a new Marxist theory. Mr. Plamenatz makes it clear that he was a different sort of man; but this is not an interesting discovery—all men are different, as well as being the same. The important thing is that he was a man of a different age. Marx was a rationalist, believing in Progress and anxious to discover its laws. He was satisfied when he showed that progress was going in the same direction as himself. Lenin belonged to the age of collective man and of the struggle for power. He himself once said that the only interesting question in life was 'who whom?' Who exploits whom? Who sentences whom to death? He was not interested in where history was going. He wanted to know how to get to the right end of a gun and stay there. This is not an attractive question for the political theorist, but it has its importance in certain societies and at certain moments. Leninism is not a political philosophy; it is a guide to political practice in the era of gangster-warfare, the sort of guide that Marx often tried to write but never succeeded. Mr. Plamenatz suggests that Lenin vulgarized Marx's theories and perverted them. But he believes this only because he prefers the age of rational individualism to that of the gangsters. Everyone can have his private tastes, but they have no place in historical study. John Stuart Mill has long been in his grave; and we have to live with the secret police, the televised politician and the hydrogen bomb. 'Who whom?' is a question that will last our time.

XXI

TROTSKY

ONE early morning, in October 1902, Mr. and Mrs. 'Richter' were still abed in their lodgings near King's Cross. There was a violent knocking at the door. Mrs. Richter, opening it, called out: '*The Pen* has arrived!' In this way Trotsky, 'the young eagle', burst—under his first pseudonym—into Lenin's life. The meeting was a symbol of their future. Lenin was orderly, quiet in speech and habit, hardly to be distinguished from his neighbours. Trotsky rode contemptuously over the conventions, knocking violently at doors and expecting them to open at the impact of his genius. He was at a loss when there was no door to force open. Lenin was to end as a sacred mummy, in the silence of death still dominating the lives of two hundred million people. Trotsky was to be murdered far from Europe and—what would seem worse to him—his very name has been erased from the history-books. Mention Bronstein, and men think you are referring to a chess player. The greatest writer and perhaps the greatest leader that revolution ever produced is forgotten; and the younger generation of readers will puzzle why a book has been devoted to him.

Mr. Deutscher has done a striking work of rehabilitation.[1] This is the story of Trotsky's triumph. It carries him through the victory of the revolution and the civil war to his highest moment, when he seemed the predestined successor of Lenin. A further volume will tell the story of his fall and of his unquenchable resistance until he was rubbed out by an ice-pick. Mr. Deutscher has mastered all the printed sources and has been the first to use extensively the Trotsky archives now at Harvard. Yet it may be questioned whether he is the right man for the subject. We can perhaps get over his ponderous style, suitable enough when he is pontificating on Bolshevism in the columns of the Astor press. But, like all Marxists—even the lapsed ones—he wants always to discover profound historical forces where there was only the will of men. He writes of the early Bolsheviks: 'Lenin's party had its roots deep in Russian soil'; this of some two or three thousand men, bewitched by an academic

1. *The Prophet Armed: Trotsky 1879–1921*. By Isaac Deutscher.

ideal. In 1917 'the whole dynamic of Russian history was impelling Lenin and Trotsky, their party, and their country towards the revolution'; when it would be truer to say that these two wrenched 'history' (whatever that may mean) violently from its course. In the most preposterous passage of all he describes the Russian working class of 1917 (who, poor chaps, had no idea what was happening to them) as

> one of history's wonders. Small in numbers, young, inexperienced, uneducated, it was rich in political passion, generosity, idealism, and rare heroic qualities. . . . With its semi-illiterate thoughts it embraced the idea of the republic of the philosophers.

The reader must put up with this hocus-pocus for the sake of the gigantic individual who overshadows it.

Trotsky himself used to claim that history was on his side. When he came to the Congress of Soviets fresh from the conquest of power, he called to the protesting Mensheviks: 'You have played out your role. Go where you belong: to the dustheap of history.' Yet no man ever chose his role in greater isolation or followed a course of more determined individualism. Trotsky carried to its peak the era of individual greatness which had begun with the French Revolution. His was a more powerful voice than Danton's, self-educated, self-made, self-advised. One could say of him as of Napoleon: 'his presence on the battlefield was worth ten divisions'. It is ironic that Trotsky, the greatest of revolutionary Socialists, should have owed his success to liberal enterprise and capitalist freedom. The age of the individual was finished when men were eclipsed by machines—and nowhere more decisively than by the machine of the great political party. In the First World War genius still counted. Lloyd George, Clémenceau, Trotsky, were each in their separate ways the saviours of their countries. It is no accident that the careers of all three ended in barren failure when the war was over. The leaders of the Second World War needed bureaucracies and party organizations. Even Winston Churchill had to become leader of the Conservative party; and only backward countries, Yugoslavia or France, could produce heroes—a Tito or a de Gaulle. Trotsky came just in time. Now he could never rise from provincial obscurity.

Trotsky had no background of Marxist training or of party experience. Mr. Deutscher writes: 'He diligently studied Marxism, which in this its golden age gave the adept a solid mental equipment.' In reality Trotsky learnt from Marxism only that capitalism was doomed—a fact which he knew instinctively already. His own writings that have survived never dealt with economic developments; they were concerned always with poiltical strategy, owing more to Clausewitz than to Marx. He never adapted himself to the needs of practical work in a party. When he first came to London in 1902 it was as a detached individual; and he stood outside the conflict between Bolshevik and Menshevik. Though himself a revolutionary, he opposed Lenin's exclusiveness; and always hoped to close the breach between the two Socialist currents. Even after the revolution of 1905, when his actions had outstripped Bolshevik theory, he kept up a tolerant association with the Mensheviks; and the outbreak of the First World War found him more solitary than ever. He joined the Bolshevik party only in the summer of 1917, some two months before he was to carry it to supreme power. The exact date is unknown; and the possession of a party-card meant nothing to him. His position in the world did not depend on the accuracy of a filing-cabinet.

In the slovenly decay of imperial Russia Trotsky's voice could fill a continent. When the revolution of 1905 broke out, he was an unknown youth of twenty-five. At St. Petersburg, knowing nobody, representing nobody, he forced himself on to the Soviet; and before it ended he was its dominating figure. At the final meeting he even ruled out of order the police officer who had come to arrest the members: 'Please do not interfere with the speaker. If you wish to take the floor, you must give your name.' In those days words were more powerful than armies. It was the same on a more gigantic scale in 1917. The Bolsheviks did not carry Trotsky to power; he carried them. Lenin made the party resolve on insurrection, but he was still in hiding when it broke out and at first could not believe in its success. The seizure of power in October was Trotsky's work; and Lenin acknowledged this immediately afterwards, with supreme generosity, when he proposed that Trotsky be put at the head of the new revolutionary government. One may even ask—what did Lenin and the Bolsheviks do during the civil war? They held on clumsily to the reins of civil power in Moscow. It was Trotsky who created the armies; chose the officers; determined the strategy; and inspired the soldiers. Every interference by the Soviet government was a mistake; and the greatest mistake was the campaign against Poland, which Trotsky opposed. The achievement was not only one of organization. It was the impact of a fiery personality, the sparks from which flew round the world.

The man of action in Trotsky was always second to the man of words, even at the greatest moments of decision. He was never happy over a victory until he had written about it; and in later years literary triumph seemed almost to atone with him for the bitterness of defeat. Bernard Shaw said that, as a political pamphleteer, he 'surpassed Junius and Burke'; what is even more to the point, he is the only Marxist who has possessed literary genius. Time and again the force of this genius posed problems that were still unperceived by others and even pointed to solutions that were unwelcome to Trotsky himself. Immediately after the revolution of 1905, when he was still in prison, he discovered the central dilemma which a victorious Russian revolution would face and which indeed the Soviet Union still faces. How was revolutionary Russia to maintain itself in a hostile world? Backwardness made revolution easy, but survival difficult. Trotsky gave already the answer to which he adhered all his life: permanent revolution. The Russian revolution must touch off revolutions elsewhere. 'The working class of Russia will become the initiator of the liquidation of capitalism on a global scale.' It was in this belief that Trotsky led the revolution of 1917, defied the German empire at Brest-Litovsk, and composed the most ringing phrases in the foundation manifesto of the Communist International. But what if the more advanced proletariat failed to respond? It was useless to maintain for long Trotsky's earliest answer: 'luckily for mankind, this is impossible'.

The impossible is what men get from events—and often at its most unwelcome. Trotsky foresaw even in 1905 the conflict that would follow between workers and peasants, if they were ever cooped up together in isolation. Once more he fell back on pious hope. The working class would remain by its very nature enlightened, progressive, tolerant. Somehow 'proletarian dictatorship' would escape the evils which other forms of dictatorship had always produced. Did Trotsky ever believe this? It seems unlikely. In the early days of doctrinal dispute he always preached toleration, despite his own sharp and wounding phrases. Lenin had an easier time of it. Both men understood the virtue of intellectual freedom. But for Lenin it was one of the many bourgeois virtues that he was prepared to discard—confident that Communism would resurrect it in a higher form. In just the same way he was ready to write off the greatest artistic achievements of the past. The very wonder of them was an embarrassment in the present. Trotsky could never bring himself to renounce European civilization. He recognized Russia's backwardness and resented being associated with it—an attitude possible for a Jew, but repugnant even to Lenin. As the net of intolerance drew tighter, as the European revolutions failed and the Russian masses became increasingly discontented, Trotsky grew more explosive.

His response was characteristic. At one bound he reached totalitarianism in its most ruthless form. His own gifts betrayed him. A dictator lurks in every forceful writer. Power over words leads easily to a longing for power over men. Trotsky could never resist a challenge. He wrote *The Defence of Terrorism* at the height of his labours during the civil war; and he justified the conquest of Georgia against the Social Democrats of western Europe, though he had himself opposed it. Now in 1921 he preached the militarization of labour and permanent dictatorship of the Communist party. Lenin restrained him. But the weapons which Trotsky forged then were soon to be turned against him by Stalin. He was to purge his betrayal of freedom by many years of resistance and exile. The glories of his revolutionary triumph pale before the nobility of his later defeats. The spirit of man was irrepressible in him. Colonel Robins, the American military representative at Petrograd, pronounced history's verdict: 'A four-kind son-of-a-bitch, but the greatest Jew since Jesus Christ.'

69 70 71 72 73 12 11 10 9 8 7 6 5 4 3

JOHN C. MILLER: Alexander Hamilton and the Growth of the New Nation TB/3057
RICHARD B. MORRIS, Ed.: The Era of the American Revolution TB/1180
FRANCIS S. PHILBRICK: The Rise of the West, 1754-1830. † *Illus.* TB/3067
TIMOTHY L. SMITH: Revivalism and Social Reform: *American Protestantism on the Eve of the Civil War* TB/1229
ALBION W. TOURGÉE: A Fool's Errand ‡ TB/3074
GLYNDON G. VAN DEUSEN: The Jacksonian Era: 1828-1848. † *Illus.* TB/3028
LOUIS B. WRIGHT: Culture on the Moving Frontier TB/1053

American Studies: The Civil War to 1900

W. R. BROCK: An American Crisis: *Congress and Reconstruction, 1865-67* ° △ TB/1283
THOMAS C. COCHRAN & WILLIAM MILLER: The Age of Enterprise: *A Social History of Industrial America* TB/1054
W. A. DUNNING: Reconstruction, Political and Economic: 1865-1877 TB/1073
HAROLD U. FAULKNER: Politics, Reform and Expansion: 1890-1900. † *Illus.* TB/3020
HELEN HUNT JACKSON: A Century of Dishonor: *The Early Crusade for Indian Reform.* ‡ *Edited by Andrew F. Rolle* TB/3063
ALBERT D. KIRWAN: Revolt of the Rednecks: *Mississippi Politics, 1876-1925* TB/1199
ROBERT GREEN MC CLOSKEY: American Conservatism in the Age of Enterprise: 1865-1910 TB/1137
ARTHUR MANN: Yankee Reformers in the Urban Age: *Social Reform in Boston, 1880-1900* TB/1247
WHITELAW REID: After the War: *A Tour of the Southern States, 1865-1866.* ‡ *Edited by C. Vann Woodward* TB/3066
CHARLES H. SHINN: Mining Camps: *A Study in American Frontier Government.* ‡ *Edited by Rodman W. Paul* TB/3062
VERNON LANE WHARTON: The Negro in Mississippi: 1865-1890 TB/1178

American Studies: 1900 to the Present

RAY STANNARD BAKER: Following the Color Line: *American Negro Citizenship in Progressive Era.* ‡ *Illus. Edited by Dewey W. Grantham, Jr.* TB/3053
RANDOLPH S. BOURNE: War and the Intellectuals: *Collected Essays, 1915-1919.* ‡ *Ed. by Carl Resek* TB/3043
A. RUSSELL BUCHANAN: The United States and World War II. † *Illus.* Vol. I TB/3044; Vol. II TB/3045
THOMAS C. COCHRAN: The American Business System: *A Historical Perspective, 1900-1955* TB/1080
FOSTER RHEA DULLES: America's Rise to World Power: 1898-1954. † *Illus.* TB/3021
JOHN D. HICKS: Republican Ascendancy: 1921-1933. † *Illus.* TB/3041
SIDNEY HOOK: Reason, Social Myths, and Democracy TB/1237
ROBERT HUNTER: Poverty: *Social Conscience in the Progressive Era.* ‡ *Edited by Peter d'A. Jones* TB/3065
WILLIAM L. LANGER & S. EVERETT GLEASON: The Challenge to Isolation: *The World Crisis of 1937-1940 and American Foreign Policy* Vol. I TB/3054; Vol. II TB/3055
WILLIAM E. LEUCHTENBURG: Franklin D. Roosevelt and the New Deal: 1932-1940. † *Illus.* TB/3025
ARTHUR S. LINK: Woodrow Wilson and the Progressive Era: 1910-1917. † *Illus.* TB/3023
GEORGE E. MOWRY: The Era of Theodore Roosevelt and the Birth of Modern America: 1900-1912. † TB/3022
RUSSEL B. NYE: Midwestern Progressive Politics TB/1202
WILLIAM PRESTON, JR.: Aliens and Dissenters TB/1287
WALTER RAUSCHENBUSCH: Christianity and the Social Crisis. ‡ *Edited by Robert D. Cross* TB/3059
JACOB RIIS: The Making of an American. ‡ *Edited by Roy Lubove* TB/3070
PHILIP SELZNICK: TVA and the Grass Roots: *A Study in the Sociology of Formal Organization* TB/1230
IDA M. TARBELL: The History of the Standard Oil Company. *Briefer Version.* ‡ *Edited by David M. Chalmers* TB/3071
GEORGE B. TINDALL, Ed.: A Populist Reader ‡ TB/3069

Anthropology

JACQUES BARZUN: Race: *A Study in Superstition. Revised Edition* TB/1172
JOSEPH B. CASAGRANDE, Ed.: In the Company of Man: *Portraits of Anthropological Informants* TB/3047
W. E. LE GROS CLARK: The Antecedents of Man: *Intro. to Evolution of the Primates.* ° △ *Illus.* TB/559
CORA DU BOIS: The People of Alor. *New Preface by the author. Illus.* Vol. I TB/1042; Vol. II TB/1043
RAYMOND FIRTH, Ed.: Man and Culture: *An Evaluation of the Work of Bronislaw Malinowski* ¶ ° △ TB/1133
DAVID LANDY: Tropical Childhood: *Cultural Transmission and Learning in a Puerto Rican Village* ¶ TB/1235
L. S. B. LEAKEY: Adam's Ancestors: *The Evolution of Man and His Culture.* △ *Illus.* TB/1019
EDWARD BURNETT TYLOR: The Origin of Culture. *Part I of "Primitive Culture."* § *Intro. by Paul Radin* TB/33
EDWARD BURNETT TYLOR: Religion in Primitive Culture. *Part II of "Primitive Culture."* § *Intro. by Paul Radin* TB/34

Art and Art History

WALTER LOWRIE: Art in the Early Church. *Revised Edition. 452 illus.* TB/124
EMILE MÂLE: The Gothic Image: *Religious Art in France of the Thirteenth Century.* § △ *190 illus.* TB/44
MILLARD MEISS: Painting in Florence and Siena after the Black Death: *The Arts, Religion and Society in the Mid-Fourteenth Century. 169 illus.* TB/1148
ERICH NEUMANN: The Archetypal World of Henry Moore. △ *107 illus.* TB/2020
DORA & ERWIN PANOFSKY: Pandora's Box: *The Changing Aspects of a Mythical Symbol. Illus.* TB/2021
ALEXANDRE PIANKOFF: The Shrines of Tut-Ankh-Amon. *Edited by N. Rambova. 117 illus.* TB/2011
JEAN SEZNEC: The Survival of the Pagan Gods △ TB/2004
OTTO VON SIMSON: The Gothic Cathedral △ TB/2018
HEINRICH ZIMMER: Myths and Symbols in Indian Art and Civilization. *70 illustrations* TB/2005

Business, Economics & Economic History

REINHARD BENDIX: Work and Authority in Industry TB/3035
THOMAS C. COCHRAN: The American Business System: *A Historical Perspective, 1900-1955* TB/1080
THOMAS C. COCHRAN & WILLIAM MILLER: The Age of Enterprise: *A Social History of Industrial America* TB/1054
ROBERT DAHL & CHARLES E. LINDBLOM: Politics, Economics, and Welfare TB/3037
PETER F. DRUCKER: The New Society: *The Anatomy of Industrial Order* △ TB/1082
EDITORS OF FORTUNE: America in the Sixties: *The Economy and the Society* TB/1015
ROBERT L. HEILBRONER: The Great Ascent: *The Struggle for Economic Development in Our Time* TB/3030
ROBERT L. HEILBRONER: The Limits of American Capitalism TB/1305
FRANK H. KNIGHT: The Economic Organization TB/1214
FRANK H. KNIGHT: Risk, Uncertainty and Profit TB/1215
ABBA P. LERNER: Everybody's Business TB/3051
ROBERT GREEN MC CLOSKEY: American Conservatism in the Age of Enterprise, 1865-1910 TB/1137
PAUL MANTOUX: The Industrial Revolution in the Eighteenth Century ° △ TB/1079

WILLIAM MILLER, Ed.: Men in Business: *Essays on the Historical Role of the Entrepreneur* TB/1081
RICHARD B. MORRIS: Government and Labor in Early America TB/1244
HERBERT SIMON: The Shape of Automation: *For Men and Management* TB/1245
PERRIN STRYKER: The Character of the Executive: *Eleven Studies in Managerial Qualities* TB/1041
PIERRE URI: Partnership for Progress: *A Program for Transatlantic Action* TB/3036

Education

JACQUES BARZUN: The House of Intellect △ TB/1051
RICHARD M. JONES, Ed.: Contemporary Educational Psychology: *Selected Readings* TB/1292
CLARK KERR: The Uses of the University TB/1264
JOHN U. NEF: Cultural Foundations of Industrial Civilization △ TB/1024
NATHAN M. PUSEY: The Age of the Scholar: *Observations on Education in a Troubled Decade* TB/1157
PAUL VALÉRY: The Outlook for Intelligence △ TB/2016

Historiography & Philosophy of History

JACOB BURCKHARDT: On History and Historians. △ *Introduction by H. R. Trevor-Roper* TB/1216
WILHELM DILTHEY: Pattern and Meaning in History: *Thoughts on History and Society.* ○ △ *Edited with an Introduction by H. P. Rickman* TB/1075
J. H. HEXTER: Reappraisals in History: *New Views on History & Society in Early Modern Europe* △ TB/1100
H. STUART HUGHES: History as Art and as Science: *Twin Vistas on the Past* TB/1207
RAYMOND KLIBANSKY & H. J. PATON, Eds.: Philosophy and History: *The Ernst Cassirer Festschrift. Illus.* TB/1115
ARNALDO MOMIGLIANO: Studies in Historiography TB/1288
GEORGE H. NADEL, Ed.: Studies in the Philosophy of History: *Essays from* History and Theory TB/1208
JOSE ORTEGA Y GASSET: The Modern Theme. *Introduction by Jose Ferrater Mora* TB/1038
KARL R. POPPER: The Open Society and Its Enemies △
Vol. I: The Spell of Plato TB/1101
Vol. II: The High Tide of Prophecy: Hegel, Marx and the Aftermath TB/1102
KARL R. POPPER: The Poverty of Historicism ○ △ TB/1126
G. J. RENIER: History: Its Purpose and Method △ TB/1209
W. H. WALSH: Philosophy of History △ TB/1020

History: General

L. CARRINGTON GOODRICH: A Short History of the Chinese People. △ *Illus.* TB/3015
DAN N. JACOBS & HANS H. BAERWALD: *Chinese Communism: Selected Documents* TB/3031
BERNARD LEWIS: The Arabs in History △ TB/1029
BERNARD LEWIS: The Middle East and the West TB/1274

History: Ancient

A. ANDREWES: The Greek Tyrants △ TB/1103
ADOLF ERMAN, Ed.: The Ancient Egyptians TB/1233
MICHAEL GRANT: Ancient History ○ △ TB/1190
SAMUEL NOAH KRAMER: Sumerian Mythology TB/1055
NAPHTALI LEWIS & MEYER REINHOLD, Eds.: Roman Civilization. *Sourcebook I: The Republic* TB/1231
NAPHTALI LEWIS & MEYER REINHOLD, Eds.: Roman Civilization. *Sourcebook II: The Empire* TB/1232

History: Medieval

P. BOISSONNADE: Life and Work in Medieval Europe ○ △ TB/1141
HELEN CAM: England before Elizabeth △ TB/1026
NORMAN COHN: The Pursuit of the Millennium △ TB/1037
G. G. COULTON: Medieval Village, Manor, and Monastery TB/1022
CHRISTOPHR DAWSON, Ed.: Mission to Asia: *Narratives and Letters of the Franciscan Missionaries in Mongolia and China in the 13th and 14th Centuries* △ TB/315
HEINRICH FICHTENAU: The Carolingian Empire: *The Age of Charlemagne* △ TB/1142
GALBERT OF BRUGES: The Murder of Charles the Good. *Trans with Intro. by James Bruce Ross* TB/1311
F. L. GANSHOF: Feudalism △ TB/1058
DENO GEANAKOPLOS: Byzantine East and Latin West: *Two Worlds of Christendom in Middle Ages and Renaissance* △ TB/1265
DENYS HAY: Europe TB/1275
DENYS HAY: The Medieval Centuries ○ △ TB/1192
J. M. HUSSEY: The Byzantine World △ TB/1057
ROBERT LATOUCHE: The Birth of Western Economy ○ △ TB/1290
FERDINAND LOT: The End of the Ancient World and the Beginnings of the Middle Ages TB/1044
MARSILIUS OF PADUA: The Defender of the Peace. *Trans. with Intro. by Alan Gewirth* TB/1310
G. MOLLAT: The Popes at Avignon: 1305-1378 △ TB/308
CHARLES PETIT-DUTAILLIS: The Feudal Monarchy in France and England ○ △ TB/1165
HENRI PIRENNE: Early Democracies in the Low Countries TB/1110
STEVEN RUNCIMAN: A History of the Crusades. △
Vol. I TB/1143; *Vol. II* TB/1243; *Vol. III* TB/1298
FERDINAND SCHEVILL: Siena: *The History of a Medieval Commune. Intro. by William M. Bowsky* TB/1164
HENRY OSBORN TAYLOR: The Classical Heritage of the Middle Ages TB/1117
F. VAN DER MEER: Augustine the Bishop: *Church and Society at the Dawn of the Middle Ages* △ TB/304
J. M. WALLACE-HADRILL: The Barbarian West: *The Early Middle Ages, A.D. 400-1000* △ TB/1061

History: Renaissance & Reformation

JACOB BURCKHARDT: The Civilization of the Renaissance in Italy. △ *Illus.* Vol. I TB/40; Vol. II TB/41
JOHN CALVIN & JACOPO SADOLETO: A Reformation Debate. *Edited by John C. Olin* TB/1239
ERNST CASSIRER: The Individual and the Cosmos in Renaissance Philosophy. △ *Translated with an Introduction by Mario Domandi* TB/1097
FEDERICO CHABOD: Machiavelli & Renaissance △ TB/1193
EDWARD P. CHEYNEY: The Dawn of a New Era, 1250-1453. * *Illus.* TB/3002
G. CONSTANT: The Reformation in England: *The English Schism, Henry VIII, 1509-1547* △ TB/314
R. TREVOR DAVIES: The Golden Century of Spain, 1501-1621 ○ △ TB/1194
G. R. ELTON: Reformation Europe, 1517-1559 ** ○ △ TB/1270
DESIDERIUS ERASMUS: Christian Humanism and the Reformation: *Selected Writings. Edited and translated by John C. Olin* TB/1166
WALLACE K. FERGUSON et al.: Facets of the Renaissance TB/1098
WALLACE K. FERGUSON et al.: The Renaissance: *Six Essays. Illus.* TB/1084
JOHN NEVILLE FIGGIS: The Divine Right of Kings. *Introduction by G. R. Elton* TB/1191
JOHN NEVILLE FIGGIS: Political Thought from Gerson to Grotius: 1414-1625 TB/1032
MYRON P. GILMORE: The World of Humanism, 1453-1517. * *Illus.* TB/3003
FRANCESCO GUICCIARDINI: Maxims and Reflections of a Renaissance Statesman *(Ricordi)* TB/1160
J. H. HEXTER: More's Utopia: *The Biography of an Idea. New Epilogue by the Author* TB/1195

HAJO HOLBORN: Ulrich von Hutten and the German Reformation TB/1238
JOHAN HUIZINGA: Erasmus and the Age of Reformation.△ *Illus.* TB/19
JOEL HURSTFIELD, Ed.: The Reformation Crisis △ TB/1267
ULRICH VON HUTTEN et al.: On the Eve of the Reformation: *"Letters of Obscure Men"* TB/1124
PAUL O. KRISTELLER: Renaissance Thought: *The Classic, Scholastic, and Humanist Strains* TB/1048
PAUL O. KRISTELLER: Renaissance Thought II: *Papers on Humanism and the Arts* TB/1163
NICCOLÒ MACHIAVELLI: History of Florence and of the Affairs of Italy TB/1027
ALFRED VON MARTIN: Sociology of the Renaissance. *Introduction by Wallace K. Ferguson* △ TB/1099
GARRETT MATTINGLY et al.: Renaissance Profiles. △ *Edited by J. H. Plumb* TB/1162
MILLARD MEISS: Painting in Florence and Siena after the Black Death: *The Arts, Religion and Society in the Mid-Fourteenth Century.* △ *169 illus.* TB/1148
J. E. NEALE: The Age of Catherine de Medici ° △ TB/1085
ERWIN PANOFSKY: Studies in Iconology: *Humanistic Themes in the Art of the Renaissance* △ TB/1077
J. H. PARRY: The Establishment of the European Hegemony: 1415-1715 △ TB/1045
J. H. PLUMB: The Italian Renaissance: *A Concise Survey of Its History and Culture* △ TB/1161
A. F. POLLARD: Henry VIII. ° △ *Introduction by A. G. Dickens* TB/1249
A. F. POLLARD: Wolsey. ° △ *Introduction by A. G. Dickens* TB/1248
CECIL ROTH: The Jews in the Renaissance. *Illus.* TB/834
A. L. ROWSE: The Expansion of Elizabethan England. ° △ *Illus.* TB/1220
GORDON RUPP: Luther's Progress to the Diet of Worms ° △ TB/120
G. M. TREVELYAN: England in the Age of Wycliffe, 1368-1520 ° △ TB/1112
VESPASIANO: Renaissance Princes, Popes, and Prelates: *The Vespasiano Memoirs: Lives of Illustrious Men of the XVth Century* TB/1111

History: Modern European

FREDERICK B. ARTZ: Reaction and Revolution, 1815-1852. * *Illus.* TB/3034
MAX BELOFF: The Age of Absolutism, 1660-1815 △ TB/1062
ROBERT C. BINKLEY: Realism and Nationalism, 1852-1871. * *Illus.* TB/3038
ASA BRIGGS: The Making of Modern England, 1784-1867: *The Age of Improvement* ° △ TB/1203
CRANE BRINTON: A Decade of Revolution, 1789-1799. * *Illus.* TB/3018
D. W. BROGAN: The Development of Modern France. ° △ Volume I: *From the Fall of the Empire to the Dreyfus Affair* TB/1184
Volume II: *The Shadow of War, World War I, Between the Two Wars. New Introduction by the Author* TB/1185
J. BRONOWSKI & BRUCE MAZLISH: The Western Intellectual Tradition: *From Leonardo to Hegel* △ TB/3001
GEOFFREY BRUUN: Europe and the French Imperium, 1799-1814. * *Illus.* TB/3033
ALAN BULLOCK: Hitler, A Study in Tyranny ° △ TB/1123
E. H. CARR: German-Soviet Relations between the Two World Wars, 1919-1939 TB/1278
E. H. CARR: International Relations between the Two World Wars, 1919-1939 ° △ TB/1279
E. H. CARR: The Twenty Years' Crisis, 1919-1939 ° △ TB/1122
GORDON A. CRAIG: From Bismarck to Adenauer: *Aspects of German Statecraft. Revised Edition* TB/1171
DENIS DIDEROT: The Encyclopedia: *Selections. Ed and trans. by Stephen Gendzier* TB/1299
WALTER L. DORN: Competition for Empire, 1740-1763. * *Illus.* TB/3032
FRANKLIN L. FORD: Robe and Sword: *The Regrouping of the French Aristocracy after Louis XIV* TB/1217
CARL J. FRIEDRICH: The Age of the Baroque, 1610-1660. * *Illus.* TB/3004
RENÉ FUELOEP-MILLER: The Mind and Face of Bolshevism TB/1188
M. DOROTHY GEORGE: London Life in the Eighteenth Century △ TB/1182
LEO GERSHOY: From Despotism to Revolution, 1763-1789. * *Illus.* TB/3017
C. C. GILLISPIE: Genesis and Geology: *The Decades before Darwin* § TB/51
ALBERT GOODWIN: The French Revolution △ TB/1064
ALBERT GUÉRARD: France in the Classical Age: *The Life and Death of an Ideal* △ TB/1183
CARLTON J. H. HAYES: A Generation of Materialism, 1871-1900. * *Illus.* TB/3039
STANLEY HOFFMANN et al.: In Search of France TB/1219
A. R. HUMPHREYS: The Augustan World: *Society, Thought, and Letters in 18th Century England* ° △ TB/1105
DAN N. JACOBS, Ed.: The New Communist Manifesto *& Related Documents. Third edition, Revised* TB/1078
LIONEL KOCHAN: The Struggle for Germany: *1914-45* TB/1304
HANS KOHN: The Mind of Germany △ TB/1204
HANS KOHN, Ed.: The Mind of Modern Russia: *Historical and Political Thought of Russia's Great Age* TB/1065
WALTER LAQUEUR & GEORGE L. MOSSE, Eds.: International Fascism, 1920-1945 ° △ TB/1276
WALTER LAQUEUR & GEORGE L. MOSSE, Eds.: The Left-Wing Intellectuals between the Wars, 1919-1939 ° △ TB/1286
WALTER LAQUEUR & GEORGE L. MOSSE, Eds.: 1914: *The Coming of the First World War* ° △ TB/1306
FRANK E. MANUEL: The Prophets of Paris: *Turgot, Condorcet, Saint-Simon, Fourier, and Comte* TB/1218
KINGSLEY MARTIN: French Liberal Thought in the Eighteenth Century TB/1114
L. B. NAMIER: Facing East △ TB/1280
L. B. NAMIER: Personalities and Powers: *Selected Essays* △ TB/1186
L. B. NAMIER: Vanished Supremacies: *Essays on European History, 1812-1918* ° △ TB/1088
JOHN U. NEF: Western Civilization Since the Renaissance: *Peace, War, Industry, and the Arts* TB/1113
FRANZ NEUMANN: Behemoth: *The Structure and Practice of National Socialism, 1933-1944* TB/1289
FREDERICK L. NUSSBAUM: The Triumph of Science and Reason, 1660-1685. * *Illus.* TB/3009
DAVID OGG: Europe of the Ancien Régime, 1715-1783 ** ° △ TB/1271
JOHN PLAMENATZ: German Marxism and Russian Communism. ° △ *New Preface by the Author* TB/1189
RAYMOND W. POSTGATE, Ed.: Revolution from 1789 to 1906: *Selected Documents* TB/1063
PENFIELD ROBERTS: The Quest for Security, 1715-1740. * *Illus.* TB/3016
PRISCILLA ROBERTSON: Revolutions of 1848: *A Social History* TB/1025
GEORGE RUDÉ: Revolutionary Europe, 1783-1815 ** ° △ TB/1272
LOUIS, DUC DE SAINT-SIMON: Versailles, The Court, and Louis XIV. △ *Introductory Note by Peter Gay* TB/1250
ALBERT SOREL: Europe Under the Old Regime. *Translated by Francis H. Herrick* TB/1121
N. N. SUKHANOV: The Russian Revolution, 1917: *Eyewitness Account.* △ *Edited by Joel Carmichael*
Vol. I TB/1066; Vol. II TB/1067
A. J. P. TAYLOR: From Napoleon to Lenin: *Historical Essays* ° △ TB/1268
A. J. P. TAYLOR: The Habsburg Monarchy, 1809-1918 ° △ TB/1187

G. M. TREVELYAN: British History in the Nineteenth Century and After: 1782-1919. △ *Second Edition* TB/1251

H. R. TREVOR-ROPER: Historical Essays ° △ TB/1269

ELIZABETH WISKEMANN: Europe of the Dictators, 1919-1945 ** ° △ TB/1275

JOHN B. WOLF: The Emergence of the Great Powers, 1685-1715. * *Illus.* TB/3010

JOHN B. WOLF: France: 1814-1919: *The Rise of a Liberal-Democratic Society* TB/3019

Intellectual History & History of Ideas

HERSCHEL BAKER: The Image of Man TB/1047

R. R. BOLGAR: The Classical Heritage and Its Beneficiaries △ TB/1125

RANDOLPH S. BOURNE: War and the Intellectuals: *Collected Essays, 1915-1919.* ‡ △ *Edited by Carl Resek* TB/3043

J. BRONOWSKI & BRUCE MAZLISH: The Western Intellectual Tradition: *From Leonardo to Hegel* △ TB/3001

ERNST CASSIRER: The Individual and the Cosmos in Renaissance Philosophy. △ *Translated with an Introduction by Mario Domandi* TB/1097

NORMAN COHN: Pursuit of the Millennium △ TB/1037

C. C. GILLISPIE: Genesis and Geology: *The Decades before Darwin* § TB/51

G. RACHEL LEVY: Religious Conceptions of the Stone Age *and Their Influence upon European Thought.* △ *Illus. Introduction by Henri Frankfort* TB/106

ARTHUR O. LOVEJOY: The Great Chain of Being: *A Study of the History of an Idea* TB/1009

FRANK E. MANUEL: The Prophets of Paris: *Turgot, Condorcet, Saint-Simon, Fourier, and Comte* TB/1218

PERRY MILLER & T. H. JOHNSON, Editors: The Puritans: *A Sourcebook of Their Writings*
Vol. I TB/1093; Vol. II TB/1094

MILTON C. NAHM: Genius and Creativity: *An Essay in the History of Ideas* TB/1196

ROBERT PAYNE: Hubris: *A Study of Pride. Foreword by Sir Herbert Read* TB/1031

RALPH BARTON PERRY: The Thought and Character of William James: *Briefer Version* TB/1156

GEORG SIMMEL et al.: Essays on Sociology, Philosophy, and Aesthetics. ¶ *Edited by Kurt H. Wolff* TB/1234

BRUNO SNELL: The Discovery of the Mind: *The Greek Origins of European Thought* △ TB/1018

PAGET TOYNBEE: Dante Alighieri: *His Life and Works. Edited with Intro. by Charles S. Singleton* TB/1206

ERNEST LEE TUVESON: Millennium and Utopia: *A Study in the Background of the Idea of Progress.* ¶ *New Preface by the Author* TB/1134

PAUL VALÉRY: The Outlook for Intelligence △ TB/2016

W. WARREN WAGAR, Ed.: European Intellectual History since Darwin and Marx TB/1297

PHILIP P. WIENER: Evolution and the Founders of Pragmatism. △ *Foreword by John Dewey* TB/1212

BASIL WILLEY: Nineteenth Century Studies: *Coleridge to Matthew Arnold* ° △ TB/1261

BASIL WILLEY: More Nineteenth Century Studies: *A Group of Honest Doubters* △ TB/1262

Literature, Poetry, The Novel & Criticism

JACQUES BARZUN: The House of Intellect △ TB/1051

W. J. BATE: From Classic to Romantic: *Premises of Taste in Eighteenth Century England* TB/1036

RACHEL BESPALOFF: On the Iliad TB/2006

R. P. BLACKMUR et al.: Lectures in Criticism. *Introduction by Huntington Cairns* TB/2003

JAMES BOSWELL: The Life of Dr. Johnson & The Journal of a Tour to the Hebrides with Samuel Johnson LL.D: *Selections.* ° △ *Edited by F. V. Morley. Illus. by Ernest Shepard* TB/1254

ABRAHAM CAHAN: The Rise of David Levinsky: *a documentary novel of social mobility in early twentieth century America. Intro. by John Higham* TB/1028

ERNST R. CURTIUS: European Literature and the Latin Middle Ages △ TB/2015

ÉTIENNE GILSON: Dante and Philosophy TB/1089

ALFRED HARBAGE: As They Liked It: *A Study of Shakespeare's Moral Artistry* TB/1035

STANLEY R. HOPPER, Ed.: Spiritual Problems in Contemporary Literature § TB/21

A. R. HUMPHREYS: The Augustan World: *Society in 18th Century England* ° △ TB/1105

ALDOUS HUXLEY: Antic Hay & The Giaconda Smile. ° △ *Introduction by Martin Green* TB/3503

ARNOLD KETTLE: An Introduction to the English Novel △
Volume I: *Defoe to George Eliot* TB/1011
Volume II: *Henry James to the Present* TB/1012

RICHMOND LATTIMORE: The Poetry of Greek Tragedy △ TB/1257

J. B. LEISHMAN: The Monarch of Wit: *An Analytical and Comparative Study of the Poetry of John Donne* ° △ TB/1258

J. B. LEISHMAN: Themes and Variations in Shakespeare's Sonnets ° △ TB/1259

ROGER SHERMAN LOOMIS: The Development of Arthurian Romance △ TB/1167

JOHN STUART MILL: On Bentham and Coleridge. △ *Introduction by F. R. Leavis* TB/1070

KENNETH B. MURDOCK: Literature and Theology in Colonial New England TB/99

SAMUEL PEPYS: The Diary of Samuel Pepys. ° *Edited by O. F. Morshead. Illus. by Ernest Shepard* TB/1007

ST.-JOHN PERSE: Seamarks TB/2002

V. DE S. PINTO: Crisis in English Poetry, 1880-1940 ° △ TB/1260

ROBERT PREYER, Ed.: Victorian Literature TB/1302

GEORGE SANTAYANA: Interpretations of Poetry and Religion § TB/9

C. K. STEAD: The New Poetic: *Yeats to Eliot* ° △ TB/1263

HEINRICH STRAUMANN: American Literature in the Twentieth Century. △ *Third Edition, Revised* TB/1168

PAGET TOYNBEE: Dante Alighieri: *His Life and Works. Edited with Intro. by Charles S. Singleton* TB/1206

DOROTHY VAN GHENT: The English Novel TB/1050

E. B. WHITE: One Man's Meat TB/3505

BASIL WILLEY: Nineteenth Century Studies: *Coleridge to Matthew Arnold* ° △ TB/1261

BASIL WILLEY: More Nineteenth Century Studies: *A Group of Honest Dcubters* ° △ TB/1262

RAYMOND WILLIAMS: Culture and Society, 1780-1950 △ TB/1252

RAYMOND WILLIAMS: The Long Revolution. △ *Revised Edition* TB/1253

MORTON DAUWEN ZABEL, Editor: *Literary Opinion in America* Vol. I TB/3013; Vol. II TB/3014

Myth, Symbol & Folklore

JOSEPH CAMPBELL, Editor: Pagan and Christian Mysteries. *Illus.* TB/2013

MIRCEA ELIADE: Cosmos and History: *The Myth of the Eternal Return* § △ TB/2050

MIRCEA ELIADE: Rites and Symbols of Initiation: *The Mysteries of Birth and Rebirth* § △ TB/1236

THEODOR H. GASTER: Thespis △ TB/1281

DORA & ERWIN PANOFSKY: Pandora's Box: *The Changing Aspects of a Mythical Symbol.* △ *Revised Edition. Illus.* TB/2021

HELLMUT WILHELM: Change: *Eight Lectures on the I Ching* △ TB/2019

HEINRICH ZIMMER: Myths and Symbols in Indian Art and Civilization. △ *70 illustrations* TB/2005

Philosophy

G. E. M. ANSCOMBE: An Introduction to Wittgenstein's Tractatus. ° △ *Second Edition, Revised* TB/1210

HENRI BERGSON: Time and Free Will ° △ TB/1021
H. J. BLACKHAM: Six Existentialist Thinkers ° △ TB/1002
CRANE BRINTON: Nietzsche TB/1197
ERNST CASSIRER: The Individual and the Cosmos in Renaissance Philosophy △ TB/1097
FREDERICK COPLESTON: Medieval Philosophy ° △ TB/376
F. M. CORNFORD: Principium Sapientiae: *A Study of the Origins of Greek Philosophical Thought* TB/1213
F. M. CORNFORD: From Religion to Philosophy: *A Study in the Origins of Western Speculation* § TB/20
WILFRID DESAN: The Tragic Finale: *An Essay on the Philosophy of Jean-Paul Sartre* TB/1030
A. P. D'ENTRÈVES: Natural Law △ TB/1223
MARVIN FARBER: The Aims of Phenomenology TB/1291
MARVIN FARBER: Phenomenology and Existence: *Towards a Philosophy Within Nature* TB/1295
HERBERET FINGARETTE: The Self in Transformation: *Psychoanalysis, Philosophy and the Life of the Spirit* ¶ TB/1177
PAUL FRIEDLÄNDER: Plato: *An Introduction* △ TB/2017
ÉTIENNE GILSON: Dante and Philosophy TB/1089
J. GLENN GRAY: The Warriors: *Reflections on Men in Battle. Intro. by Hannah Arendt* TB/1294
WILLIAM CHASE GREENE: Moira: *Fate, Good, and Evil in Greek Thought* TB/1104
W. K. C. GUTHRIE: The Greek Philosophers: *From Thales to Aristotle* ° △ TB/1008
G. W. F. HEGEL: The Phenomenology of Mind ° △ TB/1303
F. H. HEINEMANN: Existentialism and the Modern Predicament △ TB/28
ISAAC HUSIK: A History of Medieval Jewish Philosophy JP/3
EDMUND HUSSERL: Phenomenology and the Crisis of Philosophy TB/1170
IMMANUEL KANT: The Doctrine of Virtue, *being Part II of the* Metaphysic of Morals TB/110
IMMANUEL KANT: Groundwork of the Metaphysic of Morals. *Trans. & analyzed by H. J. Paton* TB/1159
IMMANUEL KANT: Lectures on Ethics § △ TB/105
IMMANUEL KANT: Religion Within the Limits of Reason Alone. § *Intro. by T. M. Greene & J. Silber* TB/67
QUENTIN LAUER: Phenomenology TB/1169
GABRIEL MARCEL: Being and Having △ TB/310
GEORGE A. MORGAN: What Nietzsche Means TB/1198
PHILO, SAADYA GAON, & JEHUDA HALEVI: Three Jewish Philosophers. *Ed. by Hans Lewy, Alexander Altmann, & Isaak Heinemann* TB/813
MICHAEL POLANYI: Personal Knowledge △ TB/1158
WILLARD VAN ORMAN QUINE: Elementary Logic: *Revised Edition* TB/577
WILLARD VAN ORMAN QUINE: From a Logical Point of View: *Logico-Philosophical Essays* TB/566
BERTRAND RUSSELL et al.: The Philosophy of Bertrand Russell Vol. I TB/1095; Vol. II TB/1096
L. S. STEBBING: A Modern Introduction to Logic △ TB/538
ALFRED NORTH WHITEHEAD: Process and Reality: *An Essay in Cosmology* △ TB/1033
PHILIP P. WIENER: Evolution and the Founders of Pragmatism. *Foreword by John Dewey* TB/1212
WILHELM WINDELBAND: A History of Philosophy
Vol. I: *Greek, Roman, Medieval* TB/38
Vol. II: *Renaissance, Enlightenment, Modern* TB/39
LUDWIG WITTGENSTEIN: Blue and Brown Books ° TB/1211

Political Science & Government

JEREMY BENTHAM: The Handbook of Political Fallacies. *Introduction by Crane Brinton* TB/1069
KENNETH E. BOULDING: Conflict and Defense TB/3024
CRANE BRINTON: English Political Thought in the Nineteenth Century TB/1071
ROBERT CONQUEST: Power and Policy in the USSR: *The Study of Soviet Dynastics* △ TB/1307
EDWARD S. CORWIN: American Constitutional History: *Essays edited by Alpheus T. Mason and Gerald Garvey* TB/1136
ROBERT DAHL & CHARLES E. LINDBLOM: Politics, Economics, and Welfare TB/3037
F. L. GANSHOF: Feudalism △ TB/1058
G. P. GOOCH: English Democratic Ideas in Seventeenth Century TB/1006
J. H. HEXTER: More's Utopia: *The Biography of an Idea. New Epilogue by the Author* TB/1195
SIDNEY HOOK: Reason, Social Myths and Democracy △ TB/1237
ROBERT H. JACKSON: The Supreme Court in the American System of Government △ TB/1106
DAN N. JACOBS, Ed.: The New Communist Manifesto *and Related Documents. Third edition, Revised* TB/1078
DAN N. JACOBS & HANS BAERWALD Eds.: Chinese Communism: *Selected Documents* TB/3031
HANS KOHN: Political Ideologies of the Twentieth Century TB/1277
ROBERT GREEN MC CLOSKEY: American Conservatism in the Age of Enterprise, 1865-1910 TB/1137
KINGSLEY MARTIN: French Liberal Thought in the Eighteenth Century △ TB/1114
ROBERTO MICHELS: First Lectures in Political Sociology. *Edited by Alfred de Grazia* ¶ ° TB/1224
JOHN STUART MILL: On Bentham and Coleridge. △ *Introduction by F. R. Leavis* TB/1070
BARRINGTON MOORE, JR.: Political Power and Social Theory: *Seven Studies* ¶ TB/1221
BARRINGTON MOORE, JR.: Soviet Politics—The Dilemma of Power ¶ TB/1222
BARRINGTON MOORE, JR.: Terror and Progress—USSR: *Some Sources of Change and Stability in the Soviet Dictatorship* ¶ TB/1266
JOHN B. MORRALL: Political Thought in Medieval Times △ TB/1076
JOHN PLAMENATZ: German Marxism and Russian Communism. ° △ *New Preface by the Author* TB/1189
KARL R. POPPER: The Open Society and Its Enemies △
Vol. I: *The Spell of Plato* TB/1101
Vol. II: *The High Tide of Prophecy: Hegel, Marx, and the Aftermath* TB/1102
HENRI DE SAINT-SIMON: Social Organization, The Science of Man, and Other Writings. *Edited and Translated by Felix Markham* TB/1152
JOSEPH A. SCHUMPETER: Capitalism, Socialism and Democracy △ TB/3008
CHARLES H. SHINN: Mining Camps: *A Study in American Frontier Government.* ‡ *Edited by Rodman W. Paul* TB/3062
BENJAMIN I. SCHWARTZ: Chinese Communism and the Rise of Mao TB/1308
PETER WOLL, Ed.: Public Administration and Policy TB/1284

Psychology

ALFRED ADLER: Individual Psychology of Alfred Adler △ TB/1154
ALFRED ADLER: Problems of Neurosis. *Introduction by Heinz L. Ansbacher* TB/1145
ANTON T. BOISEN: The Exploration of the Inner World: *A Study of Mental Disorder and Religious Experience* TB/87
ARTHUR BURTON & ROBERT E. HARRIS, Eds.: Clinical Studies of Personality Vol. I TB/3075; Vol. II TB/3076
HADLEY CANTRIL: The Invasion from Mars: *A Study in the Psychology of Panic* ¶ TB/1282
HERBERT FINGARETTE: The Self in Transformation ¶ TB/1177
SIGMUND FREUD: On Creativity and the Unconscious § △ *Intro. by Benjamin Nelson* TB/45
C. JUDSON HERRICK: The Evolution of Human Nature TB/545
WILLIAM JAMES: Psychology: *Briefer Course* TB/1034
C. G. JUNG: Psychological Reflections △ TB/2001
C. G. JUNG: Symbols of Transformation △
Vol. I TB/2009; Vol. II TB/2010

C. G. JUNG & C. KERÉNYI: Essays on a Science of Mythology: *The Myths of the Divine Child and the Divine Maiden* TB/2014
JOHN T. MC NEILL: A History of the Cure of Souls TB/126
KARL MENNINGER: Theory of Psychoanalytic Technique TB/1144
ERICH NEUMANN: Amor and Psyche △ TB/2012
ERICH NEUMANN: The Archetypal World of Henry Moore. *107 illus.* TB/2020
ERICH NEUMANN: The Origins and History of Consciousness △ Vol. I *Illus.* TB/2007; Vol. II TB/2008
C. P. OBERNDORF: A History of Psychoanalysis in America TB/1147
RALPH BARTON PERRY: The Thought and Character of William James: *Briefer Version* TB/1156
JEAN PIAGET, BÄRBEL INHELDER, & ALINA SZEMINSKA: The Child's Conception of Geometry ° △ TB/1146
JOHN H. SCHAAR: Escape from Authority: *The Perspectives of Erich Fromm* TB/1155
MUZAFER SHERIF: The Psychology of Social Norms TB/3072

Sociology

JACQUES BARZUN: Race: *A Study in Superstition. Revised Edition* TB/1172
BERNARD BERELSON, Ed.: The Behavioral Sciences Today TB/1127
ABRAHAM CAHAN: The Rise of David Levinsky: *A documentary novel of social mobility in early twentieth century America. Intro. by John Higham* TB/1028
THOMAS C. COCHRAN: The Inner Revolution: *Essays on the Social Sciences in History* TB/1140
LEWIS A. COSER, Ed.: Political Sociology TB/1293
ALLISON DAVIS & JOHN DOLLARD: Children of Bondage: *The Personality Development of Negro Youth in the Urban South* ¶ TB/3049
ST. CLAIR DRAKE & HORACE R. CAYTON: Black Metropolis: *A Study of Negro Life in a Northern City. Revised and Enlarged. Intro. by Everett C. Hughes* Vol. I TB/1086; Vol. II TB/1087
EMILE DURKHEIM et al.: Essays on Sociology and Philosophy. *With Analysis of Durkheim's Life and Work.* ¶ *Edited by Kurt H. Wolff* TB/1151
LEON FESTINGER, HENRY W. RIECKEN & STANLEY SCHACHTER: When Prophecy Fails: *A Social and Psychological Account of a Modern Group that Predicted the Destruction of the World* ¶ TB/1132
ALVIN W. GOULDNER: Wildcat Strike ¶ TB/1176
FRANCIS J. GRUND: Aristocracy in America: *Social Class in the Formative Years of the New Nation* △ TB/1001
KURT LEWIN: Field Theory in Social Science: *Selected Theoretical Papers* ¶ △ *Edited with a Foreword by* Dorwin Cartwright TB/1135
R. M. MAC IVER: Social Causation TB/1153
ROBERT K. MERTON, LEONARD BROOM, LEONARD S. COTTRELL, JR., Editors: Sociology Today: *Problems and Prospects* ¶ Vol. I TB/1173; Vol. II TB/1174
ROBERTO MICHELS: First Lectures in Political Sociology. *Edited by Alfred de Grazia* ¶ ° TB/1224
BARRINGTON MOORE, JR.: Political Power and Social Theory: *Seven Studies* ¶ TB/1221
BARRINGTON MOORE, JR.: Soviet Politics — The Dilemma of Power: *The Role of Ideas in Social Change* ¶ TB/1222
TALCOTT PARSONS & EDWARD A. SHILS, Editors: Toward a General Theory of Action TB/1083
JOHN H. ROHRER & MUNRO S. EDMONSON, Eds.: The Eighth Generation Grows Up ¶ TB/3050
KURT SAMUELSSON: Religion and Economic Action: *A Critique of Max Weber's* The Protestant Ethic and the Spirit of Capitalism. ¶ ° *Trans. by E. G. French. Ed. with Intro. by D. C. Coleman* TB/1131
PHILIP SELZNICK: TVA and the Grass Roots: *A Study in the Sociology of Formal Organization* TB/1230
GEORG SIMMEL et al.: Essays on Sociology, Philosophy, and Aesthetics. ¶ *Edited by Kurt H. Wolff* TB/1234
HERBERT SIMON: The Shape of Automation △ TB/1245
PITIRIM A. SOROKIN: Contemporary Sociological Theories: *Through the First Quarter of the 20th Century* TB/3046
MAURICE R. STEIN: The Eclipse of Community: *An Interpretation of American Studies* TB/1128
FERDINAND TÖNNIES: Community and Society: *Gemeinschaft und Gesellschaft. Translated and edited by Charles P. Loomis* TB/1116
W. LLOYD WARNER & Associates: Democracy in Jonesville: *A Study in Quality and Inequality* TB/1129
W. LLOYD WARNER: Social Class in America: *The Evaluation of Status* TB/1013

RELIGION

Ancient & Classical

J. H. BREASTED: Development of Religion and Thought in Ancient Egypt TB/57
HENRI FRANKFORT: Ancient Egyptian Religion TB/77
G. RACHEL LEVY: Religious Conceptions of the Stone Age *and their Influence upon European Thought.* △ *Illus. Introduction by Henri Frankfort* TB/106
MARTIN P. NILSSON: Greek Folk Religion TB/78
ALEXANDRE PIANKOFF: The Shrines of Tut-Ankh-Amon.△ *Edited by N. Rambova. 117 illus.* TB/2011
ERWIN ROHDE: Psyche Vol. I TB/140; Vol. II TB/141
H. J. ROSE: Religion in Greece and Rome △ TB/55

Biblical Thought & Literature

W. F. ALBRIGHT: The Biblical Period from Abraham to Ezra TB/102
C. K. BARRETT, Ed.: The New Testament Background: *Selected Documents* △ TB/86
C. H. DODD: The Authority of the Bible △ TB/43
M. S. ENSLIN: Christian Beginnings △ TB/5
M. S. ENSLIN: The Literature of the Christian Movement △ TB/6
JOHN GRAY: Archaeology and the Old Testament World. △ *Illus.* TB/127
JAMES MUILENBURG: The Way of Israel: *Biblical Faith and Ethics* △ TB/133
H. H. ROWLEY: The Growth of the Old Testament △ TB/107
G. A. SMITH: The Historical Geography of the Holy Land TB/138
D. WINTON THOMAS, Ed.: Documents from Old Testament Times △ TB/85
WALTHER ZIMMERLI: The Law and the Prophets: *A Study of the Meaning of the Old Testament* △ TB/144

The Judaic Tradition

LEO BAECK: Judaism and Christianity. *Trans. with Intro. by Walter Kaufmann* TB/823
SALO W. BARON: Modern Nationalism and Religion JP/18
MARTIN BUBER: Eclipse of God: *Studies in the Relation Between Religion and Philosophy* △ TB/12
MARTIN BUBER: For the Sake of Heaven TB/801
MARTIN BUBER: Hasidism and Modern Man △ TB/839
MARTIN BUBER: The Knowledge of Man: *Selected Essays.* △ *Edited with an Introduction by Maurice Friedman. Translated by Maurice Friedman and Ronald Gregor Smith* TB/135
MARTIN BUBER: Moses: *The Revelation and the Covenant* △ TB/827
MARTIN BUBER: The Origin and Meaning of Hasidism △ TB/835
MARTIN BUBER: Pointing the Way. △ *Introduction by Maurice S. Friedman* TB/103
MARTIN BUBER: The Prophetic Faith TB/73
MARTIN BUBER: Two Types of Faith: *the interpenetration of Judaism and Christianity* ° △ TB/75
ERNST LUDWIG EHRLICH: A Concise History of Israel: *From the Earliest Times to the Destruction of the Temple in A. D. 70* ° △ TB/128

MAURICE S. FRIEDMAN: Martin Buber: *The Life of Dialogue* △ TB/64
GENESIS: *The NJV Translation* TB/836
SOLOMON GRAYZEL: A History of the Contemporary Jews TB/816
WILL HERBERG: Judaism and Modern Man TB/810
ARTHUR HERTZBERG: The Zionist Idea TB/817
ABRAHAM J. HESCHEL: God in Search of Man: *A Philosophy of Judaism* TB/807
ISAAK HUSIK: A History of Medieval Jewish Philosophy TB/803
FLAVIUS JOSEPHUS: The Great Roman-Jewish War, *with* The Life of Josephus. *Introduction by William R. Farmer* TB/74
JACOB R. MARCUS: The Jew in the Medieval World TB/814
MAX L. MARGOLIS & ALEXANDER MARX: A History of the Jewish People TB/806
T. J. MEEK: Hebrew Origins TB/69
JAMES PARKES: The Conflict of the Church and the Synagogue: *The Jews and Early Christianity* JP/21
PHILO, SAADYA GAON, & JEHUDA HALEVI: Three Jewish Philosophers. *Ed. by Hans Lewey, Alexander Altmann, & Isaak Heinemann* TB/813
CECIL ROTH: A History of the Marranos TB/812
CECIL ROTH: The Jews in the Renaissance. *Illus.* TB/834
HERMAN L. STRACK: Introduction to the Talmud and Midrash TB/808
JOSHUA TRACHTENBERG: The Devil and the Jews: *The Medieval Conception of the Jew and its Relation to Modern Anti-Semitism* TB/822

Christianity: General

ROLAND H. BAINTON: Christendom: *A Short History of Christianity and its Impact on Western Civilization.* △ *Illus.* Vol. I TB/131; Vol. II TB/132

Christianity: Origins & Early Development

AUGUSTINE: An Augustine Synthesis. △ *Edited by Erich Przywara* TB/335
ADOLF DEISSMANN: Paul: *A Study in Social and Religious History* TB/15
EDWARD GIBBON: The Triumph of Christendom in the Roman Empire *(Chaps. XV-XX of "Decline and Fall," J. B. Bury edition).* § △ Illus. TB/46
MAURICE GOGUEL: Jesus and the Origins of Christianity. ° △ *Introduction by C. Leslie Mitton*
Volume I: *Prolegomena to the Life of Jesus* TB/65
Volume II: *The Life of Jesus* TB/66
EDGAR J. GOODSPEED: A Life of Jesus TB/1
ROBERT M. GRANT: Gnosticism and Early Christianity. △ *Revised Edition* TB/136
ADOLF HARNACK: The Mission and Expansion of Christianity *in the First Three Centuries. Introduction by Jaroslav Pelikan* TB/92
R. K. HARRISON: The Dead Sea Scrolls: *An Introduction* ° △ TB/84
EDWIN HATCH: The Influence of Greek Ideas on Christianity. § △ *Introduction and Bibliography by Frederick C. Grant* TB/18
ARTHUR DARBY NOCK: Early Gentile Christianity and Its Hellenistic Background TB/111
ARTHUR DARBY NOCK: St. Paul ° △ TB/104
ORIGEN: On First Principles. △ *Edited by G. W. Butterworth. Introduction by Henri de Lubac* TB/310
JAMES PARKES: The Conflict of the Church and the Synagogue: *The Jews and Early Christianity* JP/21
SULPICIUS SEVERUS et al.: The Western Fathers: *Being the Lives of Martin of Tours, Ambrose, Augustine of Hippo, Honoratus of Arles and Germanus of Auxerre.* △ *Edited and translated by F. R. Hoare* TB/309
F. VAN DER MEER: Augustine the Bishop: *Church and Society at the Dawn of the Middle Ages* △ TB/304
JOHANNES WEISS: Earliest Christianity: *A History of the Period A.D. 30-150. Introduction and Bibliography by Frederick C. Grant* Volume I TB/53
Volume II TB/54

Christianity: The Middle Ages and The Reformation

ANSELM OF CANTERBURY: Truth, Freedom and Evil: *Three Philosophical Dialogues, Ed., trans., and Intro. by Jasper Hopkins & Herbert Richardson* TB/317
JOHN CALVIN & JACOPO SADOLETO: A Reformation Debate. *Edited by John C. Olin* TB/1239
G. CONSTANT: The Reformation in England: *The English Schism, Henry VIII, 1509-1547* △ TB/314
CHRISTOPHER DAWSON, Ed.: Mission to Asia: *Narratives and Letters of the Franciscan Missionaries in Mongolia and China in the 13th and 14th Centuries* △ TB/315
JOHANNES ECKHART: Meister Eckhart: *A Modern Translation by R. B. Blakney* TB/8
DESIDERIUS ERASMUS: Christian Humanism and the Reformation: *Selected Writings. Edited and translated by John C. Olin* TB/1166
ÉTIENNE GILSON: Dante and Philosophy △ TB/1089
WILLIAM HALLER: The Rise of Puritanism △ TB/22
HAJO HOLBORN: Ulrich von Hutten and the German Reformation TB/1238
JOHAN HUIZINGA: Erasmus and the Age of Reformation. △ *Illus.* TB/19
A. C. MCGIFFERT: Protestant Thought Before Kant. △ *Preface by Jaroslav Pelikan* TB/93
JOHN T. MCNEILL: Makers of the Christian Tradition: *From Alfred the Great to Schleiermacher* △ TB/121
G. MOLLAT: The Popes at Avignon, 1305-1378 △ TB/308
GORDON RUPP: Luther's Progress to the Diet of Worms ° △ TB/120

Christianity: The Protestant Tradition

KARL BARTH: Church Dogmatics: *A Selection* △ TB/95
KARL BARTH: Dogmatics in Outline △ TB/56
KARL BARTH: The Word of God and the Word of Man TB/13
RUDOLF BULTMANN et al.: Translating Theology into the Modern Age: *Historical, Systematic and Pastoral Reflections on Theology and the Church in the Contemporary Situation. Volume 2 of* Journal for Theology and the Church, *edited by Robert W. Funk in association with Gerhard Ebeling* TB/252
WINTHROP HUDSON: The Great Tradition of the American Churches TB/98
SOREN KIERKEGAARD: On Authority and Revelation TB/139
SOREN KIERKEGAARD: Crisis in the Life of an Actress *and Other Essays on Drama.* △ *Trans. with Intro. by Stephen D. Crites* TB/145
SOREN KIERKEGAARD: Edifying Discourses. *Edited with an Introduction by Paul Holmer* TB/32
SOREN KIERKEGAARD: The Journals of Kierkegaard. ° △ *Edited with an Introduction by Alexander Dru* TB/52
SOREN KIERKEGAARD: The Point of View for My Work as an Author: *A Report to History.* § *Preface by Benjamin Nelson* TB/88
SOREN KIERKEGAARD: The Present Age. § △ *Translated and edited by Alevander Dru. Introduction by Walter Kaufmann* TB/94
SOREN KIERKEGAARD: Purity of Heart △ TB/4
SOREN KIERKEGAARD: Repetition: *An Essay in Experimental Psychology.* △ *Translated with Introduction & Notes by Walter Lowrie* TB/117
SOREN KIERKEGAARD: Works of Love: *Some Christian Reflections in the Form of Discourses* △ TB/122
WALTER LOWRIE: Kierkegaard: *A Life* Vol. I TB/89
Vol. II TB/90

JOHN MACQUARRIE: The Scope of Demythologizing: *Bultmann and his Critics* △ TB/134
PERRY MILLER & T. H. JOHNSON, Editors: The Puritans: *A Sourcebook of Their Writings* Vol. I TB/1093; Vol. II TB/1094
JAMES M. ROBINSON et al.: The Bultmann School of Biblical Interpretation: New Directions? *Volume 1 of* Journal of Theology and the Church, *edited by Robert W. Funk in association with Gerhard Ebeling* TB/251
F. SCHLEIERMACHER: The Christian Faith. △ *Introduction by Richard R. Niebuhr* Vol. I TB/108; Vol. II TB/109
F. SCHLEIERMACHER: On Religion: *Speeches to Its Cultured Despisers. Intro. by Rudolf Otto* TB/36
PAUL TILLICH: Dynamics of Faith △ TB/42
PAUL TILLICH: Morality and Beyond TB/142
EVELYN UNDERHILL: Worship △ TB/10

Christianity: The Roman and Eastern Traditions

DOM CUTHBERT BUTLER: Western Mysticism: *The Teaching of Augustine, Gregory and Bernard on Contemplation and the Contemplative Life* § ° △ TB/312
A. ROBERT CAPONIGRI, Ed.: Modern Catholic Thinkers I: *God and Man* △ TB/306
A. ROBERT CAPONIGRI, Ed.: Modern Catholic Thinkers II: *The Church and the Political Order* △ TB/307
THOMAS CORBISHLEY, S. J.: Roman Catholicism △ TB/112
CHRISTOPHR DAWSON: The Historic Reality of Christian Culture TB/305
G. P. FEDOTOV: The Russian Religious Mind: *Kievan Christianity, the 10th to the 13th Centuries* TB/370
G. P. FEDOTOV, Ed.: A Treasury of Russian Spirituality TB/303
ÉTIENNE GILSON: The Spirit of Thomism TB/313
DAVID KNOWLES: The English Mystical Tradition △ TB/302
GABRIEL MARCEL: Being and Having: *An Existential Diary.* △ *Introduction by James Collins* TB/310
GABRIEL MARCEL: Homo Viator: *Introduction to a Metaphysic of Hope* TB/397
GUSTAVE WEIGEL, S. J.: Catholic Theology in Dialogue TB/301

Oriental Religions: Far Eastern, Near Eastern

TOR ANDRAE: Mohammed: *The Man and His Faith* § △ TB/62
EDWARD CONZE: Buddhism: *Its Essence and Development.* ° △ *Foreword by Arthur Waley* TB/58
EDWARD CONZE et al., Editors: Buddhist Texts Through the Ages △ TB/113
ANANDA COOMARASWAMY: Buddha and the Gospel of Buddhism. △ *Illus.* TB/119
H. G. CREEL: Confucius and the Chinese Way TB/63
FRANKLIN EDGERTON, Trans & Ed.: The Bhagavad Gita TB/115
SWAMI NIKHILANANDA, Trans. & Ed.: The Upanishads: *A One-Volume Abridgment* △ TB/114
HELMUT WILHELM: Change: *Eight Lectures on the I Ching* △ TB/2019

Philosophy of Religion

NICOLAS BERDYAEV: The Beginning and the End § △ TB/14
NICOLAS BERDYAEV: Christian Existentialism: *A Berdyaev Synthesis. Ed. by Donald A. Lowrie* △ TB/130
NICOLAS BERDYAEV: The Destiny of Man △ TB/61
RUDOLF BULTMANN: History and Eschatology: *The Presence of Eternity* ° TB/91
RUDOLF BULTMANN AND FIVE CRITICS: Kerygma and Myth: *A Theological Debate* △ TB/80
RUDOLF BULTMANN and KARL KUNDSIN: Form Criticism: *Two Essays on New Testament Research.* △ *Translated by Frederick C. Grant* TB/96
MIRCEA ELIADE: The Sacred and the Profane TB/81
LUDWIG FEUERBACH: The Essence of Christianity. § *Introduction by Karl Barth. Foreword by H. Richard Niebuhr* TB/11
ÉTIENNE GILSON: The Spirit of Thomism TB/313
ADOLF HARNACK: What is Christianity? § △ *Introduction by Rudolf Bultmann* TB/17
FRIEDRICH HEGEL: On Christianity: *Early Theological Writings. Ed. by R. Kroner & T. M. Knox* TB/79
KARL HEIM: Christian Faith and Natural Science △ TB/16
IMMANUEL KANT: Religion Within the Limits of Reason Alone. § *Intro. by T. M. Greene & J. Silber* TB/67
K. E. KIRK: The Vision of God: *The Christian Doctrine of the Summum Bonum* § △ TB/137
JOHN MACQUARRIE: An Existentialist Theology: *A Comparison of Heidegger and Bultmann.* ° △ *Preface by Rudolf Bultmann* TB/125
PAUL RAMSEY, Ed.: Faith and Ethics: *The Theology of H. Richard Niebuhr* TB/129
EUGEN ROSENSTOCK-HUESSY: The Christian Future *or the Modern Mind Outrun* TB/143
PIERRE TEILHARD DE CHARDIN: The Divine Milieu ° △ TB/384
PIERRE TEILHARD DE CHARDIN: The Phenomenon of Man ° △ TB/383

Religion, Culture & Society

JOSEPH L. BLAU, Ed.: Cornerstones of Religious Freedom in America: *Selected Basic Documents, Court Decisions and Public Statements. Revised and Enlarged Edition* TB/118
C. C. GILLISPIE: Genesis and Geology: *The Decades before Darwin* § TB/51
KYLE HASELDEN: The Racial Problem in Christian Perspective TB/116
WALTER KAUFMANN, Ed.: Religion from Tolstoy to Camus: *Basic Writings on Religious Truth and Morals. Enlarged Edition* TB/123
JOHN T. MC NEILL: A History of the Cure of Souls TB/126
KENNETH B. MURDOCK: Literature and Theology in Colonial New England TB/99
H. RICHARD NIEBUHR: Christ and Culture △ TB/3
H. RICHARD NIEBUHR: The Kingdom of God in America TB/49
RALPH BARTON PERRY: Puritanism and Democracy TB/1138
PAUL PFUETZE: Self, Society, Existence: *Human Nature and Dialogue in the Thought of George Herbert Mead and Martin Buber* TB/1059
WALTER RAUSCHENBUSCH: Christianity and the Social Crisis. ‡ *Edited by Robert D. Cross* TB/3059
KURT SAMUELSSON: Religion and Economic Action: *A Critique of Max Weber's* The Protestant Ethic and the Spirit of Capitalism. ¶ ° △ *Trans. by E. G. French. Ed. with Intro. by D. C. Coleman* TB/1131
TIMOTHY L. SMITH: Revivalism and Social Reform: *American Protestantism on the Eve of the Civil War* △ TB/1229
ERNST TROELTSCH: The Social Teaching of the Christian Churches ° △ Vol. I TB/71; Vol. II TB/72

NATURAL SCIENCES AND MATHEMATICS

Biological Sciences

CHARLOTTE AUERBACH: The Science of Genetics Σ △ TB/568
MARSTON BATES: The Natural History of Mosquitoes. *Illus.* TB/578
A. BELLAIRS: Reptiles: *Life, History, Evolution, and Structure.* △ *Illus.* TB/520
LUDWIG VON BERTALANFFY: Modern Theories of Development: *An Introduction to Theoretical Biology* TB/554
LUDWIG VON BERTALANFFY: Problems of Life: *An Evaluation of Modern Biological and Scientific Thought* △ TB/521

HAROLD F. BLUM: Time's Arrow and Evolution TB/555
JOHN TYLER BONNER: The Ideas of Biology. Σ △ *Illus.* TB/570
A. J. CAIN: Animal Species and their Evolution. △ *Illus.* TB/519
WALTER B. CANNON: Bodily Changes in Pain, Hunger, Fear and Rage. *Illus.* TB/562
W. E. LE GROS CLARK: The Antecedents of Man: *Intro. to Evolution of the Primates.* ° △ *Illus.* TB/559
W. H. DOWDESWELL: Animal Ecology. △ *Illus.* TB/543
W. H. DOWDESWELL: The Mechanism of Evolution. △ *Illus.* TB/527
R. W. GERARD: Unresting Cells. *Illus.* TB/541
DAVID LACK: Darwin's Finches. △ *Illus.* TB/544
ADOLF PORTMANN: Animals as Social Beings. ° △ *Illus.* TB/572
O. W. RICHARDS: The Social Insects. △ *Illus.* TB/542
P. M. SHEPPARD: Natural Selection and Heredity. *Illus.* TB/528
EDMUND W. SINNOTT: Cell and Psyche: *The Biology of Purpose* TB/546
C. H. WADDINGTON: How Animals Develop. △ *Illus.* TB/553
C. H. WADDINGTON: The Nature of Life: *The Main Problems and Trends in Modern Biology* △ TB/580

Chemistry

J. R. PARTINGTON: A Short History of Chemistry. △ *Illus.* TB/522

Communication Theory

J. R. PIERCE: Symbols, Signals and Noise: *The Nature and Process of Communication* △ TB/574

Geography

R. E. COKER: This Great and Wide Sea: *An Introduction to Oceanography and Marine Biology. Illus.* TB/551
F. K. HARE: The Restless Atmosphere △ TB/560

History of Science

MARIE BOAS: The Scientific Renaissance, 1450-1630 ° △ TB/583
W. DAMPIER, Ed.: Readings in the Literature of Science. *Illus.* TB/512
A. HUNTER DUPREE: Science in the Federal Government: *A History of Policies and Activities to 1940* △ TB/573
ALEXANDRE KOYRÉ: From the Closed World to the Infinite Universe: *Copernicus, Kepler, Galileo, Newton, etc.* △ TB/31
A. G. VAN MELSEN: From Atomos to Atom: *A History of the Concept Atom* TB/517
O. NEUGEBAUER: The Exact Sciences in Antiquity TB/552
HANS THIRRING: Energy for Man: *From Windmills to Nuclear Power* △ TB/556
STEPHEN TOULMIN & JUNE GOODFIELD: The Architecture of Matter ° △ TB/584
STEPHEN TOULMIN & JUNE GOODFIELD: The Discovery of Time ° △ TB/585
LANCELOT LAW WHYTE: Essay on Atomism: *From Democritus to 1960* △ TB/565

Mathematics

E. W. BETH: The Foundations of Mathematics: *A Study in the Philosophy of Science* △ TB/581
H. DAVENPORT: The Higher Arithmetic: *An Introduction to the Theory of Numbers* △ TB/526
H. G. FORDER: Geometry: *An Introduction* △ TB/548
S. KÖRNER: The Philosophy of Mathematics: *An Introduction* △ TB/547
D. E. LITTLEWOOD: Skeleton Key of Mathematics: *A Simple Account of Complex Algebraic Problems* △ TB/525
GEORGE E. OWEN: Fundamentals of Scientific Mathematics TB/569
WILLARD VAN ORMAN QUINE: Mathematical Logic TB/558
O. G. SUTTON: Mathematics in Action. ° △ *Foreword by James R. Newman. Illus.* TB/518
FREDERICK WAISMANN: Introduction to Mathematical Thinking. *Foreword by Karl Menger* TB/511

Philosophy of Science

R. B. BRAITHWAITE: Scientific Explanation TB/515
J. BRONOWSKI: Science and Human Values. △ *Revised and Enlarged Edition* TB/505
ALBERT EINSTEIN et al.: Albert Einstein: Philosopher-Scientist. *Edited by Paul A. Schilpp* Vol. I TB/502 Vol. II TB/503
WERNER HEISENBERG: Physics and Philosophy: *The Revolution in Modern Science* △ TB/549
JOHN MAYNARD KEYNES: A Treatise on Probability. ° △ *Introduction by N. R. Hanson* TB/557
KARL R. POPPER: Logic of Scientific Discovery △ TB/576
STEPHEN TOULMIN: Foresight and Understanding: *An Enquiry into the Aims of Science.* △ *Foreword by Jacques Barzun* TB/564
STEPHEN TOULMIN: The Philosophy of Science: *An Introduction* △ TB/513
G. J. WHITROW: Natural Philosophy of Time ° △ TB/563

Physics and Cosmology

JOHN E. ALLEN: Aerodynamics: *A Space Age Survey* △ TB/582
STEPHEN TOULMIN & JUNE GOODFIELD: The Fabric of the Heavens: *The Development of Astronomy and Dynamics.* △ *Illus.* TB/579
DAVID BOHM: Causality and Chance in Modern Physics. △ *Foreword by Louis de Broglie* TB/536
P. W. BRIDGMAN: The Nature of Thermodynamics TB/537
P. W. BRIDGMAN: A Sophisticate's Primer of Relativity △ TB/575
A. C. CROMBIE, Ed.: Turning Point in Physics TB/535
C. V. DURRELL: Readable Relativity. △ *Foreword by Freeman J. Dyson* TB/530
ARTHUR EDDINGTON: Space, Time and Gravitation: *An Outline of the General Relativity Theory* TB/510
GEORGE GAMOW: Biography of Physics Σ △ TB/567
MAX JAMMER: Concepts of Force: *A Study in the Foundation of Dynamics* TB/550
MAX JAMMER: *Concepts of Mass in Classical and Modern Physics* TB/571
MAX JAMMER: Concepts of Space: *The History of Theories of Space in Physics. Foreword by Albert Einstein* TB/533
G. J. WHITROW: The Structure and Evolution of the Universe: *An Introduction to Cosmology.* △ *Illus.* TB/504